pe...Books

D0316367

OPENING THE BOOKS

Essays on the Social and Cultural History of British Communism

Edited by GEOFF ANDREWS,
NINA FISHMAN and KEVIN MORGAN

Pluto Press

LONDON • BOULDER, COLORADO

First published 1995 by Pluto Press
345 Archway Road, London N6 5AA
and 5500 Central Avenue
Boulder, Colorado 80301, USA

99   98   97   96   95   5   4   3   2   1

British Library Cataloguing in Publication Data
A catalogue record for this book is available
from the British Library

ISBN 0 7453 0871 6 hardback

Library of Congress Cataloging in Publication Data
Opening the books: essays on the social and cultural history of
   British communism / edited by Geoff Andrews, Nina Fishman and
   Kevin Morgan.
       p.   cm.
    Includes bibliographical references
    ISBN 0–7453–0871–6. —
    1. Communism—Great Britain—History. 2. Communist Party
of Great Britain—History. I. Andrews, Geoff, 1961–   . II. Fishman,
Nina. III. Morgan, Kevin, 1961–   .
    HX243.064   1995
 320.5'32'0941—dc20   94–42972
                                                                CIP

Designed and produced for Pluto Press by
Chase Production Services, Chipping Norton, OX7 5QR
Typeset from disk by Stanford DTP Services, Milton Keynes
Printed in the EC by WSOY, Finland

Contents

Note: works mentioned in the further reading sections at the end of every chapter are not included in the Bibliography.

Abbreviations used in Text, Notes and Index

AEU	Amalgamated Engineering Union
AG	Action Group
AITUC	All-India Trade Union Congress
AMU	Ayrshire Miners' Union
BMPL	Buckhaven and Methil Public Library
BRS	*The British Road to Socialism* (Communist Party programme)
BUA	Bristol Unemployed Association
CBC	Central Bus Committee (of the TGWU for the London buses)
CC	Central Committee (of Communist Party)
CI	Communist International (Comintern)
CND	Campaign for Nuclear Disarmament
CPA	Communist Party archives (National Museum of Labour History)
CP(GB)	Communist Party (of Great Britain)
CPI	Communist Party of India
CPSU	Communist Party of the Soviet Union
CPUSA	Communist Party of the United States of America
CUL	Communist University of London
DW	*Daily Worker*
EC	Executive Committee (of Communist Party)
ECCI	Executive Committee of Communist International
EEF	Engineering Employers' Federation
EOO	Egbe Omo Oduduwa
ETU	Electrical Trades Union
FKCMA	Fife, Kinross and Clackmannan Miners' Association
ILP	Independent Labour Party
ITUCNW	International Trade Union Committee–Negro Workers
IUS	International Union of Students
JK	Notes made by James Klugmann, Communist Party archives
JPC	Joint Production Committee

KPD	German Communist Party
KUTV	University of the Toilers of the East
LAI	League Against Imperialism
LM	*Labour Monthly*
LMCU	Lanarkshire Mineworkers' County Union
LRD	Labour Research Department
LSI	Labour and Socialist International
MELMA	Mid and East Lothian Miners' Association
MFGB	Miners' Federation of Great Britain
MM	Minority Movement
NCC	National Cultural Committee (of Communist Party)
NCNC	National Council of Nigeria and the Camerouns
NI	National Insurance
NJC	National Jewish Committee (of Communist Party)
NLC	Nigerian Labour Congress
NLR	*New Left Review*
NLS	National Library of Scotland
NMA	Nottinghamshire Miners' Association
NMM	National Minority Movement
NNFL	Nigerian National Federation of Labour
NPA	Newspaper Proprietors' Association
NR	*New Reasoner*
NSC	National Student Committee (of Communist Party)
NUJ	National Union of Journalists
NUM	National Union of Mineworkers
NUS	National Union of Students
NUSM	National Union of Scottish Mineworkers
NUWM	National Unemployed Workers' Movement
NWA	Negro Welfare Association
PAC	Public Assistance Committee
PPPS	People's Press Printing Society
PRO	Public Record Office
Profintern	Red International of Labour Unions
RILU	Red International of Labour Unions
SDF	Social Democratic Federation
SLP	Socialist Labour Party
SWMF	South Wales Miners' Federation
TGWU	Transport and General Workers' Union
TUC	Trades Union Congress
ULR	*Universities and Left Review*
UMS	United Mineworkers of Scotland

UWPP	United Working People's Party
WANS	West African National Secretariat
WASU	West African Students' Union
WCML	Working Class Movement Library, Salford
WFDY	World Federation of Democratic Youth
WFTU	World Federation of Trade Unions
WLM	Women's Liberation Movement
WWL	Workers' Welfare League of India
YCL	Young Communist League

Introduction

The history of the British Communist Party has never lacked its ironies. One is that, having nurtured as brilliant a school of historians as any this century, the party long proved incapable of addressing even the most matter-of-fact problems of its own history. With alumni like Christopher Hill, Eric Hobsbawm, E.P. Thompson, John Saville and Rodney Hilton, the CP's legendary Historians' Group put Britain at the very forefront of Marxist historical scholarship. Work on the party's own history, inauspiciously commenced in 1956, the year that most of these historians left the party, was by contrast a timid and pedestrian affair. Its first pious offerings took some twelve years to appear and, with a third but much fuller and franker volume not published until 1985, the party history was moving slower than history itself. Still, into the 1960s and 1970s, these were matters not for academic debate but for party diktat. A key witness like Palme Dutt, awkwardly Stalinist in his old age, was in 1971 forbidden by the party executive to make unauthorised disclosures about the past. Kenneth Newton, a 'bourgeois' sociologist not at all hostile to the CP, found some years earlier that party branches had been warned not to deal with him. Younger historians, Communist and non-Communist, prepared a more challenging set of essays in the late 1970s, but the project never saw the light of day. One of those involved put it down to 'Brezhnevite inertia'. The commemorative brochures that marked each passing decade were not much in the way of compensation.

A second irony is that, with the decline and disappearance of the Communist Party itself, the study of its history now seems to be in better shape than ever before. The reasons are not hard to fathom. Loyalties and anathemas are now eroded that once froze historians into rigid, unyielding postures. Mid-century certainties mean little to a more sceptical age and less than they did, perhaps, to a mellowing generation of veterans. With pride or bitterness, these older comrades put their story to a growing number of oral historians. Crucially, the main party archives are now accessible to anybody who wishes to see them. Records sent to Moscow in the inter-war years can now be examined

1

in the former party archives there. The British party's own archives, meanwhile, are now catalogued and have been deposited in the National Museum of Labour History. Old debates can at last be settled and new questions opened.

At the same time, as the study of modern British society advances, historians have brought to the twentieth century the sort of insights that CP historians tended to reserve for a more distant past. It is not surprising therefore that the history of the party itself has been enriched. The rebellion against constricting definitions of the political is reflected in the CP's historians' diminished interest in simply plotting the vagaries of the party line. The view of history from below poses questions as to the functioning of the party's authoritarian structures and the attempted construction of an all-encompassing Communist identity. Multiple allegiances obscured by institutional narratives are brought more fully into the open and the resulting complexities teased out. The different experiences of women and minority ethnic groups, so often marginalised or excluded, add insight to the diversity of the Communist experience. Cultural questions are central, freed of any glib reductionism or suggestion of superstructural froth. Labour historians explore more familiar territories but in profounder ways, eschewing facile generalisations for the specificities of gender, occupation, locality and ethnicity.

For some two decades these new emphases have been illuminating different aspects of the party's history, but not since the first wave of interest in Communist history in the late 1970s has there been any attempt to bring their exponents together. It was with this in mind that a weekend conference of historians of the CP was held in Manchester in January 1994. No particular body was identified with the event and its origins were informal. The organisers were hardly known to each other and, even had we thought a common programme desirable, we probably could not have agreed on one. Our aim in fact was quite modest: simply to provide a forum for recent work in the field that is critical, disinterested and free of any narrow partisanship. Veteran Communists were there to add the distinctive voice of their own experience, but the emphasis on this occasion was on interpretation and reconstruction rather than retrospection.

The thirteen chapters in this volume comprise half the papers given at the conference. The contributors are almost evenly divided between those first drawn to CP history in the 1970s, as Gramscianism, neo-syndicalism and second-wave feminism flourished, and those representing the revival of interest in less optimistic times. The emphasis in this book is on themes of social and cultural history which are often underplayed in stock representations of British Communism. Indigenous influences frequently predominate, but this does not imply any common depreciation by the contributors of the Soviet connections that have dominated so many accounts of the party's development. Most, indeed, would no doubt agree that another book will be needed on 'the CPGB and Moscow', the theme of the last history event organised by the party itself. But what, by the very choice of their subjects, all the contributors to this volume do assert is that the history of the British Communist Party cannot be *reduced* to any such relationship. That would involve not only a crude distortion of the party's own history, but the disregarding of the contribution that that history can make to the broader understanding of British society as a whole. Whether replicating or challenging that society's assumptions, or more often torn between the two, the very existence of a home-grown Communism poses a query as to some of the prevailing mythologies of modern Britain. It is not, perhaps, the identity of British Communism alone that is thrown into perspective by the essays that follow.

Kevin Morgan for the editors
London, August 1994

1 The Communists and the Colonies: Anti-imperialism between the Wars

John Callaghan

Formally, at least, socialist internationalism has always meant recognition of the common interests of the working class in the struggle against capitalism. Its champions demanded acts of solidarity in recognition of this commonality and envisaged concerted action across national frontiers the better to prosecute the cause of labour. Well before the Communist International (Comintern) was established in 1919 militants – such as, for example, some of the leaders of the British Chartist movement – had extended this logic of internationalism to embrace the struggles of peoples against colonialism. The distinctive contribution of Karl Marx to this question was the argument that the development of capitalism tended to homogenise the material conditions of the class struggle. From this it followed that an international organisation of the working-class movement was feasible as well as desirable. Communists saw no need to revise this judgement when national differences within European socialism became all too obvious in August 1914. Lenin attributed such divisions to imperialism and its corruption of a fraction of the working class. But in establishing the Comintern he relied on organisational measures to ensure that the new International's transnational directives on strategy and tactics would actually find implementation. In so doing he provided Communists with a simple proof of internationalism – their loyalty in words and deeds to the International's centralised command structure. In place of the imagined community of the nationalist, Communists belonged henceforth to the actual community of the International as well as the more abstract community of workers engaged in a common global struggle against capitalism. From the beginning it is fair to say that this loyalty to the Comintern was indistinguishable in the minds of most Communists from the instinctive loyalty which they felt for the Soviet Republic, the first workers' state headed, of course, by the intellectual leader of the Communist movement. Calculations concerning the appropriate international policy on any issue henceforth necessarily included this new

4

entity which must always remain, as far as Communists were concerned, the object of capitalist belligerence. Its 'unconditional defence' was therefore a matter of principle and urgency as well as a formal requirement of belonging to the new International. Furthermore since the main axis of conflict in world politics was said to pitch a small number of imperialist powers against the Soviet Republic it could be reasoned that no accurate balance of international class forces could be calculated which omitted to weigh its need for survival and development in the balance.

But if the survival of the Bolshevik Revolution depended on internationalism in these defensive forms, its prospects hinged more fundamentally on the offensive capabilities of the European working class. For not only was it threatened with military extinction or submission by starvation, thanks to the armed intervention and cordon sanitaire thrown around it; but, as the Bolsheviks repeatedly stressed, the prospects for socialism in economically backward Russia depended on a breakthrough in the West. Undoubtedly the Communist Party of Germany (KPD) carried the heaviest burden of immediate expectations in respect of the social revolution in Europe. But no section of the Comintern was more important than the tiny British party (CPGB) in the tasks of defending the Soviet Republic and promoting the anti-imperialist struggle. From the outset Soviet policy necessarily assumed the dual character of a struggle for world revolution and a struggle for survival. By 1919 it was clear that the latter involved a contest, first and foremost, with Great Britain, the largest imperialist power and the leader of the anti-Soviet coalition of capitalist states. It was obvious that a Bolshevik Germany would assist the Soviet state but it was already clear that any weakening of the British Empire was to be welcomed, in the meantime, on the same grounds.[1]

So many founding figures in the CPGB had been active in the Hands off Russia campaign since the summer of 1918 that their zeal for the defence of Lenin's state can hardly be doubted – it preceded any real familiarity with the principles of Bolshevism. What was less obvious was their capacity for anti-imperialist work: the Communist Unity Convention of 31 July–1 August 1920 had not even mentioned it. Tom Quelch of the British Socialist Party was frankly 'alarmed' by the idea that the British Communists would be required to help organise revolutionary movements in the British colonies and told the Second Congress of the Comintern that 'the average English worker would consider it treason'. Yet before the end of the congress the British delegation knew that they 'would be judged, not by their articles in favour of liberation, but by the numbers of them imprisoned for agitation in Ireland, Egypt or India'.[2] Four years later the Comintern complained that the party had done 'as good as nothing', that its attitude was 'passive' and that it had yet to declare 'unequivocally for the separation of the colonies from the British Empire'.[3]

Of course the four years in question were years when the International itself, let alone the tiny CPGB, was still finding its way. Leading individuals within the Comintern did not speak with one voice on colonial issues or through the same channel. Policies and lines of communication alike were in the process of formation. The British Communists were nevertheless well aware that they had much to prove as internationalists. Prominent socialists of the recent past, such as Robert Blatchford, H.M. Hyndman and the leading Fabians, had acquired reputations for chauvinism within the pre-1914 Second International, while reformism in the shape of the Labour Party was, *ipso facto*, tarred with the same brush. More to the point anti-imperialist agitation had yet to reach, much less attract support from, the bulk of politically active workers in Britain who remained in profound ignorance of virtually every aspect of Empire.[4] But among the British party's most energetic members were those with a strong commitment to put this right – notably R. Palme Dutt, W.N. Ewer, Robin Page Arnot and Emile Burns, all of whom served on the Labour Party's Advisory Committee on International Questions in the course of 1919 and dominated the Labour Research Department (LRD) in which Dutt also served as International Secretary until 1922.[5] From July 1921 Dutt edited the *Labour Monthly* which became the outstanding journal of the British left in its attention to imperialism, while Elinor and Emile Burns produced a succession of pamphlets from the LRD on East Africa, Malaya, China (all 1926), West Africa (1927), Egypt (1928) and the Leninist theory of imperialism (1927).

International questions were, of course, exceptionally salient in the wake of the Peace of Versailles when two versions of internationalism contended within the socialist movement. Woodrow Wilson's 'Fourteen Points' were widely seen as a crusade for democracy, the self-determination of nations, and the abolition of war. Much of the left was taken in.[6] The Communist movement, however, saw only an imperialist settlement and the seeds of future wars in the Versailles Treaty. The Comintern's propaganda focused on the hypocrisies of the peace and none was more obvious than the compatibility of the new League of Nations with the preservation and expansion of imperialism by its leading members. It should be remembered that in this battle of ideas

British Communists had to contend not only with the apologists of Empire but with the existing indigenous theories of imperialism, which like Hobson's focused on its domestic impact and its irrational roots in a psychology of jingoism, militarism and secret diplomacy. From the statements of the leaders of the Labour Party socialists might conclude that to support free trade was to be anti-imperialist; they would certainly have taken the existing international division of labour for granted and learned nothing about the nature of racism. Not the least measure of the CP's anti-imperialist impact, given this context, was its success in making Lenin's theory the common sense of much of the activist left by the late 1920s. When imperialism was understood as a structural consequence of monopoly capitalism it was not so easily conjured away by notions of 'trusteeship', the 'dual mandate' or 'colonial development' under a 'socialist inspiration'. As Pollitt's resolution before the TUC in 1925 insisted, 'the domination of the non-British peoples by the British Government' served the interests of 'capitalist exploitation'. It was a point repeatedly stressed – not least in argument with advocates of what Dutt called 'empire socialism' or the belief that a Labour government could keep the structure while 'moralising' the content of imperialism.

Britain's imperial dominion actually grew after the First World War via the acquisition of most of the former German colonies in the Middle East and in Africa. But of all its overseas possessions India remained by far the most important. The subcontinent was also of geopolitical significance to the Soviet Republic and was perceived as an 'Achilles' heel' of British imperialism in the light of the nationalist agitation which swept the country after the First World War. Obviously the prospects for building Communist parties in the colonies depended to a large extent on the existence of widespread anti-imperialist sentiment; tiny Communist cells could hardly be expected to conjure it into existence themselves. Given the almost complete absence of Communist organisation throughout the British Empire it thus made sense to focus energies where nationalist agitation had already bitten. The CPGB, moreover, could claim to possess a number of leaders with genuine expertise on Indian political economy, Clemens and Rajani Palme Dutt and Shapurji Saklatvala in particular. Indeed they had developed their own distinctive analysis of Indian political economy by 1921 to the effect that the subcontinent was embarked upon a phase of rapid industrialisation, accelerated during the war as a conscious act of British policy, with political compromise between the Indian and British capitalists inscribed at its heart. Although the advocates of this argument did not agree on every detail, all were convinced from the early 1920s that the supposed economic transformation opened up prospects for revolutionary work, rather than closed them, and strengthened the objective basis for solidarity between the workers of both countries.[7]

So it was with such expectations as these that British Communists took part in discussions in Berlin at the beginning of 1923 which led to the formation of an Indian Labour Bureau and a link to nascent trade unionism on the subcontinent. Saklatvala was prominent in the work of the bureau, a logical choice in view of his work since 1917 in the Workers' Welfare League of India (WWL) which campaigned in Britain for basic trade union rights and the protective regulation of working conditions on the subcontinent.[8] Under his secretaryship the WWL was to become the London agent of the the All-India Trade Union Congress (AITUC) from 1925. The party was also instructed to create an Oriental Seamen's Union in Britain in June 1923 on the orders of the Red International of Labour Unions (Profintern); apart from its obvious agitational functions in the London docks, such bodies – established throughout Europe in great ports such as Hamburg and Marseilles – formed a network of courier connections with Europe's colonies through which the Comintern's illegal publications could be smuggled. The Seamen's Union was later affiliated to the transport section of the Communist-sponsored Minority Movement.

As early as 1924 the CPGB was also making connections with Indian students' societies at Oxford and Cambridge universities, work which bore fruit in the 1930s in terms of recruitment. But the party's colonial work was already somewhat wider in scope than either India or the immediate priorities dictated by the Comintern's reading of the international situation, in which China figured prominently during the 1920s. Contact between the CPGB and Communist parties or revolutionary groups was established in 'most' of the colonies and Crown Dominions by 1924, according to the party executive.[9] Although this is undoubtedly an exaggeration, the effort to network the colonies was actually made and contact was registered by 1925 with Communists in Egypt, India, Palestine and China and with various revolutionary and trade union groups in Ireland.[10] James Crossley was sent to Egypt and Palestine in 1925 in connection with this work and helped to set up an Egyptian Communist Party. In the same year the party established its own Colonial Committee overseen by Clemens Dutt, with Hugo Rathbone, Dona Torr, Willie Gallacher and Walter Holmes involved in its work. Clemens Dutt also participated in the foreign bureau of the Communist Party of India (CPI), based in Berlin, where he worked alongside M.N. Roy – in the production of *Masses of India* – and Virendranath Chattopadhyaya. Meanwhile R. Palme Dutt represented the British party on the Comintern's Colonial Bureau in Paris from 1924 and Ralph Fox held responsibility for Indian work in Moscow from September 1925. The Labour Party's International Department, by contrast, did not employ a single permanent official to specialise on colonial affairs until 1949.

It was through this network of overseas organisations that steps were taken to promote a Communist Party in India. Roy actually declared its formation at Tashkent in 1920 but it was little more than a name for his immediate entourage. In 1924 the Fifth Congress of the Comintern insisted that 'very close contact' had to be established with the nationalists. This was against Roy's advice and his predilections for bypassing the nationalists altogether.[11] In reality small unconnected propaganda groups were all that existed on the Marxist left and further progress – massively exaggerated by Roy in any case – was nipped in the bud by the Cawnpore Conspiracy Case of April 1924. Indeed when Percy Glading reported the results of his 1925 reconnoitre of the Indian left he was adamant that there were no Communist groups operating in India.[12] Responsibility for establishing such groups and making connections with the nationalists now devolved to the CPGB. At a colonial conference held in Amsterdam in July 1925 the party reported that its Colonial Committee had created an 'East–West Circle' with a view to convening a conference of nationalists and socialists. Invitations had been sent to Indian nationalists and to radicals in Egypt, Syria, Palestine and Morocco. Though the forthcoming 'Oriental Conference' was dismissed as 'futile' by Roy, the project of bringing colonial nationalists and European socialists together was realised in Brussels in February 1927 under Willi Munzenburg's directing genius at the Congress of Oppressed Nationalities.[13]

The British party also understood that its colonial work involved a responsibility to get into the British colonies and conduct its work on the spot. The Amsterdam meeting heard that 'just as in the case of India, so also in the case of Egypt, Syria, and Palestine ... it is absolutely necessary for a representative of our Party to be in continual residence in these places'.[14] A number of emissaries attempted to live up to these expectations. Guy Horniman and George Allison were deported from India before Philip Spratt and Ben Bradley established themselves there in 1927 to begin trade union work and the construction of a Workers' and Peasants' Party as a legal cover for the Communist movement.[15] By the time they were joined by Lester Hutchinson in September

1928 they had transformed the nominal CPI from a directionless group of 15–20 members to an effective force in the unions. Saklatvala's much-publicised tour of the country in 1927, and his argument with Congress leaders over the need to adopt a programme of demands tailored to the interests of the workers and peasants, could only have helped them. The party now had a presence inside the Indian National Congress, dominated the leadership of the AITUC and held a strong base in the textile unions of Bombay where 71 mills were closed down in the six-month-long strike of 1928. The Indian Communists could also claim a presence in the jute mills and paper mills of Bombay, among the railway workers – Bradley was vice-president of the Indian Railways Union – and in the Madras branch of the Burma Oil Company. By the end of 1928 Workers' and Peasants' Parties had been established in Delhi, Meerut, Gorakhpur, Jhansi and Allahabad and the time had arrived to place them on an all-India footing.

What the Communists could do in the colonies depended on a variety of factors. The two that stand out most clearly are the level of development of local politics and the policies of the Comintern. Most of black Africa, for example, was exceptionally difficult to penetrate politically between the world wars because economic development had given rise to neither a nationalist nor a class movement on any appreciable scale. Of course this did not prevent Communists from associating themselves with the cause of Africa – in publicising the general strike in Nigeria in December 1929, for example, or the construction by forced labour of the Congo–Ocean Railroad in French Equatorial Africa during which 20,000 labourers reportedly died before the workforce embarked on a general uprising in 1928. But while the Communist Party of France was able to make some progress in relation to West Africa – assisted by the fact that Paris was an important centre of African pressure groups – the CPGB was unable to emulate it. There was no equivalent in London of groups such as Tovalou Houenou's Paris-based *Ligue universelle pour la défense de la race noir* and its Communist-oriented successors, though the formation of the West African Students' Union in 1925 was a step, albeit a conservative one, in this direction. Communists had to form their own organisations and use whatever else was available; for example, Saklatvala, Walton Newbold, MacManus and Gallacher were remembered by Claude McKay as speakers at the International Club in London where he learned about Marxism. After a British branch of the League Against Imperialism (LAI) was formally established in June 1928, important work of propaganda and lobbying in relation to African colonies was undertaken. The point remains, however, that outside of South Africa and the Maghreb the circumstances were not conducive to party work and Paris eclipsed London as a centre for Pan-African agitation in the 1920s.[16]

But where nationalism was aroused – as in India – the question was what to do with it and the answer was far from straightforward. The abrupt changes of Comintern tactics have naturally attracted most attention as the biggest limitation imposed by policy on Communist colonial work. But this should not be allowed to imply that a clear-cut colonial policy was ready to hand if only principle had triumphed over Soviet foreign policy. In reality there was plenty of scope for different estimations of the relationship between colonial nationalism and the Comintern's ultimate goals, which included the defence of the Soviet Republic as well as socialist revolution. Different estimations of such issues surfaced in the first Comintern debate on the colonial question in 1920. Then there was the related question of the level and pace of economic development in the colonies – a question on which the British Communists held a distinctive view in relation to India and on which they were defeated at the sixth congress of the Comintern in 1928. This in turn raised questions about the economic and class relationships between the colonial power and the nationalist movement and the balance of class forces within the nationalist movement itself. Finally there was the vexed question of the tactics to be derived from all of this and the extent to which a single tactical line could be appropriate throughout the colonial world. When Philip Spratt received his briefing for India, for example, the prospect put before him was emulation of Communist tactics in China[17] – an orientation that almost extinguished the Chinese Communists twelve months later but which had been initially successful as a springboard for the party in Indonesia where the 'bloc within' was first fashioned.[18]

Until 1928, however, Communist colonial policy broadly encouraged a close working relationship with the nationalists. The prevailing perspective was summed up by Munzenburg's League Against Colonial Oppression, which was launched in Berlin at the beginning of 1926 as 'a vast … grouping of all the anti-imperialist forces in the colonies and in the leading colonising countries'. Its British section was organised by Reginald Bridgeman, a former official of the diplomatic service, but in common with its French counterpart it never got beyond the committee stage.[19] The league was effectively relaunched in February 1927 after the Brussels Congress of Oppressed Nationalities which fulfilled the ambitions of the British party's 'East–West Circle' in bringing colonial nationalists together with European socialists and Communists. Appropriately enough one of the largest European delegations at the Brussels congress was the British, with Fenner Brockway, Ellen Wilkinson, Raymond Postgate and John Beckett MP among the non-Communist members of the contingent. But more important was the success, as Brockway recalled, of establishing the first international coordination of anti-imperialist forces by bringing together 'nearly all the known leaders in Asia and Africa' including Jawaharlal Nehru, Mohammed Hatta of Indonesia's Saraket Islam, representatives from the African National Congress, from French North Africa, from Indo-China, French Antilles, Egypt, Syria, Palestine, Persia, Korea and China.[20]

In the manifesto issued by the Brussels congress – *Against Imperialism: For National Liberation* – the Soviet Republic featured as an 'historical example of the free union of nations and races constructed on the ruins of imperialism' and as 'the guiding star' of the anti-colonial movements throughout the world. One of the enduring attractions of the Bolshevik state among subject peoples was the belief that it was based on racial equality and that it had demonstrated in practice that it was possible to overcome economic backwardness – Soviet Central Asia was often cited in support of this view – once racism and imperialism were eliminated. Needless to say Soviet propaganda assiduously promoted this image of multiracial equality but so too did leading black political activists such as Paul Robeson and George Padmore – the latter continuing to do so even after his break with the Communist movement and drawing further credibility from his long residence inside the Soviet Union. There seems little reason to doubt that such views were held sincerely; they were certainly taken for granted inside the Communist parties. It is hard to believe, in the light of this, that the political culture of the Communist Party was unaffected by the constant trumpeting of the Soviet Union as a land of race equality and harmony of national minorities. Communists, moreover, were conscious of belonging to a world party composed of many different nationalities. The party press, which formally reserved a relatively large proportion of its space for international and colonial affairs, constantly regaled its readers with Soviet success stories in the development of the previously backward corners of the Tsarist Empire. They were at least as frequently reminded of the hardships and struggles of their comrades abroad in the fight against imperialism in China or Indonesia or India. This does not mean that the Communist parties were free of racism – the example of the Communist Party of the USA (CPUSA) is enough to dispel that illusion. But Communists were required to combat racism, as again the example of the CPUSA attests; and even under conditions of tremendous repression

– as in South Africa – the Communist movement stood unwaveringly for racial equality. In Britain, where black Communists could be counted on one hand in the 1920s, the party was never really put to the test on the issue of race equality within its own ranks, though there were of course leading party members of Jewish or Indian background. But it can certainly be said that the ordinary member was more aware of the international dimensions of the struggle for socialism than his or her counterpart in any of the other organisations of the working class.

In 1927 the League Against Imperialism was born at the Brussels congress – tactics at this stage being informed by the 'united front' which in Otto Kuusinen's phrase involved the creation of an organisational 'solar system' with the party at its centre.[21] Nehru, a convert at the congress to Lenin's theory of imperialism, persuaded the Indian National Congress to affiliate. Non-European branches were also established in Brazil, South Africa, Cuba, Nicaragua, Mexico and Argentina. The British section was set up provisionally in April 1927 with Bridgeman as its secretary. The LAI immediately incurred the wrath of imperial governments and the Labour and Socialist International (LSI). Its literature was banned in India, its leaders imprisoned by colonial governments and denounced as Communist stooges by the LSI. It was all the more embarrassing to the LSI because socialists like Lansbury were associated with the league while Brockway and Maxton of the Independent Labour Party (ILP) served on its executive. Indeed when the LSI decided to boycott the league the ILP was the only affiliated organisation which continued to allow its members to participate on an individual basis[22] and Maxton actually presided over its Frankfurt congress in July 1929. By this time, however, the league was obliged to adopt the sectarian 'Class Against Class' analysis unveiled the previous year by the sixth congress of the Comintern, and former allies from the non-Communist left – including the likes of Nehru – were driven out. There can be no doubt that the league was reduced, by the end of 1929, to its Communist membership apart from the few, like Bridgeman, who held no party card but faithfully supported its politics. Any serious estimation of the LAI's work has to take account of this and the fact that party membership fell to as little as 2,555 by 1931.

Africa and the 'Negro Question' had been one of the themes discussed at Brussels but the second world congress of the LAI at Frankfurt in July 1929 gave these issues a new prominence, as did the decision to organise an International Congress of Negro Workers involving such black militants as George Padmore, Jomo Kenyatta, Frank Macauley of the Nigerian Workers' Party, I.T.A. Wallace-Johnson of Sierra Leone and E.F. Small representing Gambia's labour unions. The congress was scheduled to convene in London – *Labour Monthly* announced it in June 1930 – but was forced to turn to Hamburg when the Labour government banned it. It was dominated by black Americans and delegates from Communist organisations such as the Paris-based *Ligue universelle pour la défense de la race noir*, but it could also claim delegates from the Caribbean, Nigeria, Sierra Leone, the Gold Coast, Gambia and South Africa. The guiding hand here was the International Trade Union Committee–Negro Workers (ITUC–NW) which the Profintern had established in 1928, along with the journal *Negro Worker*. Of course the black activists involved had to work with their comrades in Britain – Padmore's job was in any case to coordinate the whole initiative. But it is also true that when Kenyatta became the representative of the Kikuyu Central Association in London in 1929 it was the British section of the League Against Imperialism to which he turned for political and financial assistance.[23] Padmore and Kenyatta also contributed articles to *Labour Monthly* from June 1930 covering such issues as 'the revolt in Haiti', 'British Finance Capitalism in West Africa', 'Forced Labour in Africa', 'Labour Imperialism in East Africa', 'Left Imperialism and the Negro Toilers' and 'Hands Off Abyssinia'.

The Profintern's central direction of this initiative accounts for the attention given to the exploitation of black workers by the Minority Movement in Britain in 1931 and the appearance of a pamphlet by Palme Dutt – *Free the Colonies* – which tried to advance the demand for a workers' charter for Africa. Padmore's *The Life and Struggles of Negro Toilers* (1932) was also published under its auspices. The annual conference of the British section of the LAI in 1931 reflected the new emphases with its discussions of colonialism in relation to black workers in Britain as well as in Africa. Much of the LAI's work involved lobbying Parliament – on behalf of the Kikuyu Central Association, for example, and on the question of land rights in East Africa – and providing detailed questions and information to sympathetic MPs. Another example is the campaign waged during 1934–6 for constitutional reform in the Gold Coast on behalf of the Aborigines Rights Protection Society founded by the Gold Coast lawyer Kobina Sekyi, one of Padmore's contacts. The league also established the Negro Welfare Association in 1932 with the ubiquitous Bridgeman as chairman. The LAI published its own *Anti-Imperialist Review* and distributed journals produced by the other national sections such as the *Indian Front*, *Zipnima*, the Cypriot monthly, *L'Orient Araba*, *Emancipation* (which was printed in Chinese), as well as the English-language monthly review of the Chinese struggle *China News*. The British section acquired the reputation of being one of the most active divisions of the organisation and despite what he described as the very unfavourable circumstances in which it operated Padmore many years later was able to refer to its 'excellent work of enlightenment'.[24] No doubt this was all very rudimentary but it could not be otherwise; in December 1928 *Negro Worker* – with its grandiose design of drawing black workers everywhere 'into revolutionary class struggle' – was still forced to appeal for contacts in West, Central and East Africa 'for the purpose of linking up the workers there with the South African centre'.[25] In other words, as we have already observed, the only functioning Communist party south of the Sahara was in the Republic of South Africa.

It can be no surprise, therefore, that China and India occupied the bulk of the LAI's work. It campaigned for trade union rights on the sub-continent and exposed the TUC's inaction in this area – a matter of some embarrassment given that Walter Citrine was chairman of the International Federation of Trade Unions at the time when the AITUC was applying for membership. It also campaigned for the removal of British troops from China and against Japanese imperialism, and it publicised the trial of the Meerut prisoners and lobbied the TUC through the Meerut Prisoners' Defence Committee. Again Citrine was rattled. The Meerut defendants – 31 of them, including Spratt and Bradley – were accused of seeking to 'deprive the King-Emperor of his sovereignty of India' because of their temerity in organising and campaigning for the economic and social rights of Indian workers. The trial dragged on for nearly four years – much of it during the second Labour government – and finally resulted in exemplary sentences; twelve years transportation for Spratt and ten years for Bradley. Long afterwards the National Council of Labour admitted that the prosecutions had been 'indefensible'. But throughout the proceedings it had been the LAI and Communist Party which had continually brought the case before the Labour and trade union conferences. In the general elections of 1929 and 1931 the party even ran one of the Meerut prisoners – Shaukat Usmani – as its candidate. Usmani received but a few hundred votes, in Spen Valley, but the protracted Meerut campaign undoubtedly caused consternation at the highest levels of the Labour Party and TUC.[26]

It is impossible to know how effective such work was in disabusing activists of any illusions they may have had concerning the British Empire. What can certainly be said is that the party provided information which the already-sceptical among the members of the Labour Party and trade unions would not obtain from their own organisations.

Subhas Bose was right when he said in 1933 that 'the more one lives in Europe, the more one realises the great want of propaganda on behalf of India'; and what was true of India was true of all the other European dependencies. Given the prevailing climate of ignorance and indifference the Communists had their work cut out simply in pressing the issue of colonialism before audiences of organised labour.

But the LAI was particularly assiduous in exposing the realities behind the image of a benign imperium. It promoted 'workers' theatres' which focused on conditions in the colonies, created a youth section, sponsored an international students' conference, targeted colonial students in Britain, published pamphlets and set up debates and study circles. Its Negro Welfare Association worked with Harold Moody's League of Coloured Peoples in community politics in London and in the organisation of black seamen in the Cardiff docks. The latter brought it into collision with the National Union of Seamen in 1933 when the union supported discrimination against the employment of black seamen. It campaigned to expose racism in the US, especially in connection with the Scottsboro boys[27] on whose behalf it formed a defence committee in 1933. This was the year when the LAI was forced to abandon its Berlin headquarters and move to London, where Bridgeman orchestrated its work on issues relating to India, China, Palestine, Afghanistan and, of course, the fascist invasion of Abyssinia. In 1934–5 the league did what it could to publicise and oppose repressive legislation in the Gold Coast where civil liberties and the freedom of the press had been curtailed by the governor. The league's work continued until 1937 when it was replaced by a Colonial Information Bureau. It was folded, according to Ben Bradley, because its work had been 'seriously hampered' by the hostility of official Labour. As a proscribed organisation, reduced to 'a small group of people interested in the colonial struggle', in Bradley's words, the LAI, like the party itself, had been impeded by the sectarianism of the Communist movement since 1928. With the inauguration of the Popular Front policy in 1935 the banned organisation was to be liquidated in the interests, so it was claimed, of bringing colonial politics before a wider working-class movement.

The decision to disband the ITUCNW in August 1933, followed by the Soviet Union's entry into the League of Nations in 1934 and the gradual shift in Comintern policy towards the campaign for collective security against fascism and war, led some leading black activists to leave the Communist movement with a sense that the anti-imperialist cause had been betrayed. Lack of progress in colonial matters under a Popular

Front government in France and allegations of continued Soviet trade with Italy after the invasion of Abyssinia in 1935 strengthened these suspicions, as did the failure of the Spanish Popular Front to liberate the Spanish colonies. What was certainly true was that anti-fascism eclipsed anti-colonialism at the highest levels of the Comintern and the CPGB was left to its own devices in relation to the colonies. Padmore and Kenyatta turned their attention to Pan-Africanism, establishing the International African Friends of Abyssinia in London. The LAI supported the new organisation financially, however, and cooperated with the India League and the Pan-African Federation during the 'Unity Campaign's' peak year of 1936–7. For all their espousal of Pan-Africanism as against Communism, Marxist reasoning remained dominant within this group up to and including the fifth Pan-African Congress of 1945 and Padmore for one continued to think in terms of Comintern categories.

The real context of the party's anti-colonialism between the wars is better gauged when it is remembered that 'almost all British writers in this period believed that social and economic advance [in the colonies] must precede political independence'; indeed the most influential among them, Sir Frederick Lugard, argued within the framework of social Darwinist notions of racial hierarchy.[28] The dominant Eurocentric assumptions of social evolution and racial hierarchy also permeated the Labour Party leadership, as did the equation made between British national interests and the preservation of Empire which was the real basis for talk of 'the dual mandate' and watered-down notions of 'trusteeship'. In 1923 Philip Snowden had given voice to the prevalent realism when he declared: 'the British Empire is a fact ... and having incurred the responsibility, we cannot lightly cast it off; indeed, we cannot cast it off at all.'[29] Labour had talked of 'the moral claims upon us of the non-adult races' in its election manifesto of 1918; 40 years later the paternalism of its colonial experts was more guarded but it is remarkable that on the eve of the formal Empire's rapid dismantling Rita Hinden, secretary of the Fabian Colonial Bureau, still believed that the end of colonial poverty 'may be sooner cured by *prolonging* imperial rule' while Arthur Creech Jones opined, in defence of delaying independence, that 'the extension of political freedom is an indifferent objective if the economic basis for the operation of that freedom is not properly laid'.[30]

Against these conventional wisdoms the Communists insisted that political independence was the only basis upon which economic independence could possibly be founded - a case which included the territories of sub-Saharan Africa. The Communists maintained that it was part of the imperialist rationale to stress the inherent backwardness of

African peoples and that it was a mark of the political backwardness of British labour that it believed it. They had argued in the 1920s and 1930s that what was required from those who really cared about this issue was a concerted campaign to promote the social, economic and political rights of Africans. Imperialism, they insisted, arrested the development of the colonies while proclaiming that their independence depended on economic advance. The hypocrisy of imperialism was evident. Land reform, a free press, trade union rights, access to education: these were all eminently feasible reforms yet they elicited little enthusiasm among the defenders of Empire – the very people who were content to say that freedom for Africans would only produce chaos. The Communists argued that freedom was a historical process and

> in this process what appear to be insuperable barriers between different nationalities, religions and languages which militate against the growth of solidarity necessary not only to gain independence but to organise the independent state will be found to have been broken down.[31]

The problem – contrary to official propaganda – was that the colonial authorities were not preparing Africans for self-government but rather placing obstacles in their path.

But the problem for the Communists is also evident; in the absence of strong, indigenous campaigns for independence they were reduced to the propaganda and lobbying activities already described. It cannot be said that this propaganda was always consistent, let alone that it addressed the full complexities of colonialism. The party's colonial work reflected certain priorities – first and foremost of which was the agenda set by the Comintern. From its inception the Communist movement had made a virtue of its monolithicity in action. By degrees, however, the Comintern increasingly reflected Soviet state interests. To make matters worse, the latter were construed according to the dictates of a brutal and unstable faction of the Communist Party of the Soviet Union. The wild swings in Comintern policy of 1928 are inexplicable without reference to Stalin's domestic preoccupations. But there were, none the less, certain continuities. One dominant consideration was the maturity of the anti-colonial struggle in any given dependency. Thus the attention given to India was determined by the scale of the nation-alist movement there, which in turn affected the scope for building the party and weakening the British ruling class both economically and strate-gically. The subcontinent was also a subject, as we have seen, on which certain party members could claim expertise, though this was to some extent a function of its prolonged centrality in British anti-colonial politics. For all these reasons India was the subject of 36 articles in *Labour Monthly* in the years 1928–35, while the whole of Africa occupied only 16. In the same period, however, the journal found space for an additional 37 essays on other colonial territories and issues. After the Popular Front turn, the twin themes of fascism and war preoccupied Dutt's journal; but while no less than 60 articles were published on these subjects in the years 1936–9, in the same period over 40 articles focused on colonial issues – with India once again dominant.

Indeed the party's agitation for complete independence for India continued unabated as the Second World War approached. There was, after all, no Popular Front government in Britain and no earthly reason for restraint. Indeed, in Communist invectives the National government appeared time and again as the main fascist threat in Britain. Almost everything it did was interpreted in this light. Not surprisingly then the CPGB campaigned for a complete boycott of the 1935 constitution for which the Simon Commission had paved the way in India. It agitated for the affiliation of workers' and peasants' organisations to Congress; and for the adoption by Congress of a radical social and economic programme to serve these interests. Palme Dutt also privately advised Nehru in 1936 on the need for an agrarian revolution which, if sufficiently broadbased and supported by workers' struggles in the towns, would represent 'the decisive force which would swamp British rule and sweep it away'.[32] There was no suggestion that the quest for collective security affected the vigour with which Indian independence should be pursued. In Britain itself party leaders were prominent in the series of Indian political conferences staged to promote the cause. They spoke on the same platforms as visiting nationalists such as Nehru and Bose throughout the 1930s – many of whom could see, of course, that their own cause was indissolubly connected to the defeat of fascism. Certainly Communist influence among Indian students in Britain had never been stronger – according to British intelligence the London branch of the Indian National Congress was 'completely under the influence of Saklatvala' and the League Against Imperialism by the end of the 1920s.[33] So was the University Students Group which Saklatvala helped to set up in the summer of 1931; and from 1930 the party worked so closely with the India League, under V.K. Krishna Menon's management, that Krishna Menon was himself regarded as a Communist,[34] though this did not prevent the league's parliamentary committee growing from just 30 MPs in the mid-1930s to almost 100 by 1945.[35]

By this time the days of British rule in India were numbered. But while the Communists had likened British wartime policy in India to one of the worst military fiascos of the period, the realists in Cabinet still toyed with the idea of undermining the nationalists with post-war schemes for the economic development of the subcontinent under British auspices. Though a non-starter if ever there was one, such hopes lingered on into the peace – a final testament perhaps to the decisive role of the extra-parliamentary forces in finally bringing about Indian independence. The swing of international opinion against imperialism nevertheless failed to dislodge it elsewhere and in the conditions of the Cold War a new round of battles commenced, on a bloodier basis and with the odds even more firmly stacked against internationalism.

Notes

1. It was for this reason that Bukharin, at the eighth congress of the Russian Communist Party in 1918, urged the delegates to support 'the most outright nationalist movement' if it 'contributes to the destruction of English imperialism'. See J. Degras (ed.), *Documents of the Communist International, 1919–1943*, vol. 1, 1919–22 (Cass, 1971), p. 139.
2. Ibid., p. 139; Quelch is quoted in S. MacIntyre, 'Imperialism and the British Labour movement in the 1920s', *Our History*, 64, Autumn 1975.
3. See E.T. Wilson, *Russia and Black Africa Before World War Two* (Holmes & Meier, New York, 1974), p. 140.
4. P. Fryer, *Black People in the British Empire* (Pluto Press, 1988), p. 55.
5. See the minutes and agendas of the Labour Party Advisory Committee on International Questions in Labour Party Archives, National Museum of Labour History.
6. A.J. Mayer, *Political Origins of the New Diplomacy* (Yale University Press, New Haven, Conn., 1959) p. 25.
7. S. Saklatvala, 'India in the Labour world', *LM*, November 1921, pp. 400–51; R. Palme Dutt, *Modern India* (CPGB, 1926).
8. M. Squires, *Saklatvala* (Lawrence & Wishart, 1990), p. 147.
9. Central Executive Committee *Report* to CPGB sixth congress, May 1924, p. 24.
10. J. Klugmann, *History of the Communist Party of Great Britain*, vol. 1 (Lawrence & Wishart, 1969), p. 136.

11. J.P. Haithcox, *Communism and Nationalism in India* (Princeton University Press, New Jersey, 1971), p. 39.
12. HMSO, *Communist Papers*, Cmd. 2682, 1926, pp. 83–4.
13. Ibid., pp. 85, 101.
14. Ibid., p. 97.
15. S.R. Chowdhuri, *Leftist Movements in India 1917–1947* (South Asian Books, Calcutta, 1976), p. 17.
16. On pan-Africanism see P.O. Esedebe, 'A history of the Pan-African movement in Great Britain 1900–1948' (University of London, PhD, 1968) and J.A. Langley, 'West African aspects of the Pan-African movements 1900–1945' (University of Edinburgh PhD, 1968). The best published account is I. Geiss, *The Pan-African Movement* (Methuen, 1974).
17. J.P. Haithcox, *Communism and Nationalism,* pp. 56–7.
18. R.T. McVey, *The Rise of Indonesian Communism* (Cornell University Press, New York, 1965), pp. xiii and 82.
19. See A.J. Mackenzie, 'British Marxists and the Empire: anti-imperialist theory and practice' (University of London, PhD, 1978), p. 44.
20. F. Brockway, *The Colonial Revolution* (Hart-Davis, 1973), p. 35.
21. See J. Jones, *The League Against Imperialism* (Socialist History Society, forthcoming).
22. *International Information*, 20 July 1929.
23. H. Tinker, *Men Who Overturned Empires* (Macmillan, 1987), p. 219.
24. G. Padmore, *Pan-Africanism or Communism?* (Dobson, 1956), pp. 328–9.
25. *Negro Worker*, December 1928, p. 2.
26. See A.J. Williams, *Labour and Russia* (Manchester University Press, 1989), p. 83.
27. The nine defendants were accused of rape in 1931.
28. P. Hetherington, *British Paternalism and Africa 1920–1940* (Cass, 1978), pp. 4–5.
29. Quoted in J. Saville, 'Britain: internationalism and the Labour movement between the wars' in F. Van Holtoon and M. Van Der Linden (eds), *Internationalism in the Labour Movement 1830–1940* (E.J. Brill, Leiden, 1988), p. 570.
30. R. Hinden, 'Socialism and the colonial world' and A. Creech Jones, 'The Labour party and colonial policy 1945–51' in A. Creech Jones (ed.), *New Fabian Colonial Essays* (Hogarth Press, 1959), pp. 13 and 25.

31. H. Rathbone, 'The problem of African independence', *LM*, March
    1936, p. 166.
32. See J. Callaghan, *Rajani Palme Dutt: A Study in British Stalinism*
    (Lawrence & Wishart, 1983), p. 158.
33. A.J. Mackenzie, 'British Marxists and the Empire', p. 136.
34. K. Vijay, 'British Opinion and Indian independence' (University
    of London, MPhil, 1970), p. 285.
35. Ibid., p. 288.

Further Reading

Documentary material relating to the League Against Imperialism can
be found at the International Institute for Social History, Amsterdam:
among the Reginald Bridgeman papers at the Brynmor Jones Library,
University of Hull; in the Labour Party archive (National Museum of
Labour History) in the file on 'Ancillary Organisations of the Communist
International', ref. 10/CI/36/5vi. Six copies of *Anti-Imperialist Review*
are held at the Working Class Movement Library in Salford where there
is also a file of papers concerning R. Palme Dutt. Most of Dutt's papers
are housed in the British Library and in the Communist Party archive.

2 'Divisions in the Movement': the National Unemployed Workers' Movement and its Rivals in Comparative Perspective

Richard Croucher

This chapter deals with questions of division and unity, uniformity and diversity in organisations of the unemployed in Britain between the wars. Its first purpose is to reassert that there was more than one such organisation. British labour historians have largely focused on the history of the principal one: the Communist-led National Unemployed Workers' Movement (NUWM). The NUWM led a continuous agitation against unemployment and its effects which spanned the inter-war years. Its tenacious and often effective action on local and national levels give it prominence among British and indeed world unemployed movements.[1] Yet even if our aim was to be limited to understanding the nature of the NUWM, some serious consideration of alternative organisations would be required. There is a sense in which British unemployed organisations shared certain characteristics, and therefore it is relevant to look at the whole range rather than at one particular case. In fact our aims ought to be wider to encompass an understanding of the nature of all unemployed bodies, as important non-trade union developments within the working class.

My first aim, then, is to assert historical diversity. I begin by looking at the nature and origins of the historiography, and then sketch a wider picture of the history. An ultimate aim should be for labour historians to reconstruct a still wider picture, which would include the history of such organisations as the National Council for Social Services (whose local centres were often an important attraction for the unemployed in the 1930s) and the churches. However, we do not examine the history of non-labour movement bodies here. The NUWM had two types of rival within the labour movement at the local level: bodies linked to the TUC through trades councils (probably the larger grouping, comprising 52 associations in 1935)[2] and those that were not. The second category has not been researched adequately, but was almost certainly smaller than the TUC affiliates. They tended to have important representative, social and 'collective self-help' activities and frequently had ex-servicemen as activists. Although this chapter takes a brief excursion to look at the nature of one of these local bodies, I concentrate on giving an account of the local origins of the TUC's unemployed associations, the NUWM's principal rival.

My second purpose is to examine the different aims and characteristics of the NUWM and the TUC affiliates. In the process, it is hoped that relevant questions will be raised in connection with the concept of 'divisions' in the working-class movement.

It will be argued that the existing historical writing has tended itself to reflect the historical division between Communist and 'reformist' unemployed organisations. This position is not felt to be helpful for two reasons: first, it has concealed an element of complementarity between the different types of organisation in terms of their usefulness to the unemployed, and second it has tended to suppress the extent to which the NUWM itself was like the other bodies in its approach to the daily existential needs of the workless and their families.

The historiographical tradition ought briefly to be described. The discussion has two types of argument. The first has important insights to offer in describing the position of the majority of the unemployed. It suggests that in this period the unemployed were apathetic in that they sought individual solutions to their collective problems. Stressing the misery of people's positions, historians describe such collective activity as there was as being supplicant, requesting and petitioning. It is sometimes allowed that 'self-help' activity occurred, but this is generally portrayed as being individual rather than collective. The assertion of the dignity and integrity of the unemployed in response to the negative images projected on to them is identified as the principal focus of collective activity. This could be called the 'Jarrow Crusade' school, but such assumptions underlie some descriptions of the hunger marches run by the NUWM.[3] The other strand focuses more on the NUWM as an organisation making demands on government and the Labour movement. This strand has made a useful contribution in establishing that there was a range of collective activity by the unemployed which went beyond the supplicant. More recent historians in this strand have analysed the origins of the various forms of protest.[4]

This slow and underdeveloped discussion has obscured much activity which was neither protest nor supplication. More importantly for our purposes here, it has focused attention on the NUWM on the one hand and the Jarrow Town Council and Ellen Wilkinson on the other. The

problem of division has consequently largely been viewed from the perspective of a mid-1930s Communist Party of Great Britain (CPGB)
desperate to achieve 'unity' and overcome division within the working-
class movement. This desperation had not always existed. But my central
point here is that this 'maximum unity' (of the employed and
unemployed, of the different organisations of unemployed, in fact of the
'widest forces') is very much a CPGB view of the political requirements.
There were others which need to be recognised.

If the history of unemployed organisation had been approached on
an *international comparative* level, then important questions would immediately have been raised about the nature of unemployed movements.
For example, if a comparison with the German case had been seen as
relevant, then the issue of 'division' might have been approached more
rigorously, given the historical consensus around the importance of the
political divisions on the left in Germany in allowing the Nazi seizure
of power in 1933.[5] If a comparison with the US had been used, then
'self-help' would have been examined more closely given the great extent
of self-help organisations in America.[6] This is the generally important
issue of the rather ironically national focus of labour historians.

Returning more directly to our theme, one must recognise that
unemployed organisation did not begin with the NUWM. There was
a tradition of unemployed agitation going back to the 1880s and
beyond, and this re-emerged immediately after the First World War.
The Social Democratic Federation, the pre-war 'Right to Work'
movement, the Labour Party (especially in London) and Sylvia
Pankhurst's Workers Socialist Federation all had a part in building this
tradition. After the war many ex-servicemen's organisations sprang up
and these were at local level either closely linked with groups of
unemployed or themselves contained such groups prior to the formation
of the NUWM in 1920. Some continued to operate after the NUWM
was formed. These groupings were described by Wal Hannington, the
leader and first historian of the NUWM, as basically begging bodies
which derived a militant perspective from the NUWM.[7] Some of the
evidence allows a slightly different view. They often *combined* the
'demanding' and 'practical support' perspectives, sometimes linked
with the use of ex-service networks through officers and the newly
formed British Legion. There was, then, an association with 'unacceptable' attitudes and people as far as the left was concerned. They could
be of little interest to labour historians.

Yet militancy and ex-servicemen's organisations were no strangers.
At the end of the war, the Discharged and Demobilized Soldiers and

Sailors Association was described by the Home Secretary as 'insistent on its demands and most aggressive' [8] and this was typical of a number of similar remarks. Nor were other unemployed groupings necessarily 'begging' or 'campaigning'. In Coventry, for a short time in the summer of 1921, a non-NUWM body appeared as a competitor. Led by the Reverend J.J. Armitage, the Church's Industrial Messenger (a fanatical anti-Communist), this grouping called for more relief, no eviction for rent arrears, priority in job allocation to Coventry residents, soup kitchens and rabbits from the local gentry. Armitage organised marches and meetings in the early 1920s. [9] Such evidence tends to suggest that neither the ex-servicemen's movements, nor the other unemployed groupings, were all quite as Hannington depicted them. At the time the movement's own newspaper described the unemployed prior to the NUWM as 'whining, mimping groups, totally un-class conscious, and material for blacklegging'. [10] Yet Hannington's own account of the formation of the NUWM acknowledges that it was in part a work of coordination of existing groups, an enterprise only possible within a certain shared set of aims. Our main point here is not to describe the nature of a wide range of unemployed committees, but simply to point out that the NUWM was built from a previous base. It was a base which the NUWM later described in an unflattering way, but which did bring with it a certain heritage of its own. The task for the new movement was to attempt to justify its national title, and to establish some hegemony as *the* organisation of the unemployed, and these were two reasons for the NUWM's own rapid reinterpretation of history.

The movement's key strength in building itself was also its main weakness. The support of the CPGB meant that a national network of politically conscious working-class militants was available as a framework. In fact it is questionable whether without this skeleton it would have been possible to sustain the NUWM, given the unfavourable position of its constituents. But the support of the CPGB increasingly meant that the mainstream of the labour movement kept their distance. There was a point in 1923 when the TUC established a joint committee with the NUWM, but the TUC had become a reluctant partner long before the committee's formal dissolution in 1928. This division meant that the Labour Party from 1923 and the TUC from 1928 made efforts to develop their own unemployed organisations. At local level, there were others – sometimes explicitly politically motivated like anarchist Henry Georgeites and the followers of Sylvia Pankhurst – sometimes not, like Harry Goldthorpe of Leeds, who had some success in building local organisations.[11]

There were a number of town-based organisations of the workless between the wars in Britain. They could certainly be numbered in tens, although a comprehensive survey to reach a more exact figure would be welcome. Why did they exist on this scale? First, it was because systems of relief and charity were administered at local level. Until the 1930s, the national system of relief was regulated by local boards of guardians, elected by ratepayers. Even during the 1930s, when the guardians had been abolished, the Public Assistance Committee (PAC) was still organised regionally. In addition, church and municipal authorities still retained considerable functions in relevant matters such as charity, public health, transport, public works and so on. Because unemployment was concentrated in the industrial regions it was often seen as a local problem, and government policy in terms of resettlement encouraged this view.[12] Second, the workless themselves related more easily to a local than a national body. Transport was difficult: not everyone was prepared to walk or cycle hundreds of miles to attend meetings of the NUWM's national bodies, as some people incredibly did in the early 1920s. Access to telephones was also difficult. The question could therefore be reversed, and one could ask the rhetorical question (since we do not intend to pursue it seriously): how could one build a *national* movement under these conditions?

Seen from the point of view of the leadership of the NUWM, this was a real question both internally and externally: internally because there were difficulties in maintaining contacts with branches and drawing them into national activities, and externally because non-CPGB forces were often interested in trying to bring together local unemployed groups to compete with the NUWM on a national scale. Sylvia Pankhurst attempted such a project through her Unemployed Workers' Organisation in 1923–4; the Independent Labour Party (ILP) attempted to set up groups all over Britain soon afterwards, and the TUC launched its own distinctive initiative in 1932. The CPGB and NUWM saw all three as significant threats, and spent some time and energy trying to stop them.[13] They succeeded in the cases of the first two alternatives, and although they were unsuccessful in the third, the TUC was not trying to create a national organisation *per se*. Such a body would not have been tolerated by TUC-affiliated trade unions, who would have seen it as a rival. The key point here is that such a task posed large political and practical problems which only the NUWM could even claim to have solved. The forces militating in the local direction were strong.

The TUC's attempt to sap the NUWM by building its own links with the unemployed came during the mass unemployment of the early 1930s. The trade unions were concerned about loss of contact with many ex-members from 1920 onwards. Initially, too, they were concerned about the possibility of mass blacklegging by the unemployed. But prior to the eye of the Depression in 1930–3, the trade union leaders did not regard the level of unemployment as a major threat to their organisations. Members' contributions were raised, so that throughout the 1920s income to national funds was never less (and sometimes considerably more) than twice its 1914 level. Mass blacklegging had not actually occurred (partly, no doubt, due to the activities of the NUWM).[14] Amalgamations strengthened many unions as institutions. Thus, although the TUC established a joint committee with the NUWM which conducted some activity during 1925, there was no great pressure on the TUC from individual unions to develop this collaboration. For the NUWM the collaboration was a huge success in terms of membership. As a recent detailed study of NUWM membership trends shows, the collaboration doubled the rate of recruitment in 1925 and brought a high point in total membership, not subsequently exceeded before 1930.[15] The TUC for its part complained that it had come under attack for its policies during joint events. The main motives of the TUC in collaborating were to show its general social concern, and to exercise some control over the NUWM itself.[16] This period can be characterised as one of 'weak unity' between the TUC and the NUWM.

Both the NUWM and the TUC played their part in the shift from weak unity to mutual hostility which developed from late 1924 onwards. The Zinoviev Letter, the defeat of the General Strike amidst criticism from the CPGB and the Minority Movement and the growth of ideas of 'industrial peace' within the TUC on the one hand met the international communist movement's increasingly anti-reformist policies on the other. Eventually the TUC announced the end of the joint committee in 1928, citing a lack of practical proposals from the NUWM and doubts as to their bona fides.[17]

Hannington took a critical stance within the CPGB towards the 'Class Against Class' policy, reflected in his later account in *Unemployed Struggles*. Incidentally, his attitude was well known in Comintern circles and it may well be that this condemned him to remain outside of the CPGB leadership elite despite his record as a mass leader.[18] On the whole, the 'Third Period' has been viewed critically by labour movement historians, as increasing the isolation of the Communist left and reducing its influence during the period of crisis and mass unemployment between 1930 and 1933. There have been few dissenting voices among the historians. Yet, although there can be little doubt that this is true, the NUWM was able to build its organisation quite effectively in the Third Period. This occurred despite attempts to build alternative organisations.

The most important attempt of the inter-war years occurred in Bristol. The local unemployed organisation was interested in forming a national grouping of unemployed associations. It attracted the interest and support of the TUC, within which there were those who were anxious to use the local form of organisation as a model which could be more widely applied. Bristol was therefore much more than just another locality; it was a cockpit around which stakes were raised to a high level.

The Bristol Unemployed Association (BUA) was formed in 1924, and from the first had an association both with the Trades Council and the Labour MPs elected to the first Labour government. The BUA gained the right to represent individuals to the Board of Guardians on the strict condition that there would be no further unemployed demonstrations. In 1924 the MPs pursued cases of disqualification from benefit on behalf of the local unemployed, with some considerable success.[19] In 1927 the BUA was reorganised to bring it under the direct control of the Trades Council. Its committee was reconstituted on the basis of representation from city councillors, the churches and the Board of Guardians as well as the unemployed. It was evident from numerous reports of its activities that the BUA did have some genuine involvement from the unemployed. The object of the association was said by Walter Baker MP to be to pressurise the government to help local authorities, without taking any political stands.[20] The General Council of the TUC supported this initiative, and recommended to Congress in 1928 that similar associations be set up more widely, with the aims of taking up relief questions, organising meetings and arranging social and educational activities. Unusually, the General Council's recommendation was referred back. Davies of the Miners Federation moved the reference back, arguing that 'People who are doing nothing else but trying to render the unions in twain, will be given an opportunity to do it.' He was especially concerned at the apparent lack of any control over the associations. In this he was supported by Dukes of the General and Municipal Workers.[21] The key issues, then, were the potential for allowing the NUWM a field of operation and control over the associations.

The Bristol NUWM had already given the opponents of the TUC scheme some evidence of their activities within the BUA, whose meetings they attended. At the same time they were able to build their own branch. The year 1932 saw a peak in their activity – in January they led a large demonstration which ended in fighting with the police, and in February they organised another big demonstration on the NUWM's National Day of Struggle.[22]

Yet neither the BUA nor the Bristol NUWM were simply, or even mainly, demonstrating or marching bodies. The BUA, it will be recalled, had given up its right to demonstrate against the guardians in return for the right to represent individuals to them. In doing so, they did not rule out use of the public sphere. Quite the contrary. They made use of Parliament and the services of their Labour MPs to challenge rulings of the National Insurance Commissioners. Since the National Insurance (NI) system was still in an early stage of development, and the influence of MPs was perhaps rather greater during the first Labour government than was later the case, it was possible to achieve some success. The BUA's strategy could, then, partly be described as 'constitutional'. In this, it took account of an important social consideration: that public demonstrations had the potential for identifying individuals as 'troublemakers' who were not suitable for employment. But they also behaved in ways that were not typically trade unionist, in recognising that the disbursement of relief both through the guardians and charities *could* be influenced by sympathetic individuals within the local churches and municipal authorities who were predisposed for religious or political reasons to feel sympathy for the unemployed. A particular case in point was that of ex-servicemen, who had been prominent among the active elements of the Bristol unemployed. There was a strong argument for retaining the ability to influence the authorities through this particular complex of arguments and associations throughout the inter-war years.

The local NUWM, who embraced more expressly radical societal and political aims, were scornful of the BUA's approach. During 1932, for example, they were fiercely critical of the BUA's refusal to join them in demonstrations; but they, too, found themselves increasingly drawn into representational work,[23] the development of which was part of a wider national trend in the organisation. The NUWM had obviously been largely excluded from representing individuals to the guardians through the BUA agreement, but the situation shifted greatly in their favour with the abolition of the guardians in the late 1920s. This gave rise to a new situation in that the potential for representation on non-NI matters became practically non-existent. The possibility of advising the unemployed in their dealings with, for example, the regional officials of the PACs of course remained. On NI questions, however, the position of the NUWM was greatly strengthened in the late 1920s.

The NUWM was formally recognised in 1930 as being an association of the unemployed with the same rights as a trade union by a decision of the National Insurance Umpire communicated to local NI officials in Circular 5809/30. The NUWM therefore had the right to make representations on individuals' behalf, provided it could be shown that the people concerned were in fact NUWM members. The NUWM could thus remind the unemployed that a clear contribution card protected their right of appeal; NI officials actually assisted in this by asking to see people's cards before allowing representation. For the first time the NUWM had an 'official' place in the system.[24] They used it to great effect. Many of the Communists who did this type of work were working-class intellectuals with considerable knowledge of the system, and the confidence and ability to engage in an argument about finer points within it. Their record was literally almost twice as good as the average for the generality of appellants.[25]

The result of the two patterns of representational work developed by the BUA and the NUWM was that the NUWM was to some extent able to take up where the BUA left off. The BUA's channel through the local MPs was cut off after the 1931 election, although of course it could still work through the NI system. But at this time the NUWM was strengthening its own NI position. In terms of the two organisations, then, the balance in this particular field swung towards the NUWM, except in Bristol. Although the NUWM branch was able to organise sizeable demonstrations in the peak period of unemployment, the BUA continued to thrive and to provide a beacon for the TUC.

In other areas, too, the NUWM was unable to establish itself conclusively as the sole legitimate representative of the workless. The trade unions continued to assert their role in representing the unemployed, and some Trades Councils were active in trying to further their interests. In some areas the TUC was able to call on considerable loyalty despite its lack of a strong regional structure. In Northampton, for example, the Trades Council remained intensely loyal to the TUC line despite regular challenges from the left, and formed a TUC Unemployed Association when TUC policy allowed.[26] In 1932 the TUC adopted Unemployed Associations under the supervision of Trades Councils as part of their national policy and proceeded to build similar bodies throughout Britain.[27]

The continued interest of a section of the Bristol unemployed, and that of their counterparts in other localities in non-NUWM organisations, requires explanation. It would seem that little remained of the representational possibilities which had provided a good deal of the rationale for adhesion in the 1920s, although it does seem probable that charitable benefits would be more likely to flow towards the more 'respectable' organisations. Equally, such organisations were more likely generally to be able to influence local Labour councillors in most areas. But these were almost certainly not the only explanations, since others are likely to lie with the atmosphere and norms reigning within the two different types of organisation. It is at this point that it is perhaps most relevant to talk in terms of a 'division' between the NUWM and others.

The NUWM tended to be dominated by the Communists with their studious habits, their peculiarly coded language of Cominternese, their devotion to the struggle (frequently at the expense of their families), their relegation of the individual in favour of the interests of the working class, their (public at least) opposition to alcohol on hunger marches, their loyalty to a far-off foreign country and its interests and not least their desire to focus on the misery of the unemployed.[28] The NUWM in particular was determined to define itself against the 'lumpenproletariat' and took regular action including expulsions to ensure that such 'elements' were excluded. In short, it had a very specific culture, which between 1929 and 1933 and 'Class Against Class' became particularly hostile to that of mainstream Labour politics. With the tremendous growth in unemployment, and its undoubted advantages in many areas, the NUWM expanded its membership very greatly in these years. Nevertheless, the new members did not stay very long, and this gives us a clue as to the reasons for the persistence of the BUA and its equivalents elsewhere.[29] The regular demonstrations, marches and actions of this period, which often left many people hurt or even dead, were not events in which everybody wanted to play a part. Many people felt a need in themselves to overcome the isolation brought by unemployment by joining an organisation. But in order to overcome their isolation effectively they wanted to mix with people who shared their culture. This is a field which needs more research, but we can discern some obvious differences. In particular, they wanted to *forget* their position as unemployed rather than to focus on it as a central feature of their lives. Organisations like the BUA and the TUC's unemployed associations often helped them to do this by organising sporting, educational and social events. This brought devastating scorn and hostility from the leaders of the NUWM in the form of violent diatribes against the 'scab' organisations. The very use of the scab label offers a window into a whole vocabulary and use of language on the part of the CPGB which could also be further examined. We may note here that the scab term contained a trade union analogy which may well have appeared foreign to many of the unemployed, who had either not retained union membership or had not had it in the first place. Further, we can speculate that to a considerable extent the CPGB was in its rhetoric frequently dealing with an *imaginary* body of unemployed, who were more collectively- and protest-oriented than the *actual* unemployed. Be that as it may, at local level the sporting and social events run by the scab bodies frequently brought the flattery of imitation from NUWM branches. Such imitation was of course limited by the vigilance of the leadership, anxious as ever to maintain the movement's commitment to struggle.

At this point, we make a brief excursion to look at an organisation whose activities were not directly condemned in this way. The Bury St Edmunds Unemployed Association had a link with the NUWM, but it also had a particular orientation which might otherwise have brought it NUWM condemnation. The politics of the town was typical of many in the sense that the Labour movement in any guise had to adopt a stance which recognised a seemingly indefinite and profound hostility from the Conservative local authorities and employers. This may have been one of the reasons for the NUWM's relatively friendly stance towards the association. In any case the association's leader, George Freezer, adroitly exploited the possibilities, apparently without the help of the TUC. An ex-serviceman in his thirties who had worked in local industry, Freezer gathered a group of unemployed activists and local professionals around him to form an association claiming some 700 members in the early 1930s. Taking some care to keep explicit politics at arm's length despite his known Labour Party and then (probably less well known) CP membership, he was able to draw in Dr Stork, the local Medical Officer of Health, Dr Skinner, the Methodist head of Culford School, and other local dignitaries. Activities included asking the local landed gentry for money and then distributing it as vouchers to unemployed people for use in local shops, frequent representational work to the Court of Referees in Ipswich and parties for the unemployed and their children. Hannington was asked to speak locally. So successful was Freezer in effectively splitting the local elite down the unemployment fault line that he earned both the public praise of Alderman Sidney Oliver, chair of the local Conservative Party, and perhaps the ultimate private praise in the post-war years of being told that the local Conservatives (clearly over-optimistically and to Freezer's great amusement) hoped to recruit him to their ranks.[30]

Freezer's prescription for success almost certainly ruled out too open or close an association with the NUWM, despite the existence of some contact. One of the values of the case as such is that it illustrates the way in which the space for an unemployed organisation could be created in even the most unfavourable circumstances. The NUWM was never successful in East Anglia; the only branch it was able consistently to sustain there was in Norwich. Given such failure, it may well have been the case that the Bury St Edmunds perspective was the only viable one under the circumstances. In any case, it seems possible that the leadership of the NUWM was sufficiently astute to recognise that there was a sort of complementarity involved here: if one could not have an NUWM branch because the local circumstances were unfavourable, then the Unemployed Association was better than nothing. From a pragmatic point of view, the social and political context of unemployed protest had to be taken into account. In many respects it was and had to be the art of the possible given the lack of power of the unemployed in other than social or political senses.

How the NUWM absorbed the values of these sorts of activity is an interesting question. They may simply have learned from their own experience, or that coupled with the transmitted experience of local unemployed associations. It may have been both of these factors combined with the rival attractions of local National Councils for Social Services in the later 1930s. But the NUWM itself had long been involved in trying to meet the existential needs of the workless in terms of social activities such as brass bands, football teams, Children's Socialist Sunday Schools and so on, even if they generally drew the line at asking for money. It appears that these activities were developed in the 1930s, possibly because of the increasingly dire state of the unemployed themselves. Some of the examples are really quite striking in their size. In 1934, for example, the Greenock branch opened a fund for a children's outing to which over £100 was subscribed. This paid for nearly 5,000 Clydeside children to have a day out, with food, in Battery Park.[31] Regular holiday camps were also organised during the 1930s.[32] This kind of activity has perhaps hitherto been underestimated partly because it involved many 'invisible' women rather than the men who made up the overwhelming majority of the movement's local and national leadership. But it was an important and probably underplayed aspect of the movement's work, which marked it off internationally from, for example, the German KPD-run unemployed activities, which have been criticised for their unremitting orientation towards struggle, often to ends irrelevant to many of the workless themselves.[33] Perhaps we can speculate that one of the reasons for the violent verbal outbursts from the NUWM and particularly the CPGB prior to their change of line around 1935 was a realisation of the extent of the 'unsound' practice of their activists, which the Comintern had viewed with a jaundiced eye for some time.

The NUWM leadership's vituperation against the unemployed associations is interesting from the point of view of our principal theme. We have touched on the use of the scab label already. Neither the TUC nor members of the associations would be prepared, after such language, to recognise the NUWM as a body with which they wanted to cooperate. The CP leadership of the NUWM had described the TUC's creation of unemployed associations as 'divisive', and they then tried to ensure that a durable division actually occurred. This was a process which Hannington, the leader of the movement, did not acknowledge, since he largely passed over the 'Class Against Class' policy itself in his own influential historical writing.

Thus it was hardly surprising that, in the 'Popular Front' period during the later 1930s in which the NUWM tried to develop its links with the unemployed associations and even to dissolve itself into them, it often found its approaches rejected. In fact, the latter 1930s saw some disarray in CPGB policy with regard to the very necessity for a NUWM at all. Some agreed with Lewis Jones of South Wales that dissolution was required if maximum unity was to be obtained. This was not a view shared by the NUWM leadership, but it was one which damaged the NUWM. During the late 1930s the TUC claimed a steady expansion in its associations despite a secular fall in unemployment, whilst the NUWM declined. It would seem possible to argue that the TUC's perspective was in fact proving fruitful, and that the NUWM's downward trajectory in these years was not solely due to falling unemployment. In Norwich, for example, the NUWM branch split during the 1935 agitations, with a group of unemployed veterans leaving the NUWM branch to form a rival association.[34] It appears that some Communists later drew lessons from such developments. In discussions held in 1942 and 1943 concerning the future of the NUWM after the war, the view that 'maximum unity' meant the rejection of the NUWM finally defeated a current of thought which favoured retention of a shell organisation ready for later use.[35] The successful argument flowed logically, of course, from Communist politics of the time. But it was supported by an awareness of the relative success of the TUC in the pre-war years.

In conclusion, it is also important for us to look at the light that all these cases throw on the question of unemployed organisation as a whole, when viewed in a wider context. There is a need for this not only because organisational history is unfashionable *per se*, but also because discussion of the history of Labour movement institutions has focused almost exclusively on trade unions and political parties. Such issues are central, too, to the history of Communism between the world wars. Yet the problems of running an unemployed movement have hardly been revisited since Paul Mattick first raised them, systematically but rather unsatisfactorily, in 1969.[36] Perhaps here we can restrict ourselves to looking at the question of how an unemployed movement sustains its *contact* with the workless. In all of the British organisations mentioned above, this was done by representational work at a minimum, usually supplemented by social activities of one sort or another. This was usually sufficient to allow the organisation to sustain itself as such. In an international context, this may be seen as a specific formula rather than an unexceptional description. In the German and Austrian unemployed movements the situation was quite different. These movements were organised along party lines, by Communists, Social Democrats, religious denominations and so on. The Communist movements in particular, as we have already noted in the German case, placed great emphasis on *party* objectives such as supporting the employed in their disputes with employers. Moreover, their demands in relation to the workless have been widely criticised in different contexts by historians as irrelevant to the unemployed themselves.[37]

It was certainly the case that even before 1933 the German and Austrian unemployed movements had degenerated from being quite large to a state of almost total collapse.[38] Again, many reasons may be advanced for this, such as, for example (as Peter Wilding says in the Austrian case), a massive disparity between the movement's demands and the actual, dramatically worsening situation of the mass of workless.[39] But it may also be (and Wilding's conclusion would apparently allow this argument) that there was a problem for them in terms of the nature of their contact with the workless.

In the British case the key development was the official decision to allow representation within the system to organisations. In other words, it had less to do with the Labour movement than with the structure established by the state. But the opportunity still had to be taken, and here the traditions of workplace representation of British skilled workers was important. In any event it does seem important to develop further discussion about the different types of organisations of unemployed which existed between the wars in a comparative direction if we are to understand Communist activity more fully.

What further conclusions can we draw from this history in relation to our themes?

Generally speaking both the leaders of the NUWM and the historians have rarely referred to the non-NUWM unemployed bodies. To this extent, this chapter has been concerned to set the NUWM in a wider context as the biggest but not the only unemployed organisation. At the time, however, it was not possible for Hannington and his comrades to simply ignore other bodies. Both they and some historians closely concerned with the unemployed at local level have referred specifically to these as being divisive and to this as having had damaging effects on the unemployed movement.[40]

The idea of the existence of rivals to the NUWM as being divisive makes the assumption that the unemployed movement would have been more effective had it been united. (Cunningham uses the argument in relation to Norwich for example.) This is, of course strictly counterfactual and cannot be tested. In any case, it rather begs the question where different bodies with different aims are concerned. The bodies originated precisely because of these different aims. The claim that division led to a reduction in effectiveness might therefore be criticised as a *partisan* argument.

The history of unemployed organisations between the wars has tended to be written from precisely such a partisan point of view. However, an alternative model may be proposed. This model takes as its starting point the fact that the majority of workless did not join any *any* unemployed organisation between the wars. In general, as droves of sociologists have continually pointed out, the majority of the unemployed were atomised and demoralised by the experience of worklessness. Their isolation meant that they did not join organisations. In the case of the NUWM, at least, it is known that many joined and then left very soon afterwards. It could be necessary, as we have already shown, to join the NUWM in order to be represented, and then to leave when one's case had been resolved. Indeed, this would seem to have been the case for many people. For those who did not have an *ideological* commitment to the NUWM nor to any other organisation this was a perfectly rational instrumental response to the situation, especially when the costs of membership are taken into account.

An alternative model, then, would take the viewpoint of the individual unemployed person and ask: why join any organisation? Since the unemployed tended to take an individualised view of their position, one answer might be to obtain redress against injustices done to them as individuals. Another, as we have tried to indicate, might be to take immediate and practical action to improve their morale and their material position. On the other hand, since the national system for relieving unemployment was in a state of flux and negotiation, another might be to try to influence the government through collective action.

It was positively helpful to the individual actually to have a choice in the matter. To the unemployed individual, whether one organisation or another was more useful would rather depend on his or her specific needs at the time. In other words, it might be a 'trade union' rather than a political question. Organisations of the unemployed were divided along political lines. Yet British trade unions were not and British trade unionists, when unemployed, might be expected to recognise immediate benefits in organisations before political considerations. In this perspective, political divisions were not the primary problem.

As we have already noted, divisions were seen as undesirable by the NUWM and others. Yet on this level, too, it is not axiomatic that the existence of different forms of organisation actually constituted a problem from either the NUWM or the non-NUWM point of view. The NUWM's official attitude to other organisations varied, as we have seen, according to the vagaries of the heavily CPGB-influenced politics of the leadership. At times it recognised the value of other organisations, at others not.

Yet is possible to see considerable elements of complementarity between the NUWM and non-NUWM organisations. Perhaps the most important had to do with the immense amount of effort required to launch and sustain national and regional hunger marches. Hannington and others often drew attention to this – Hannington refused to contemplate a march after 1923 because of the lack of infrastructure to support one – and during the period 1930–6 there was little respite for many branches from organising around marches. This meant that local representational activity in some branches on the march route had to be curbed for considerable periods, and this was the background to a debate around the relationship between the two forms of activity in the early 1930s. There may have been recognition of the *de facto* division of labour between the NUWM and the unemployed associations. Such forms of tacit agreement may have existed at local level, but further research is required on this point. Any which did exist might be obscured by using NUWM or CPGB sources, which would often ignore or discount such 'compromise'.

We may also assert the *similarities* in a day-to-day sense between the activities of the unemployed associations and the NUWM branches. These similarities have to a large extent been obscured by Hannington and those who found it convenient for political reasons to accept his depiction of the NUWM as a 'fighting organisation', much of whose work was symbolised in the very public statement of the hunger march. These similarities asserted themselves increasingly as the inter-war years proceeded and the problem of maintaining a continuous association of the atomised unemployed was understood. There was in other words a learning process which had to be undergone by all organisers of the workless after the initial militancy of the early 1920s subsided.

To return to the 'division' issue. If the unemployed associations had a function, so, too, did the NUWM. National action through hunger marches generally brought positive results in one form or another. In the majority of cases they brought concessions from government. Many of these concessions took the form of the suspension or dropping of particular measures which would have worsened the position of the unemployed, but they were nevertheless retreats which presumably would not otherwise have been made.

What has been described is a case in which the 'division' idea has been overplayed. Originating in the Communist politics of unity, it has tended to obscure the plurality of unemployed organisations. It has also tended to emphasise the political rather than the trade union, cultural and existential concerns of both the workless and their organisations. The concept of a *positive plurality* could be counterposed to that of division. The use of the two concepts in tandem could help us to see beyond the 'division–unity' dichotomy which has afflicted writing on the more politicised topics in labour history.

Notes

1. See my 'Communist unemployed organisations between the world wars: international patterns and problems', *Archiv für Sozialgeschichte*, Band XXX, 1990.
2. Alan Clinton, *The Trade Union Rank and File* (Manchester University Press, 1977), p. 163.
3. The classical study of unemployment in the 1930s which initiated this tradition was Marie Lazarsfeld-Jahoda et al., *Die Arbeitslosen von*

Marienthal (Österreichische Wirtschaftspsychologische Forschungstelle; first edn 1933). The authors' English translation is *Marienthal: The Sociography of an Unemployed Community* (Tavistock, 1974). These ideas were picked up and reinforced by major studies of the origins of the welfare state in Britain. See, for example, the widely read history by Maurice Bruce, *The Coming of the Welfare State* (Batsford, 1961). Peter Kingsford's *The Hunger Marchers in Britain: 1920–1940* (Lawrence & Wishart, 1982) is a very different kind of book, written with a great deal of sympathy for the marchers.

4. Paul Bagguley, *From Protest to Acquiescence? Political Movements of the Unemployed* (Macmillan, 1991). My own book, *We Refuse to Starve in Silence: A History of the NUWM 1920–46* (Lawrence & Wishart, 1987) is to some extent in the same tradition.

5. See, for example, Siegfried Bahne, *Die KPD und das Ende von Weimar: Das Scheitern einer Politik 1932–1935)* Campus Verlag, Frankfurt am Main/New York, 1976), or the important study of the KPD by Hermann Weber, *Die Wandlung des deutschen Kommunismus: Die Stalinisierung der KPD in der Weimarer Republik*, 2 vols (Europäische Verlaganstalt, Frankfurt am Main, 1969).

6. Earl Browder even looked forward to the point at which the unemployed could feed themselves. See his review 'One year of struggle of the unemployed in the USA', *Inprecorr*, 15, 1932, p. 292. Howard Zinn in his *A People's History of the United States* (Harper & Row, New York, 1980) asserts that there were 330 self-help organisations in 37 states by late 1932 (p. 385). Further bibliographical information is given in my article in *Archiv für Sozialgeschichte*.

7. Wal Hannington, *Unemployed Struggles* (Lawrence & Wishart, 1936, 1979 edn), pp. 17–18.

8. PRO, CAB. 24. 71, GT 6427.

9. Frank Carr, 'The formation of the Communist Party in Coventry' (University of Warwick, unpublished MA dissertation, 1971), pp. 33–5.

10. *Out of Work*, no. 48.

11. See my *We Refuse to Starve in Silence*, for numerous references to these other organisations.

12. See H.J. Bush, 'Local, intellectual and policy responses to localised unemployment in the inter-war period' (Nuffield College, Oxford, unpublished PhD thesis, 1980).

13. On the Unemployed Workers' Organisation, see *Workers' Dreadnought*, 7, 21 July 1923; on Sylvia Pankhurst's role see S. Franchini,

Sylvia Pankhurst 1912–24: Dal Suffragismo alla Rivoluzione Sociale (ETS Università, Pisa, 1980), especially pp. 269–70. On the ILP, see *Daily Herald*, 20 and 23 June 1924. On the TUC and the NUWM reaction see Wal Hannington's pamphlet, *Crimes Against the Unemployed* (NUWM, 1932).

14. See the interesting discussions in S. Shaw, 'The attitude of the TUC towards unemployment in the inter-war period' (University of Kent, unpublished PhD thesis, 1979), especially pp. 309–11.
15. Sam Davies, 'The membership of the NUWM, 1923–1938', *Labour History Review*, 57, part 1, 1992.
16. S. Shaw, 'The attitude of the TUC', p. 313 and *passim*.
17. TUC Congress *Report*, 1928, p. 113.
18. See P. Kingsford, *The Hunger Marches in Britain*, p. 113.
19. Robert Whitfield, 'The Labour movement in Bristol: 1910–1939' (University of Bristol, unpublished MLitt thesis, 1979), pp. 200–1.
20. Ibid., pp. 221–8. *Western Daily Press*, 30 September 1927.
21. TUC Congress *Report*, 1928, pp. 111–13.
22. National Administrative Council, NUWM, *Report on Demonstrations on National Day of Struggle* (Wal Hannington Papers, Marx Memorial Library, London), p. 1.
23. *Weekly Worker*, 27 February 1932.
24. *NUWM Constitution and Rules* (nd, green) (Wal Hannington papers, CPGB, A3b). National Administrative Council, NUWM, *Report*, 7-8 May 1932.
25. National Administrative Council, NUWM, *Report*, p. 6.
26. Undated letter from Northampton branch NUWM to Northampton Trades Council (Northampton Trades Council records, Northamptonshire Record Office).
27. A. Clinton, *The Trade Union Rank and File*, p. 163.
28. Some idea of this culture is given by Phil Abrahams in an interview with Hywel Francis quoted in *Miners Against Fascism, Wales and the Spanish Civil War* (Lawrence & Wishart, 1984), p. 50. The whole interview is to be found in the South Wales Miners' Library, but Hywel Francis's quotation is itself revealing:

    We had an opinion in those days that the Communist Party was the vanguard of the workers. You had to be honest, sober, industrious, a good citizen: these were the qualities we were looking for, and of course everybody doesn't come into that.

29. S. Davies, 'The membership of the NUWM'.

30. Transcript of an interview with George Freezer by Roger Spalding and Mike O'Sullivan. I am grateful to the interviewers for their kind cooperation in giving me a copy.

31. *Unemployed Leader*, September 1934.

32. *Unemployed Leader*, September 1935.

33. Arne Andersen, *Lieber im Feuer der Revolution sterben, als auf dem Misthaufen der Demokratie verecken! Ein Beitrag zur Bremer Sozialgeschichte* (Minerva, Munich, 1987).

34. Paul Cunningham, 'Unemployment in Norwich during the 1930s' (University of East Anglia, unpublished PhD thesis, 1990).

35. Memo of National Headquarters Committee Meeting, 24 April 1943 (Wal Hannington papers, CPGB, A2f).

36. Paul Mattick, *Arbeitslosigkeit und Arbeitslosenbewegung in den USA 1929–1935* (Campus Verlag, Frankfurt am Main, 1969, first edn. 1933). I describe his statement of the problems as rather unsatisfactory because it seems to me to be overstated on occasions. For example, he describes the unemployed as having 'nichts zu opfern, weder Zeit, noch Geld' ('nothing to sacrifice, neither time nor money') (p. 109). The history of unemployed protest world-wide provides ample evidence that this is going too far.

37. See, for example, A. Andersen, *Lieber im Feuer der Revolution sterben*; Eve Rosenhaft, *Beating the Fascists? The German Communists and Political Violence 1929–1933* (Cambridge University Press, 1983), particularly pp. 49–53; Rose-Marie Huber-Koller, 'Die kommunistische Erwerbslosenbewegung in der Endphase der Weimarer Republik', in *Gesellschaft. Beiträge zur Marxschen Theorie* (Frankfurt am Main, 1977).

38. E. Rosenhaft, *Beating the Fascists?* p. 51; A. Andersen, *Lieber im Feuer der Revolution sterben,* p. 219.

39. Peter Wilding, *…für Arbeit und Brot' Arbeitslose in Bewegung* (Europaverlag, Vienna, 1990), p. 299.

40. See, for example, P. Cunningham, 'Unemployment in Norwich'.

Further Reading

An important starting point for the history of the National Unemployed Workers' Movement is the book written in the mid-1930s by its leader, Wal Hannington, *Unemployed Struggles* (Lawrence & Wishart, 1936). Hannington's racy narrative is an account of the struggles in which he was involved, written from the CP's perspective of the time. My own

We Refuse to Starve in Silence (Lawrence & Wishart, 1987) is a brief history of the organisation itself, whilst Peter Kingsford's *The Hunger Marches in Britain* (Lawrence & Wishart, 1982) is a sympathetic treatment of its subject. Those interested in an international perspective on the NUWM should read my article in the German journal *Archiv für Sozialgeschichte* cited in note 1.

3 The Communist Party in the Scots Coalfields in the Inter-war Period

Alan Campbell

The political significance of the Scottish miners in the inter-war period was well recognised both by the Communist Party (CP) and by the Communist International (CI). It was in Scotland that the major attempt was made to establish a Communist-led 'red union' in Britain, the United Mineworkers of Scotland (UMS), and two out of the three Communist MPs elected in the inter-war years represented seats in the Scots coalfields. There was extensive coverage of Scottish miners' affairs in the party press and the failure of the CPGB to initiate the formation of the UMS before 1929 was a major complaint laid against the British party by the leadership of the CI and the Red International of Labour Unions (RILU).[1] Margaret McCarthy, who worked in the apparatus of the RILU in Moscow in the 1930s, recalled the UMS as 'that most important sphere of Communist influence in the industrial life of Britain' and consequently the responsibility of the senior member of the Anglo-American section.[2]

The Scots miners therefore provide an ideal case study of the development of a regional Communist tradition. The principal aim of this chapter is to examine those factors which either nurtured or impeded this process. In the first section we briefly outline structural aspects of the mining industry and variations in the composition of the workforce in the regions of the Scots coalfields; in the second we examine the influence of these structural factors on Communist support; finally we consider the role of political agency: how the CP's cadre, organisation and policy assisted or hindered the implantation on this tradition.

The Regions of the Scots Coalfields

Although geologically linked, the Scottish coalfields do not constitute one homogenous unit but rather four distinct 'regions': Ayrshire; the large West–Central field based on Lanarkshire but which spreads north into Stirlingshire and westward into West Lothian; Fife and Clackmannan; and Mid- and East Lothian. In delineating them, we shall consider the factors suggested by Philip Cooke to explain variations in the geography of class relations.[3]

The productive base

The modern exploitation of the Scots coalfields was both chronologically and geographically uneven. Each decade after 1830 witnessed new areas being opened up in Ayrshire and the West–Central field. The eastern coalfields experienced a later expansion, both the Lothians and Fife being intensively developed after 1890. By the 1920s and 1930s, the structural decline of the western fields was reinforced by the cyclical depression in the markets of steel, engineering and shipbuilding. Between 1919 and 1935 the numbers employed in the West–Central field more than halved and the centre of gravity shifted eastwards.

Contingent upon the geology of the coalfields was the spatial distribution and size of the productive units. In Ayrshire a pattern of scattered mining developed along the coal seams exposed by deeply entrenched rivers. The few large mines were geographically separate and mining settlements were dispersed throughout a largely rural environment. In Lanarkshire there were many small mines surrounding a significant number of large ones which were concentrated in the urban archipelago of the central Clyde valley. Fife's large pits were also densely concentrated in two geographical areas: in central and east Fife; the scattered small mines extending west of Dunfermline and into Clackmannanshire were located in more rural areas. In the Lothians large and small collieries were located in the countryside south and east of Edinburgh.

The labour process

Mechanisation proceeded much more rapidly in Scotland than elsewhere in Britain after 1900; by 1925 50 per cent of Scotland's output was cut by machine, compared with a British figure of only 20 per cent. Within Scotland mechanisation was most extensive in the larger modern mines in the east, least so in Ayrshire.[4] For the miners the consequences of mechanisation were deskilling and intensification of labour. However, a further corollary of intensively mechanised cutting and conveying was the physical concentration of different grades of underground workers in closely supervised units which generated common grievances. The miners' resistance to these pressures on wages and working conditions was evidenced by Scotland being one of the most strike-prone areas in the British coal industry.[5]

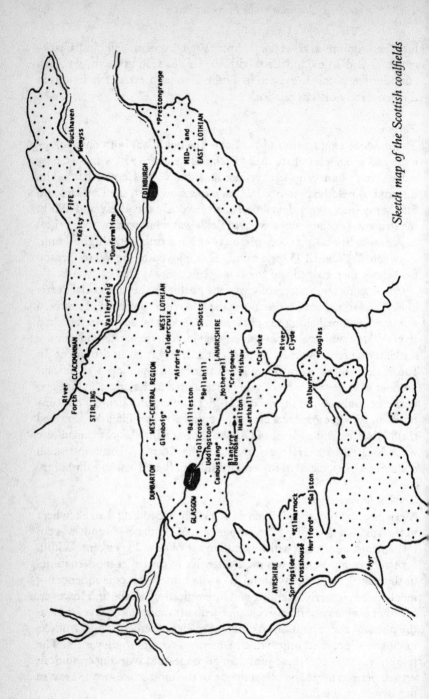

Sketch map of the Scottish coalfields

The ownership of capital

The structure of the Scots coal industry displayed considerable regional variation, even the largest companies tending to exhibit a strong regional bias in the location of their colliery operations. One company, William Baird, dominated Ayrshire, employing almost half the mineworkers in the county in 1927. In the West–Central region piecemeal development created a more fragmented structure. By 1939 there were five major companies each with a total annual output of more than a million tons, but almost two-thirds of the region's output was produced by a host of smaller companies owning one or two mines. Fife and Clackmannan were largely controlled by four companies while in the Lothians there was a larger number of medium-sized firms.[6]

Specific social relations

While there were some generally similar social relations common to all the regions – for example, a rigid gender segregation – there is space here only to indicate two important lines of differentiation. The first concerns the ethnic and religious composition of the mining populations of the regions. The intensive exploitation of the Ayrshire and West–Central fields had coincided with the peak years of Irish immigration and ethnic and sectarian disturbances were widespread in the nineteenth century.[7] Religious divisions persisted in the western coalfields into the twentieth century. Even during the early months of 1926 the solidarity of the miners in Lanarkshire was balanced precariously on the potential of sectarian division, as A.J. Cook recognised when he urged the Hamilton miners not to 'allow religious differences to divide them where their bread and cheese were concerned. The issues were not theological but economic'.[8] Catholics remained a much smaller minority in Fife. Abe Moffat recalled that 'You never had the problems with Catholics and Protestants as you had in Lanarkshire. They were all in one place [in Fife]. Valleyfield and Blairhall ...'.[9]

The second variable concerns the willingness of the miners to engage in violent social disorder. We have already commented on the industrial militancy of the West–Central region. In the turbulent and densely populated mining communities of Lanarkshire this militancy was often accompanied during major disputes by sabotage and civil disorder; there were mass pickets, riots and attacks on pitheads during strikes in 1887, 1894, 1912 and 1921. By the 1920s some Fife miners were also willing to engage in violent protest. The seven-month-long lockout following the General Strike of May 1926 highlighted a division between the more peaceable regions of Ayrshire and, to a lesser extent, the Lothians, and the West–Central and Fife coalfields. In Ayrshire the Chief Constables of Ayr and Kilmarnock reported in early November that not one case of intimidation or assault had arisen in the county during the dispute.[10] In Fife and Lanarkshire the miners were ferocious in their prosecution of the dispute. As well as numerous demonstrations, mass pickets and attacks on blacklegs, which frequently ended in police baton charges, the militants also engaged in quasi-guerilla warfare involving arson and the use of explosives to sabotage colliery machinery and railway lines.[11]

Institutional specificities

Union density rapidly increased after 1900, reaching 80 per cent of the Scottish mining workforce by 1913, but the fragmented pattern of seven county-based unions (covering Ayrshire, Lanarkshire, Stirlingshire, West Lothian, Fife and Clackmannan, Mid- and East Lothian, and until 1927, Dumbarton) persisted. In the West–Central field there were thus four separate unions (until 1927), while in contrast the large employers in the region were organised by the Lanarkshire Coal Masters' Association. The autonomous county unions were loosely linked in the Scottish Miners' Federation until 1914, thereafter equally loosely in the federal National Union of Scottish Mineworkers (NUSM). In response to this fragmented structure and the increasingly bureaucratic and undemocratic practices of the national and county unions there emerged industrial unionist Reform Committees in Lanarkshire, Fife and the Lothians during the First World War. Associated with the Reform Committees was the movement for Marxist education classes organised by John Maclean and the Scottish Labour College which was particularly active in the West–Central and Fife regions.[12]

The foregoing analysis is intended to demonstrate the regional specificities of the four coalfields. All shared some of the characteristics common to the mining industry, but the particular configurations of their social and economic structures gave each its own identity and influenced the willingness of their miners to support the CP.

Communist Support in the Scots Coalmining Regions

The formation of the CPGB in January 1921 could scarcely have come at a less auspicious moment in the history of the Scots miners. The three-month-long national lockout from April to July left the miners' unions weak and demoralised, with wages and membership in sharp decline: union density in Lanarkshire and Fife was 79 per cent and 89 per cent in 1921: it dropped to 45.7 per cent and 42.6 per cent in 1922. In Ayrshire and West Lothian a number of branches broke away from the county unions.[13] The fledgling Communist Party struggled to establish itself in an often hostile environment. At Galston in central Ayrshire it was reported that prior to the 1921 dispute there had been an 'ardent group' of Communist supporters 'who owing to victimisation have been scattered or unemployed'. At the end of 1923 the East Fife group of the CP reported that their 'strength was now only eight'.[14]

As well as the objective situation of the coal industry there were also political obstacles to recruiting left-wing miners to the CP. This was largely due to the influence of John Maclean and his 'first lieutenant' James D. MacDougall which had been built up among the Lanarkshire and Fife miners before and during the First World War. Maclean's refusal to join the CP, the party's wrecking tactics towards his activities and his brief membership of the Socialist Labour Party (SLP) delayed the entry of a cohort of radical young miners into the CP. William Allan, for example, a full-time student of Maclean's at the Scottish Labour College in 1920–1 and a member of the CP's Central Committee by 1927 was an SLP member as late as 1923. William Pearson, later a leading Lanarkshire Communist and miners' official, organised a Deleonite miners' industrial union in Lanarkshire that same year. By January 1924, however, the majority of left-wing elements in Scotland set up a Scottish Miners' Minority Movement under CP leadership.[15]

Despite protests from the CP leadership party members in Fife joined forces with other left-wing union members to form a breakaway Mineworkers' Reform Union in 1923 in opposition to the undemocratic tactics of the right-wing leadership of the Fife, Kinross and Clackmannan Miners' Association (FKCMA).[16] This involvement in the Reform Union was an important proving ground for Communist militants in the mid-1920s and helped build a significant following for the party in Fife. In Lanarkshire Communists remained within the Lanarkshire Mineworkers' County Union (LMCU) and by persistent agitation built up a popular base for the Minority Movement (MM). When William Allan, by then a CP member, stood unsuccessfully for the post of General Secretary of the LMCU in 1925, he nevertheless secured 42.4 per cent of the vote.[17]

During the 1926 lockout Communists in the Scots coalfields played a major role in organising pickets, poor relief demonstrations and soup kitchens.[18] Miners and their families flocked to join the party and CP membership in Scotland almost doubled from 845 in June 1925 to a peak of 1,560 in September 1926, although there was some loss of membership after the lockout: by September 1927 the Scottish membership was 1,321. In Fife there were over 600 members in 1927 and the Shotts and Blantyre CP branches in Lanarkshire had 58 and 40 members respectively. Party membership continued to decline, however: by 1930 there were only 78 members in Lanarkshire, 68 in Fife, 26 in Ayrshire and 14 in the Lothians.[19] We do not possess an occupational breakdown of these figures, but given the occupational structure of these counties it is likely that many were miners. Even on this assumption, however, CP membership after 1927 was, to say the least, modest.

There are a number of explanations for this failure to sustain a larger membership. In 1928 a memorandum to the Political Bureau of the CP suggested the fall in party membership in the Scots coalfields was due to victimisation, unemployment and movement away to other areas in search of work.[20] The halving of the workforce in the West–Central field was clearly significant, while victimisation, and the fear of it, also seems to have been a major factor. David Proudfoot, a leading party member in Fife, wrote in early 1927:

> At present the Party in Fife is practically an unemployed Party, very few members have been restarted and the result is that some have left the Party, and others are failing to put in an appearance at Party meetings, due to the bright and handy idea that membership of the Party is the reason for them not being employed. The new Party membership is being tested now, and events are proving that we have picked up a good number of 'Strike Communists'.[21]

At Shotts in 1930 fear of victimisation was such that the UMS collector was afraid to be seen publicly entering a CP meeting.[22]

However, CP *support* was greater than the modest membership figures suggest, as the performance of CP candidates in union elections in 1927 demonstrated. In the Lanarkshire and Fife unions CP and left-wing candidates made significant gains, while the CP candidates William Allan and John Bird won the posts of secretary and president in the NUSM elections. In part these events represented the culmination of the efforts of a generation of young militants radicalised by the First World War and its aftermath; for example William Allan was only 27 years old in 1927; John Bird, who defeated the 70-year-old veteran Robert Smillie, was 31.[23] But age and generation alone cannot fully explain these Communist victories because the pattern of union electoral support for the CP was spread unevenly through the Scots mining regions. We must therefore consider the circumstances of each region in turn.

The Lothians

Here, Communist influence was at its weakest. There was no CP local outside Edinburgh in the county of Midlothian, and the local in East Lothian fluctuated between seven and 14 members in the early 1930s. In the Mid- and East Lothian Miners' Association (MELMA) the CP appears to have influenced only the Prestongrange branch in East Lothian where 'Communist activities' were reported to be causing 'some difficulty' in 1929. When the MELMA executive recommended that no member of the association who was a member of the CP be permitted to hold any official position at branch or district level it received overwhelming support from the branches.[24] The more favourable market position of the Lothians coalfield and its scattered rural settlements appear to have proved infertile grounds for Communist implantation.

Ayrshire

In Ayrshire the CP leadership had higher hopes. A memorandum to the Political Bureau in 1928 claimed the party and MM had the support of about one-third of the men. In contrast James Brown, the veteran right-wing leader of the Ayrshire Miners' Union (AMU), stated that only the

> Galston, Hurlford, Drongan and Springside [branches] can be looked upon as communist, in respect that the Delegates representing them at the [AMU Annual] Conference were avowed communists, but in none of these with the possible exception of Hurlford, would they have anything like a majority if a ballot vote were taken.[25]

The records of the AMU indicate some support for the CP's assessment. Although in votes on the AMU Delegate Board to determine the union's support for candidates for the president and secretary of the NUSM, the MM nominees received only four and five votes against 14 and 15 for the right-wing candidates, on occasion the CP delegates secured greater support on the board – a motion to support CP affiliation to the Labour Party was narrowly defeated by ten votes to nine. A clearer indication of the political views of rank-and-file AMU members was provided by a ballot vote for the post of county agent in 1928. The contest was between James Brown and George Gilmour, a left-wing candidate, who though not a party member was supported by the CP. Gilmour secured 32.5 per cent of the vote, receiving majorities (but very large ones) in only five out of the 22 branches: Galston, Hurlford, Drongan, Springside and Crosshouse, suggesting a greater degree of support in these branches for their Communist delegates than Brown had allowed.[26] Although AMU branches were based on villages rather than individual mines, it is noteworthy that none of the mines listed in these five areas belonged to the giant firm of William Baird, and four of the five villages were within a five-mile radius of the large manufacturing town of Kilmarnock where the only CP local in Ayrshire was situated. The corollary of this explanation is that the power of the blacklist in the pits owned by Baird and the difficulties involved in politically mobilising miners living in scattered rural settlements restricted the potential for CP support in Ayrshire.

West Central

In this region the Lanarkshire union displayed the strongest Communist support. Unlike Ayrshire its union branches were usually based on single collieries. The ballot results of individual branches in the elections of 1925 and 1927 provide data for a comparative analysis of MM support. Those branches where support was 5 per cent or more above and below the mean MM vote in both 1925 and 1927 were identified.[27] Fifteen branches were found in the first category, that is displaying strong Communist support, and 22 in the latter, that is displaying weak Communist support. What does a comparison of the two groups reveal? First, it is clear that MM support tended to be stronger in the larger collieries; the average workforce in the strongly Communist group was 476 compared with 200 in the weak group. The collieries where Communist support was strong were also more industrially militant, having an average of 5.9 disputes during the period 1921–36, compared with 1.2 disputes in the weak group.

This greater militancy does not seem to have been a function of the possibly harsher industrial relations policies of larger firms since there was no clear relationship between the size of the companies and MM support. Nor did mechanisation appear to have been a significant influence on MM support, since the large majority of mines in both groups were using coal-cutting machinery, according to the government's List of Mines for 1927 (although the list does not indicate the *number* of machines in use).

Yet one variable which goes some way to distinguish between our two groups is that of geography: eleven of the strongly Communist branches were in the central Clyde valley; five of the weakly Communist branches were in Larkhall, four in Wishaw, five in a band stretching through Tollcross/Baillieston/Airdrie. This suggests that what we need to consider is what made Blantyre and Burnbank a qualitatively different kind of community from Larkhall, what social processes created a political culture in Bothwell which was different from that in Baillieston?

Space does not permit the extensive comparison required fully to answer these questions, but we can note that one significant difference between the various localities was the religious composition and ethnic identity of their workforces. Religious sectarianism had been given a new impetus with the rise of Sinn Fein and rebellion and civil war in Ireland. Andrew Fagan, an Irish-born Labour College tutor from Blantyre, was jailed for six months on suspicion of smuggling arms to the IRA.[28] His case was not an idiosyncratic one, for the militants in the Lanarkshire union took a strongly pro-Republican line on the Irish question. The association between the CP's trade union militants and militaristic republicanism may also have contributed to the violent disorders and the use of explosives associated with the industrial disputes of 1919, 1921 and 1926. Literary evidence of this connection can be gleaned from the novel *The Morlocks*, written by James C. Welsh, an agent and Vice-President of the LMCU, which was published in 1924. The book's plot is set against the rise of the MM in Lanarkshire (thinly disguised as 'The Morlocks' secret society). Its climax involves riots and the dynamiting of pits in Blantyre by a group of miners led by a hunchback named Barney Blades who introduces himself to the hero: 'I'm Irish though born in Blantyre … Bein' Irish, I'm always agin the government. I'm a revolutionary anarchist.'[29] Against such grotesque caricature we should note also the confidential judgement of the Inspector of Mines for Scotland in 1926 that the 'dangerous people prepared to do much destruction' were 'Communist and Irishmen'.[30] The political significance of the Irish in Lanarkshire is suggested by accounts of the election of J.T. Walton Newbold as the Communist MP for the Motherwell and Wishaw constituency in 1922. Although the reasons underlying the election of Britain's first Communist to Parliament were complex, his own account allowed the Irish Catholics a major role and he spoke of his 'alliance of the Marxists with the Irish'.[31]

The support for republicanism by the Reform Committee and Communist activists generated considerable hostility from militant Protestantism and the link between 'Sinn Fein and Bolshevism' in the miners' union became a significant theme in the rhetoric of Lanarkshire Orangeism in the 1920s. In 1921 a predominantly Protestant body calling itself the 'Scottish National Trade Union Association' was set up in opposition to the LMCU.[32] The new body seems to have been ephemeral, but its significance lies in the evidence it provides of the depth of feeling by Protestants against the leftward movement in the LMCU. If Protestants were leaving the official union, it helps further to explain the steep decline in membership after 1921. We can glean some information on the religious composition of the various mining communities from the form of religious service recorded in the civil marriage registers. The religious affiliation of mineworkers married in the Blantyre, Larkhall and Craigneuk districts of Lanarkshire between 1920 and 1925 were examined. (Craigneuk, lying between Motherwell and Wishaw and known locally as 'Little Moscow', was regarded as the centre of Newbold's electoral support.) It is apparent that Protestantism was strong in Larkhall where Communist support was weak: 91.6 per cent of miners there were married in Protestant churches. The reverse was the case in Blantyre and Craigneuk, with 48.1 per cent and 64.6 per cent of the miners marrying according to Catholic rites.[33] Other fragmentary evidence also suggests an association between Catholicism and the areas of strong MM support. The adjacent mining villages of Stane and Dykehead in the Shotts district were regarded as being, respectively, predominantly Catholic and Protestant.[34] This division may have underpinned the MM vote of 87 per cent in the Stane branch in 1927, and of only 14 per cent at Batonrigg near Dykehead.

Fife

In Fife the situation in 1927 was extremely complex. The reform union amalgamated with the FKCMA at the beginning of the year. In the elections to the NUSM and for two posts of full-time union officials in the summer of 1927 all the official Communist candidates were successfully elected while William Adamson, the FKCMA's right-wing General Secretary, was voted off the executive of the NUSM on which he had sat since 1908.[35]

Branch voting records are available only for the second of three exhaustive ballots. From these records have been identified branches which consistently displayed the strong support for Communist and right-wing candidates. A clear geographical division is apparent: all the Communist strongholds were in central and east Fife, while all but one of the right-wing strongholds were found in west Fife and Clackmannan. Support for the CP was found in the larger branches and, although FKCMA branches were based on residence not workplace, the CP was strongest in areas where there was a concentration of large mines; right-wing strength was in the smaller mines and more scattered rural settlements.[36]

From this survey of events in 1927 we can get a clear picture of the geography of CP support in the Scots mining regions. Never uniform, it was strongest in the two largest county unions of Lanarkshire and Fife. The CP's hold on the fragmented and declining mining population in Lanarkshire was less secure than in Fife. Although party members held office as president and general secretary of the LMCU, and could on occasion win ballot votes of the decimated membership, the CP remained in a minority on the LMCU Executive Committee. Events in the Lanarkshire union in 1928 alternated between stalemate and chaos. Moreover, as the coal industry in Lanarkshire collapsed, union membership went into sharp decline. After a visit to Blantyre at the end of 1928 David Proudfoot, a leading Fife Communist, reported that 'the prevalent feeling [among party members] in Lanarkshire is that there is no union to save, that we should immediately set about the formation of a new union'.[37] Such attitudes need to viewed against the background of growing support within elements of the CP for the CI's ultra-left 'new line': J.R. Campbell complained that some rank-and-file members had returned from the sixth World Congress of the CI held in the summer of 1928 with 'a new union complex'.[38] In Fife the CP was divided on the question of forming a new 'red' union, support being greatest in central Fife, while in east Fife David Proudfoot and John McArthur were presciently anxious of the dangers of sectarian isolation from the organised mineworkers of Britain.[39]

In response to a combination of CI pressure, the recognition by the Miners' Federation of Great Britain of a breakaway Fife union led by the defeated right-winger William Adamson and the threat of the NUSM to disaffiliate the now Communist-controlled FKCMA, the CP arranged for the inaugural conference of the UMS to be held in April 1929. The county affiliations of the 132 delegates generally followed the geographical distribution of Communist support analysed above: 64 were from Lanarkshire, 47 from Fife, eight from Ayrshire, six from West Lothian, four from Stirlingshire, three from Mid- and East Lothian.[40] The union was launched with a desperate optimism, with William Allan, its first General Secretary, claiming that the UMS represented 'the only line of salvation, of helping the unions to recover those tens of thousands of trade union members who have broken with County trade unionism in disgust ...'.[41] The desire for one union was to prove wishful thinking (there were three unions in Fife alone in 1929) and the increasingly ultra-left sectarianism of the CP led to bitter inter-union rivalries. It is to the political questions of policy, organisation and cadre quality raised by the experience of the UMS that we now turn.

Communist Party Policy and Cadre
in the Scots Coalfields

Both Branson and Macfarlane have summarised the combination of manoeuvres by the right-wing union bureaucracy and growing support for the 'new line' which meant the formation of the UMS was 'inevitable' and 'irresistible'.[42] Macfarlane goes on to suggest that 'but for the "new line", however, wiser counsels might have prevailed'.[43] This conclusion fails to take account of the fissiparous tendencies within the Scots miners' unions – CP activists in Fife had already defied the party leadership in the formation of the reform union, which had been merged with the FKCMA for barely a year. Macfarlane also neglects the extent to which the internal conflicts within the Scots miners unions were themselves deployed by advocates of the 'new line' as evidence of the 'very definite leftward swing among the masses': for example by Page Arnot before the British Commission of the Ninth Plenum of the CI.[44]

Of further significance was a persistent ultra-leftist tendency within the Scottish CP since its formation, over which the 'new line' exerted considerable support. Martin Durham has convincingly demonstrated the likelihood of an unauthorised, secret armed group within the party in Scotland in 1920–1 and even the much more pragmatic David Proudfoot was allegedly willing to authorise the dynamiting of a pithead in 1926.[45] Proudfoot was nevertheless highly critical of the ultra-leftism of '100 per cent new liners' such as Bob Selkirk, sub-district organiser in central Fife, who in 1929 wrote to *Workers' Life* criticising party propaganda for failing to 'prepare the workers for British civil war conditions', citing Lenin's 1905 exhortation for 'our workers to be trained for the mass production of bombs'.[46] Proudfoot complained that Selkirk was 'not alone in this as some of his close associates are also imbued with this particular bug' and had produced a pit paper called the *Red Guard* at the Mary Colliery 'with crossed rifles and bayonets as the design on the title. Some bloody design on a pit paper'.[47] The following year the Political Bureau despatched William Gallacher to Fife after a group of expelled members, including Selkirk, accused the CPGB of 'opportunism' and attempted to set up a new CP local loyal to the CI.[48]

In Lanarkshire also there was a strong ultra-left current: 'we have to fight the right wing with our fists, our heads and our boots', declared Ed McLaughlin of Blantyre before the party's tenth Congress.[49] Yet the Lanarkshire members were also severely criticised for 'constitutionalism' in their fight for control of the LMCU. J.R. Campbell castigated the 'weakness and poor quality' of the party membership there, confessing to the Plenum of RILU that 'our greatest failure in Lanarkshire was that we did not see the necessity of the Party conducting independent economic struggles in the coalfield ... [the situation] degenerated into a fight between communists and reformists over union jobs'.[50] In response to such criticisms the Lanarkshire Communists endeavoured to foment strikes at all costs. The UMS executive, in its report to the union's Second Annual Conference, called for:

> the complete elimination of the bad mistake of hurriedly calling for strike action without serious preparation ... The blunders made at Blantyre in the latter part of 1929 in this connection should serve as an object lesson to every member of the union. Here the mistake was made of mechanically bringing the men on strike on an issue entirely unrelated to the previous circumstances in the locality and the immediate demands of the miners which brought about a strike defeat.[51]

The consequences of such tactics (and the tensions within the party which they generated) were privately recorded by David Proudfoot when he was despatched to Shotts where there was 'one hell-of-a mess':

> This in spite of the many reassuring reports of big additions to the Party, YCL and UMS. The usual line of keeping us in the dark until everything has gone phut, then in a panic deciding that some 'Right Winger', 'Social Democrat', 'Federalist', 'Pessimist' or 'Non-believer in the Radicalisation theory' etc, like myself is then pitchforked in to attempt in a few weeks to build up after clearing away the bloody mess created by the political purists who draft resolutions in the approved 10th Plenum etc manner without understanding what they are drafting or how to apply the decisions some of them are so glib at yapping about.[52]

There were only five members of the CP left in the district and the UMS was described as 'exceptionally weak' with less than a 100 members, and 50 per cent of those were unemployed. Proudfoot also blamed 'the bad heritage of the "Strike", "Strike" continually "Strike" slogan of our Lanarkshire comrades' and complained that 'Party members seen with their pockets bulging with lit[erature], pamphlets, D[aily] W[orker] or leaflets are chaffed by the average worker about having another pocketful of bombs'.[53]

In Fife, although the UMS was more securely rooted in the pits, the CP faced the opposite problem of 'constitutionalism' within the union. Among the obstacles to building Committees of Action in 1930

Proudfoot included local UMS officials being in 'the orthodox trade union rut'. Many of them, Proudfoot argued, believed that the union reforms which had long been campaigned for were now incorporated within the UMS constitution and this encouraged passivity or worse:

> they are now realising the class nature of the UMS and have no desire to be identified with it. They now recognise that the 'reforms' in the Rules and Constitution do not constitute the victory they previously had in mind and are now looking for a getaway.[54]

Moreover, 'the syndicalist approach' of the West of Scotland representatives, who had drafted the rules and had insisted on 'rank and filers only' on the UMS executive, excluded the most experienced militants who worked as organisers: 'it is the most awful dud E.C. that I have ever come across' lamented Proudfoot.[55]

These conflicting and destructive tendencies within the CP and UMS were inherent within the contradictory policy of attempting to build 'a revolutionary union in a non-revolutionary situation' (to paraphrase Macfarlane's famous epigram). These tensions were exemplified in the objects of the union which combined conventional trade union goals with mobilising the Scottish miners 'for the overthrow of the capitalist system and the establishment of a Revolutionary Workers' Government'.[56]

In addition to these policy-derived difficulties, the union was also bedevilled by maladministration and a shortage of funds. In December 1930 the Political Bureau of the CP decided that Proudfoot should replace Allan as General Secretary. Proudfoot was himself overwhelmed by 'the almost unbelievable mess' of the union's affairs and resigned from both his position and the party in September 1931.[57] He was replaced by Abe Moffat who remained in post until the party liquidated the UMS in 1936. Under Moffat's leadership, and in step with the CPGB leadership's shift towards 'revolutionary pragmatism', the emphasis within UMS activities focused more on the objects of militant trade unionism than on revolutionary class struggle.[58]

That both Moffat and Proudfoot came from Fife reflected the decline of the party's strength in Lanarkshire. A party commission noted that the union had become 'overall a Fife union': from October 1929 to November 1930 the contributions from Fife branches had increased from 52.2 per cent to 64.5 per cent of the union's total income. Although it was regarded as essential not to concentrate on Fife, and it was intended that Allan return to Lanarkshire 'where his previous influence lies' to rebuild the organisation there, this was not to be. Mass unemployment, fear of victimisation, movement away from the West–Central field and the party's ultra-leftism all contributed to this decline and the consolidation of the UMS's strength in Fife. By 1932 approximately 70 per cent of the union's income came from Fife.[59] In part this was due to the obverse of the reasons which explain the decline in Lanarkshire. The larger companies operating the more modern pits of the Fife region were better placed than those in the west to survive the economic crisis of the 1930s. The workforce in Fife was also less fissured by sectarianism. A key element in Gallacher's victory in 1935 over the former Labour MP, William Adamson of the FCKMU, was the support given by the UMS to striking miners at Valleyfield in the months preceding the election. Valleyfield, with one of the few large Catholic communities in Fife, also elected Abe Moffat as its county councillor in 1938.[60]

These successes also reflected the quality of the party's local cadre in Fife. There are unfortunate echoes of the popular Scottish stereotype of the 'feckless Glasgow Irish' in John McArthur's critical appraisal of his Lanarkshire comrades:

> Allan, in spite of his enormous ability, suffered from what I always felt was a weakness common to most people that I knew in the Lanarkshire movement. That was a lack of serious sense of responsibility, a go-easy, devil-may-care, sometimes flippant and jocular attitude to organisational questions and the solving of problems ... It showed a big difference in the mental approach to trade unionism, to strike activity and so on between the Fife comrades and many of our Lanarkshire colleagues.[61]

Nevertheless, it may contain an element of truth. In Fife, 'probably ... because of our Calvinistic Scots upbringing', the CP sought to develop a cadre with a strong sense of Bolshevik morality and seriousness.[62] The CP and UMS in Fife built a solid base as militant trade unionists, waging defensive strikes in 1931 and 1932, and in the following years instituted a systematic programme of statutory pit safety inspections. The reputation of this Fife cadre was reflected in later years by the election of Abe Moffat as NUSM President in 1942 and of McArthur as an official of the Fife area of the NUM in 1946.

Notes

1. For example see *Inprecorr*, 9, 57, 1929, p. 1229.
2. M. McCarthy, *Generation in Revolt* (Heinemann, 1953), p. 169.

3. P. Cooke, 'Radical regions? Space, time and gender relations in Emilia, Provence and South Wales', in G. Rees et al. (eds), *Political Action and Social Identity: Class, Locality and Ideology* (Macmillan, 1985) and 'Class practices as regional markers: a contribution to labour geography', in D. Gregory and J. Urry, *Social Relations and Spatial Structures* (Macmillan, 1985).

4. P. Long, 'The economic and social history of the Scottish coal industry; 1925–39' (University of Strathclyde, unpublished PhD thesis, 1978), p. 130.

5. For a fuller discussion of mechanisation in Lanarkshire see A. Campbell, 'Colliery mechanisation in Lanarkshire', *Bulletin of the Society for the Study of Labour History*, 49, autumn 1984; for Fife see S. McIntyre, *Little Moscows: Communism and Working-class Militancy in Inter-war Britain* (Croom Helm, 1980), p. 153. Scotland's strike propensity is discussed in R. Church et al., 'British coalmining strikes 1893–1940: dimensions and distributions', *Discussion Paper Series, School of Business and Economic Studies, University of Leeds*, April 1989, p. 11.

6. *List of Mines*, 1927; P. Long, 'Economic and social history' pp. 84, 88.

7. A.B. Campbell, *The Lanarkshire Miners: A Social History of Their Trade Unions, 1775–1874* (John Donald, 1979), ch. 7.

8. *Motherwell Times*, 19 February 1926.

9. P. Long, 'Abe Moffat, the Fife miners and the United Mineworkers of Scotland: transcript of a 1974 interview', *Scottish Labour History Society Journal*, 17, 1982.

10. Letters from Chief Constables of Ayr and Kilmarnock to Scottish Office, 2 November 1926, HH 56/22, Scottish Record Office.

11. For examples see *Glasgow Herald*, 6 July, 13 October and 15 November 1926.

12. A. Campbell, 'From independent collier to militant miner: tradition and change in the trade union consciousness of the Scottish miners; 1874–1929', *Scottish Labour History Society Journal*, 24, 1989, pp. 8–23.

13. Calculated from figures in P. Long, 'Economic and social history', p. 509; *Miner*, 27 September 1923; *Communist*, 15 November 1921.

14. *Workers' Weekly*, 11 July 1924; copy of letter, 25 December 1923, in Letter Book, apparently of East Fife group of CP, 'CP, MM, RILU and YCL', G032, *Proudfoot Collection*, Buckhaven and Methil Public Library (BMPL).

15. For Maclean's relationship with the CP see R. Challinor, *The Origins of British Bolshevism* (Croom Helm, 1977), pp. 250–1; *Socialist*, May and December 1923; *Workers' Weekly*, 1 February 1924.

16. *Communist*, 27 January 1923.

17. *LMCU Minutes of Council Meetings*, 1925, Deposit 227 (41), National Library of Scotland (NLS).

18. I. MacDougall, *Militant Miners* (Polygon, 1981), pp. 141–2; I. MacDougall, 'Some aspects of the 1926 General Strike in Scotland', in I. MacDougall (ed.), *Essays in Labour History* (John Donald, nd); P. and C. Carter, 'The miners of Kilsyth in the 1926 General Strike and lockout', *Our History*, pamphlet 58, spring 1974.

19. *Workers' Life*, 4 and 25 March 1927; Notes made by the late James Klugmann at the Institute Marxism-Leninism, Moscow, Folders 4, 9, 13, 16, deposited in the CPGB Archive, London (JK).

20. Memorandum, 'The mining situation in GB', signed 'JRC, [J.R. Campbell] for Political Secretariat', Folder 2, JK.

21. Letter from David Proudfoot to G. Allen Hutt, 27 January 1927, *Proudfoot Collection*, BMPL. (Letters in this collection will be cited as 'Proudfoot Letter'.)

22. Proudfoot Letter, 11 October 1930.

23. See A. Campbell, 'Tradition and generational change in the Scots miners' unions: 1874–1929', in A. Blok et al., *Generations in Labour* (International Institute of Social History, 1989) for a discussion of the generational aspect of CP support.

24. *MELMA Minutes of Board Meetings*, 11 May, 7 and 29 June 1929, Accession 4312 (13), NLS.

25. 'The mining situation in GB', Folder 2, JK; *Forward*, 11 August 1928.

26. *AMU Minutes of Delegate Meetings*, 29 October 1927; 23 and 30 August 1928; 27 April 1929, Deposit 258 (1), NLS.

27. *LMCU Minutes of Council Meetings*, 1925 and 1927, Deposit 227 (41) and (43), NLS.

28. I. MacDougall (1981), *Militant Miners*, pp. 35–6.

29. J.C. Welsh, *The Morlocks* (Herbert Jenkins, 1924), p. 198.

30. J.W. Peck to P.J. Rose, 20 November 1926, HH 56/28, Scottish Record Office.

31. 'Autobiographical material relating to Newbold's life' (unpaginated), *Newbold Papers*, John Rylands Library, Manchester; *Workers' Weekly*, 11 December 1923. For an account of Newbold's election see R. Duncan, '"Motherwell to Moscow": Walton Newbold, revolutionary politics and the Labour movement in a Lanarkshire Con-

stituency 1918–1922', *Journal of the Scottish Labour History Society*, 28, 1993.

32. *Motherwell Times*, 15 July and 12 August 1921.

33. For Craigneuk see, for example, *Motherwell Times*, 17 November and 1 December 1922; data calculated from civil marriage registers, 1920–25, Register House, Edinburgh.

34. R. Duncan, *Shotts miners, conflicts and struggles: 1919–1960* (Motherwell District Libraries, 1982), p. 21.

35. For a detailed account of these developments see D. Proudfoot and J. McArthur, *Barriers of the Bureaucrats* (National Minority Movement, nd [1929]), p. 6.

36. 'Ballot returns re appointment of 2 Agents' and 'Ballot returns re appointment of 5 for National Executive', FKCMA, A/118, *Proudfoot Collection*, BMPL.

37. Proudfoot Letter, 25 December 1928.

38. Cited in N. Branson, *History of the Communist Party of Britain 1927-1941* (Lawrence & Wishart, 1985), p. 40.

39. Proudfoot Letter, 25 December 1928 and S. McIntyre, *Little Moscows*, p. 166.

40. Political Bureau, CPGB, 6 March 1929, Folder 2, JK; *Worker*, 19 April 1929.

41. W. Allan, 'The position of the Scottish miners', *Labour Monthly*, 11, 1929, p. 284.

42. N. Branson, *History*, pp. 14, 41–3; L.J. Macfarlane, *The British Communist Party: its Origins and Development until 1929* (MacGibbon & Kee, 1966), pp. 265–73.

43. Ibid., p. 274.

44. *Communist Policy in Great Britain: The Report of the British Commission of the Ninth Plenum of the Comintern* (CPGB, 1928), pp. 108, 126, 179.

45. M. Durham, 'The origins and early years of British Communism, 1914–24' (University of Birmingham, unpublished PhD thesis, 1982); interview with J. Boyle, Methil, 6 August 1986.

46. *Workers' Life*, 23 August 1929.

47. Proudfoot Letter, 2 September 1929.

48. Political Bureau, 12 June 1930, Folder 9, JK.

49. Conference report, Folder 6, JK.

50. *Inprecorr*, 9, 57, 1929.

51. Executive Committee Report to 2nd Annual Conference, UMS, 12 October 1930, F008, *Proudfoot Collection*, BMPL.

52. Proudfoot Letter, 27 September 1930.

53. Ibid., 11 October 1930.
54. Ibid., 2 and 8 February, 1930.
55. Ibid., 28 February 1930.
56. *United Mineworkers of Scotland: Constitution and Rules*, F001, *Proudfoot Collection*, BMPL.
57. Political Bureau, 23 December 1930 and 'Report on situation in UMS by Harry Pollitt, 31 December 1930', Folder 9, JK; Proudfoot Letter, 14 February and 13 September 1931.
58. For discussion of 'revolutionary pragmatism' see N. Fishman, *The Communist Party and the Trade Unions, 1933–45* (Scolar Press, 1994).
59. 'Report on situation in the UMS'. M. Sime, 'The United Mineworkers of Scotland', p. 22. I am grateful to Martin Sime for allowing me to photocopy this unpublished paper.
60. A. Moffat, *My Life with the Miners* (Lawrence & Wishart, 1966), pp. 35, 55.
61. I. MacDougall, *Militant Miners*, pp. 133–4.
62. Ibid., p. 143.

Further Reading

Ian MacDougall's *Militant Miners* (Polygon, 1981) is an invaluable sourcebook. The first section consists of the memoirs of John McArthur; the second transcribes dozens of letters written by David Proudfoot to George Allen Hutt during the period 1924 to 1926. These provide a unique insight into the views of one of the Scottish CP's most dedicated, articulate and perceptive militants. Many more unpublished letters covering the period 1927–36 are held with Proudfoot's collection of UMS and other union records in Buckhaven and Methil Public Library.

4 Women and Communism: a Case Study of the Lancashire Weavers in the Depression

Sue Bruley

A Communist Party has no meaning or significance without working-class involvement. Consequently historians of British Communism have been keen to discern the dynamics of the relationships between 'party and class'. Regrettably, little interest has been shown regarding gender divisions within the working class and their implications for those attempting to build the CP as a mass working-class party. Similarly, labour historians have traditionally concentrated on what they have perceived as the most 'advanced' sections of the working class, rarely considering why these are almost always male or attempting any analysis of working women within their own network of social and economic relations. As a corrective to this dominant historiography, this chapter examines the CP's role in the mass movement of women cotton workers against rationalisation, wage cuts and unemployment in the years 1928–32. This represented a high point of industrial militancy for the period and was arguably, after the General Strike, the most significant episode in inter-war labour history. Moreover, the introduction of the 'more looms' system, whilst an attempt by the cotton employers to reduce the overall wage bill, was also clearly aimed at dividing the workforce by offering the male weavers higher-paid jobs at the expense of female weavers. The episode therefore throws much light on the CP's orientation towards working women and the efforts of a key group of them to retain their jobs and living standards.

In their understanding of the oppression of women, Communists adhered to a Marxist tradition resting largely on the ideas of Engels and his *Origins of the Family, Private Property and the State*. For Engels the road to emancipation began with the proletarianisation of women; women must leave their privatised family units and participate in the capitalist economy as men do. Lenin was more explicit in developing a strategy for women. He argued that complete emancipation for women could only be achieved in a post-revolutionary society when the socialisation of all household duties would at last free women from domestic drudgery. Lenin made it clear that he envisaged the state nurseries, dining-rooms, laundries and so on to be staffed mainly by women. For him it was socialisation of labour that was the main point, not an attack on the sexual division of labour as such.[1]

Official Communist policy on women emanated from the resolution passed at the Comintern's third congress in 1921. Written largely by the German Communist Clara Zetkin, it argued that women's position in society was determined by class not gender: 'There is no specific woman question' and no 'specific women's movement'.[2] Movements like the pre-war suffrage movement were dismissed as 'bourgeois feminist'. Class-conscious women belonged inside the party, where men and women would work together in complete equality. It was recognised that many women would not be accessible through the party's normal methods of propaganda and recruitment. Therefore special women's sections would have to be formed, not as autonomous groups or committees but under strict party control.

In fact, there is little evidence in Britain of serious and systematic work among women and very few party women's groups ever got off the ground. Women's membership varied from area to area, but was typically not much more than 10 per cent of the total. Very few industrial women were recruited. The National Minority Movement, a rank-and-file movement in industry inaugurated by the CP in 1924, made no specific appeal to women workers. This lack of orientation towards women in industry is linked to the social composition of the CP. The party had established itself most successfully in mining, heavy engineering and transport. These occupations were characterised by a high degree of sexual segregation. Amongst such men the issue of equal pay did not arise since women, by informal or formal means, were excluded. The Amalgamated Engineering Union, for example, excluded women, but Communists in the union do not appear to have seen this as a particular problem. Very often women recruits to the party were the wives of party activists. Branch meetings were largely a male affair, held in the pub during the evening. Women's sections, where they existed at all, were composed largely of 'party wives' and met in the afternoons. Typically, they concentrated on fund-raising and organising party socials and failed to raise political demands relating to women.

The Lancashire cotton districts provided something of an exception to this overall picture. Cotton had been a key sector of the British economy since its initial take-off in the late eighteenth century and production was still expanding in the years up to 1914. With some 40 per cent of world textile production, it was Britain's largest manufacturing employer and provided a quarter of the country's total exports. The spinning and weaving processes were virtually separate industries, with great spinning towns like Oldham and Bolton located in the south of the county and weaving towns like Blackburn and Burnley towards the north-west. Even before 1914 the industry was falling behind the US technologically. Both horizontal and vertical integration seemed beyond the cotton employers, who appeared to have developed little since the heyday of the industrial revolution. The industry remained dominated by small, specialist firms, often family businesses, in intense competition with each other.

The supremacy of the English cotton industry and the complacency of the cotton masters rested firmly on the possession of Empire and exceptionally favourable market conditions. Conflict in Europe in 1914 hastened the inevitable growth of foreign competition and with the rise of indigenous cotton industries in Asian countries the English cotton industry never regained its pre-war position. The brief boom of 1919–20 produced large profits, but few firms used these to modernise and mills were recapitalised at grossly inflated values. When the bubble burst, firms became incapable of repaying debts and turned to the banks for large overdrafts. By the mid-1920s the industry was in serious difficulties as the employers desperately undercut each other in the struggle to retain their markets and keep up with the interest charges. This they aimed to achieve through more efficient production techniques and wage reductions.

For over a century the people of Lancashire had been imbued with the vernacular and the skills of the cotton industry. In 1913 the industry employed over half a million people, more than half of whom were women. There was a marked tendency for women to continue to work after marriage. Low fertility and birth control practices also reduced time away from work. The ideology of the single male 'breadwinner' failed to gain the dominant hold which it had attained in other industries. It was a highly differentiated labour force whose numbers included several small bodies of highly paid, male craftsmen exercising strict regulation into the trades. The largest single group were the weavers and ancillary trades. Although not recognised as skilled work, it took twelve years to become a fully established weaver. Weaving had a long tradition of collective action. In 1914 the Weavers' Association numbered 200,000 and was the second largest union in the country. It had long been established as a predominantly women's trade. Men did enter weaving but with aspirations to gain promotion to the role of overlooker or tackler. After 1914 this move became increasingly difficult. Women were excluded from becoming tacklers, although most could maintain their looms as well as any tackler.

Cotton weaving was unusual in British industry in that piecework rates were exactly the same for women as for men. In practice men frequently earned more. When demand was high they were more likely to take on extra looms and the better-paid, wider looms were usually allocated to men. Nevertheless, women weavers were nearer to enjoying equal pay with men than any other section of women workers. They were also the country's best organised group of women. Jill Liddington and Jill Norris have carefully documented the political involvement of these women in the pre-war suffrage movement.[3] The relatively equal status of women at the workplace also appears in some districts to have carried over into the home and a fairly egalitarian family structure. Bessie and Harold Dickinson, of the weaving town of Nelson, recalled a custom known as 'Mary Ann night', usually Thursday, when women and men would get down to the cleaning together.[4] The weaver from Great Harwood who stood up at the TUC in 1932 and said, 'My wife and I are permanently unemployed' must have struck an unfamiliar note among delegates who typically inhabited a more sexually segregated world, where husbands did nothing inside the home and wives were not encouraged to regard themselves as part of the labour force.[5]

Despite these traditions of equality amongst weaving families, the formal union apparatus was heavily male dominated. Like the other cotton unions, the Weavers' Amalgamation had no record of women organisers and, although women did gain representation on local committees, no woman had ever served on its executive.[6] Many unofficial barriers existed to exclude women and union meetings held in the evenings were more likely to deter women than men. Although rarely members of mill committees before 1914, women did become house collectors for union subscriptions.[7] Among rank-and-file weavers there were marked differences from area to area. North-east Lancashire, which had a long history of labour organisation, had the strongest traditions of female organisation and it is from here that we hear most later on about shared housework and birth control. In Preston, however, women weavers seem to have been relatively conventional and complacent both at home and at work, despite far outnumbering the town's male weavers. Michael Savage maintains that the crucial distinction is to be found in the work process itself. Where skill transmission was directly from worker to worker, women weavers were more likely to build up a capacity for collective action. Where the overlooker played a much greater part in the transmission of skills, in contrast, the work process was heavily patriarchal and women did not generally develop autonomous activity.[8]

After 1918 the situation was somewhat modified. Many men left weaving during the war never to return, leaving only north-east Lancashire with significant numbers of male weavers. In some mills men were absent altogether except for tacklers and other members of the labour elite. These all-women weaving sheds precluded assertions of male dominance and built up feelings of female solidarity. By the time of the employers' offensive in the late 1920s women like Emily Hoctor, president of the Ashton weavers, were at last making inroads into the union hierarchy.

In the immediate post-war boom of 1919–20 industrial action by cotton workers had secured both wage rises and a reduction in the working day. However by 1922 these advances had been clawed back by the employers. By 1928, with trade worsening further, employers began to agitate again for a large wage reduction for all cotton workers. At the same time a group of Burnley mill owners planned a twelve-month 'experiment' in which 4 per cent of the looms in twelve mills would be worked on an 'eight loom' per weaver basis. Although the 'more looms' weavers were to be paid an increased rate of 50s, it meant that four other weavers in each mill were displaced. The mill owners believed that by reducing the loom speed slightly and providing cheaper labour to perform ancillary functions a weaver could operate twice as many looms for a modestly increased wage, much less than the earnings of two four-loom weavers. Ultimately, they hoped, the scheme could reduce their total wage bill by 20–40 per cent without any outlay on costly new machinery.

When the scheme started in the designated Burnley mills in April 1929 it was with the initial agreement of the Weavers' Amalgamation. This attitude, soon to be reversed, reflected the gender divisions within the workforce. The 'more looms' scheme was more than just a cost-cutting exercise, it was also an attempt to play men and women weavers off against each other. Traditionally the weavers' union had aimed to gain recognition as a skilled trade and for male weavers, like other male skilled workers, to earn enough for their wives to become full-time housewives. It was hoped that new technology could be harnessed towards this end, but with scarcely any male weavers in some areas this patriarchal outlook had become less appropriate since the war. Except perhaps in Nelson there were too few male weavers to hope to make eight-loom weaving an exclusive all-male craft. Nevertheless, it does seem to have been union policy to employ men where possible. Alan Fowler argues that the leadership was apparently

> prepared to make a deal with the employers on the basis that the more-looms weaver would receive adequate remuneration to replace a family wage ... it was even suggested that unmarried women in the textile districts should seek work as domestic servants.[9]

Many of the 'more looms' agreements therefore incorporated a policy of favouring married men. A survey of one mill estimated that under the eight-loom system the 107 male weavers would be reduced to 101 and the 200 female weavers to 49, with the female work force evidently taking the brunt of the redundancies.[10] Even 'Red Nelson', with its record of militancy and sex equality, which also had a large number of relatively well-paid male weavers, implemented an anti-women 'more looms' policy. In July 1931 Sir Amos Nelson, owner of Valley Mills, secured an agreement with the Weavers' Amalgamation to raise the wages of the upgraded male weavers at the expense of the 37 per cent of the workforce who were married women. These were all sacked.[11] Unemployment figures also indicate that women weavers were more prone to be displaced than men.[12]

There were several grounds for opposition to 'more looms'. In the early days it was often held in the press and even amongst weavers' union officials that the system was unworkable and would eventually fizzle out. Sometimes this view took a sexist form with the assertion that women weavers were not capable of operating eight looms and stories abounded of women fainting at their looms under the new system. There is little evidence that women themselves took this view but many resented the intensification of existing work practices. Even with extra help, working six or eight looms for a few more shillings a week was a heavy burden to bear. Weaving was already a strenuous occupation in a noisy, hazardous environment. Worn out by hard work, inadequate nourishment and lack of medical care, women now faced even greater exploitation. The resentment of working women, however, was nothing compared to the anger of the unemployed.

Ultimately resistance to the 'more looms' system was inextricably bound up with the general struggle against wage cuts. In 1929 the employers won an across-the-board wage reduction after both sides had agreed to arbitration. This did nothing to alleviate the industry's deepening crisis and as unemployment rose opposition to the new system mounted. The employers responded with a seven-week lock-out in early 1931 which involved 113,203 members of the Weavers'

Union. The workers remained solid and, in the teeth of a vigorous press campaign, a union ballot produced a two-to-one majority against negotiations on 'more looms'. Eventually, faced with such strong opposition and divisions in their own ranks, the employers reopened the mills without insisting on the new terms. The weavers' victory proved to be shortlived, however, as individual mills tried to introduce different variations on the theme of 'more looms'.

Cohesion among employers had broken down and recognised agreements were suspended as employers, desperate to cut costs, offered weavers looms at the lower 'more looms' rate but without extra looms. In some areas unemployment was approaching 50 per cent and many workers were too desperate to resist. Mass pickets attempted to deter these 'blackleg' or 'knobstick' workers and violent scenes were commonplace where non-unionised weavers were bussed in to mills to work at below union rates. Great Harwood Mill, near Blackburn, was one such. Early in 1932 one of the buses was met there by a crowd of 2,000 'booing and jeering'. Police escorts were necessary to get the workers into the mill. Two days later a crowd of 3,000 had gathered and the occupants of one of the buses were given what the *Cotton Factory Times* described as 'a rough time'. The Earby Mill, near Blackburn, was another centre of discontent where police frequently made baton charges against pickets. Many allegations were made of police harassment.[13]

By this time the employers still trying to operate a recognised system were resorting to another round of wage reductions, since agreement on 'more looms' seemed a futile pursuit. In June 1932 they announced the suspension of all previous agreements on wages and conditions. A union ballot resulted in a majority for strike action against wage cuts. Predictably, Burnley weavers came out first at the end of July, but at the end of August the union leadership called for a county-wide stoppage of all cotton workers. This was one of the biggest disputes of the inter-war period and was characterised by exceptionally militant picketing and many violent incidents. The Burnley Labour Party alleged that '200 charges of unprovoked brutality could be brought against the police'.[14] Many women involved in picketing were brought up before local magistrates. Charges of verbal abuse, disorderly behaviour and breaches of the peace were common. Evelyn Foulds, mother of six children, had an infant with her when she engaged in 'booing and shouting' during a picket in Burnley in August 1932. The police constable described her as 'more conspicuous than anyone else'. The magistrate fined her 5s and told her firmly that as a mother the picket was 'the last place she should have been'.[15]

The strike ended after five weeks with the Midland Agreement of 24 September. Exhausted and demoralised, the cotton workers were forced to agree to further wage cuts, bringing down their average wage to a little over 30s. The agreement failed to solve the 'more looms' problem and promised only to reopen negotiations on the question. The workers were defeated, but with the exception of the miners they had resisted wage cuts more tenaciously than any other group of workers in this period.

Turning now to the response of the left to these events, we look first at the Labour Party. The period in which the crisis had developed was that of the second minority Labour government of 1929–31. Initially the election of the government had been greeted by jubilation amongst Labour supporters in Lancashire. Unlike the Independent Labour Party, the Labour Party had until well into the 1920s taken little interest in policies specifically geared towards the needs of women and in the cotton areas the overlapping categories of union and Labour Party officialdom were normally stalwart supporters of the family wage policy. Nevertheless, by 1929 many women cotton workers were beginning to join the Labour Party, reflecting the rise of female consciousness and the growth of the Labour Party nationally as a mass social democratic party. Disillusionment quickly set in, however, as it became clear that the government's attitude to the cotton workers was indistinguishable from that of the previous Conservative administration. Margaret Bondfield, ex-trade union official, now Minister of Labour, pursued a policy, started earlier in the 1920s, of promoting 'homecraft centres' for unemployed women and girls. In addition, the government introduced the Anomalies Act of 1931. Heavily discriminatory in character, this served to deny married women unemployment benefit, whatever their National Insurance contributions. It is not surprising that support for Labour in Lancashire fell off dramatically, especially among women. Its 1931 electoral humiliation was particularly disastrous in the cotton districts and even 'Red' Nelson and Colne fell to the Tories.

We should be careful, however, not to regard Labour as a homogenous entity, for the policies of the MacDonald government were deeply offensive to many Labour supporters in Lancashire. Encouraged by a minority of the leadership which kept up a commitment to socialist politics, many of the activists in the disputes of this period were, and remained, loyal to the Labour Party. Selina Cooper, for example, veteran of the radical suffrage movement, Nelson JP and a Labour councillor, was a vigorous supporter of the cotton workers. She fought on the bench for the right of striking families to secure relief and in 1931 marched under a banner which read, 'Unemployed Can't Get 4 Looms – What About 8 Looms?'.[16]

As for the Communist Party, it had by this time adopted the Comintern's ultra-left positions of the so-called 'Third Period', announcing the final breakdown of the capitalist system and the increasing radicalisation of the masses. Its 'Class Against Class' manifesto for the 1929 election refused support for Labour's 'social fascists' and called for a 'Revolutionary Workers' Government'. Its industrial emphasis shifted to unorganised workers who were urged to bypass the official trade unions and form 'Revolutionary Trade Union Committees'. These policies were inappropriate for a working class demoralised by the outcome of the General Strike and, from a high point of 10,000 members in 1926, party membership sank to less than 3,000 at the height of the slump.

In 1929 the party launched, through the National Minority Movement, a minimum programme for the cotton industry. Its demands included a 40-hour week, a minimum wage, abolition of fining and compensation for bad material.[17] The aim was to build a Textile Minority Movement on the basis of affiliations from rank-and-file committees. In practice the struggle developed on the basis of opposition to the 'more looms' system and demands for relief for striking and unemployed cotton workers. The offensive demands of the minimum programme, including the slogan of a Revolutionary Workers' Government, were hopelessly inappropriate for what was essentially a defensive battle. Party militants did, however, throw themselves wholeheartedly into the struggle and played an important role in linking the resistance to wage cuts and 'more looms' disputes with the unemployed movement. Moreover, the CP-led Workers' International Relief organised a solidarity network of soup kitchens and food parcels for strikers and their dependants.

During 1929 the party concentrated on general agitation, but in the course of 1930–1 there were signs of an increased sensitivity to the way that the crisis in the industry was affecting men and women in different ways. As 1931 progressed a new emphasis on the recruitment of women is apparent and the Textile Minority Movement published Bessie Dickinson's anonymous pamphlet *Women and the More Loom System*. The fact that mill owners were attempting to hire men for the new system and to sack women was clearly stated. Dickinson pointed out that, despite the majority of women in the weavers' union, there were very few women on local committees. 'Women workers, particularly,' she wrote, 'must make up their minds to fight as an organised body inside the Trade Unions and not be bluffed by the fine talk of the officials.' What is interesting here is that the sexual divisions which the party usually glossed over were brought to the fore. The *Cotton Strike Leader,* which was launched during the 1932 strike, and continued for almost a year as the *Cotton Workers' Leader,* also paid a good deal of attention to women cotton workers. The paper urged the necessity to maintain mass picketing and promoted the rights of women as workers, demanding, 'every weaver her looms back' and 'full rights of women within the trade unions'.[18]

It does appear that militant women weavers had pushed the CP into a new orientation towards women. The Communist Party, in this situation, could not be 'leading the cotton workers' unless it was a vigorous promoter of the women's demands. This contrasts strongly with the party's strategy during the early phase of the dispute when the male exclusivity of the mule spinners and other elite groups in cotton was conveniently overlooked. Prior to this new orientation, which occurs around the same time as the 'more looms' strike, the sexual divisions among the cotton workers were not acknowledged. But if the party was taking its lead from women in weaving what was happening in spinning?

Here a rigid sexual division of labour operated to the disadvantage of women. Unlike men, who were relatively well paid and highly organised, the 'women's jobs' in spinning were poorly paid and very few women were organised. Solidarity between men and women was conspicuously absent. Without any organised pressure from women themselves to raise their pay or to gain access to male preserves, the CP was not likely to promote the interests of women in spinning. It does appear that when men and women workers had conflicting interests the party promoted the interests of the most class-conscious organised group, which was invariably the men. In the situation of 1930–1, with thousands of women weavers fiercely defending their right to work, this tendency was reversed. The party had no option but to support the women weavers, which meant publicly denouncing rationalisation schemes which gave preference to male workers as 'breadwinners'.

Who were the women activists in the cotton disputes? Lily Webb, Margaret McCarthy and Rose Smith were all nationally-known Communist activists. Lily Webb was born in 1897 and grew up in a cotton household near Ashton-under-Lyne in south Lancashire. She neglected her schooling in order to carry dinners, run errands and childmind for mill workers. She entered a mill at 14 and after seven years left Lancashire. As a Communist she became active in the 1920s in the unemployed movement. Soon after the 1929 election she was sent to stand as Communist candidate in a by-election in Preston. Due to lack of funds she ran as a 'demonstrative' candidate but although her name was not on the ballot paper she organised a vigorous campaign and held many meetings outside cotton mills. In 1932 she came back to Lancashire to assist in the Women's National Hunger March.[19]

Margaret McCarthy was brought up by her widowed mother, a weaver, in very poor circumstances. She started work at a weaving mill in Accrington and by the late 1920s was a leading cadre of the Young Communist League and a delegate to international youth congresses. She was unemployed in the period 1929–30 and threw herself into the agitation against the 'more looms' system. Like Lily Webb, she was subsequently involved in the hunger marches and also spent time in the Soviet Union.[20]

Rose Smith was originally from Mansfield, Notts. During the 1920s she built a reputation as a CP speaker and organiser and in 1929 came with her two young sons to take up the post of full-time organiser in Burnley. Her active involvement in the 'more looms' picketing, particularly outside the Spencer mill, led to a prison sentence of three months in October 1930. Although it was intended that she should run as a candidate in the 1931 General Election, the idea was dropped due to adverse publicity and she was replaced by Jim Rushton, a leading local Communist and weavers' union activist.

We know far less about the women rank and file who supported the Communist Party in these years. Only by means of oral history have a handful of activists been documented in any detail.[21] One, Bessie Smith, was born in 1904 into a weaving family of parents and seven children. It was a socialist household and Bessie used to collect her father's copy of *Justice*, weekly paper of the Social Democratic Federation, a forerunner of the Communist Party. Robert Blatchford's *Merrie England* and *Britain for the British* were the first books which she read. She entered the mill at twelve and worked as a tenter for half a crown a week. From 1922 she was active in the Young Communist League (YCL). She married Harold Dickinson in 1926 and Bessie Dickinson rapidly became a leading cadre in Blackburn, where they lived. She stood as a party candidate in the Blackburn municipal elections in 1928 and 1930. She also wrote the pamphlet *Women and More Looms* and contributed to the party press on the labour movement in Lancashire.

Like other activists, Bessie and Harold were unemployed for much of the period 1929–32 and took part in many of the mass pickets in the

Burnley and Blackburn areas. Pickets at the Haigntons factory in Barrowsford, where a 'more looms' system was in operation, were kept up for twelve months. Rose Smith, among others, spoke at public meetings organised for the pickets. Jim Rushton organised a march to Preston from Barrowsford to claim relief for the strikers and their families. The CP was also active in the picketing of the Imperial factory in Burnley, which had introduced a six-loom system. When Amy Hargreaves, an unemployed weaver and a Communist, was arrested, 'crowds of people' followed her to the police station.[22] She subsequently received a fine of £8. Bessie and Harold Dickinson were also arrested and each received a three-month prison sentence for 'watching and besetting'.[23] In 1929 Hargreaves had stood for election to the Burnley Weavers' Committee and mustered 220 votes as against the successful candidate's 557.[24]

Until late into the 1930s there is no evidence of any women's sections of the Communist Party in the cotton districts. The struggle against 'more looms' brought 'women's issues' to the forefront of party work and with a tradition of women working after marriage there was no rationale for separate groups meeting in the afternoon. With a small membership and mass activity around them, both men and women threw themselves into 'mainstream' party work. Bessie Dickinson could not recall women's sections playing a big part. Both she and Evelyn Howley were aware that some Communist men preferred their wives to keep away from party work. As Bessie remarked, 'They like their home comfort don't they ... they don't want the women out. They wouldn't have kept me in, away from it.'[25]

It does appear that many Communists in north-east Lancashire enjoyed marriages which were genuine partnerships. Besides Harold and Bessie Dickinson and Evelyn Howley and her husband Jack, there is the example of George and Bertha Jane, who were both active in the unemployed movement. George looked after their two small daughters when Bertha served a month's prison sentence in 1930 after refusing to refrain from marches and demonstrations for a year. This tendency for a close, sharing relationship was very evident in the reminiscences of the Dickinsons and Evelyn Howley. At one time the Howleys both wanted to enrol for an evening class in economics at the Labour College, but were faced with a babysitting problem:

So we decided that we'd go, and one week Jack would look after them ... and t'other week I'd stop in and he could go. And that's how, more or less, that we got some fundamental understanding, shall we say, about socialism.[26]

It would be interesting to know if any Communist men in mining or engineering would have been willing to go in for such an arrangement. Besides party couples there were also examples of women on their own, such as Rose Smith and Maggie Nelson, both divorced single parents, but there is little evidence of a 'housewife' element in the party in Lancashire.

Another agitation linked with the resistance to 'more looms' and wage cuts was that of the unemployed. The authorities' reaction to single women out of work was to attempt to channel them into domestic service, army canteens or seasonal work in Blackpool. Minister of Labour, Margaret Bondfield, felt that domestic work was a 'great' occupation for women and that the loss of domestic servants during the war meant that a 'crusade' was necessary to persuade women to return to domestic labour.[27] Margaret McCarthy's recollection was very different: '"Service" to the independent Lancashire factory girl was a form of employment deeply tainted with the stigma of genuine servitude. No self-respecting girl would go "into service".'[28] Some mill girls would 'gang up together' and pretend to be ignorant of domestic work.[29] Others simply refused to take up work in Blackpool.[30] During 1931 conditions for the unemployed changed considerably for the worse with cuts in benefit, the hated Means Test and Anomalies Regulations depriving thousands of married women of benefit.

How did the Labour movement respond to all this? The idea of enforced domestic work for single mill women was received with 'widespread indignation' and many weavers' associations spoke against it. As the Nelson Weavers protested to the government:

> Our women and girls are entitled to live in their own homes and not to be compelled to live in lodgings in other people's houses where they have generally to live in a station of inferiority to the remainder of the household.[31]

On the question of married women's benefit, feelings were more mixed. The *Cotton Factory Times* provided detailed advice for women on how to avoid having benefit withdrawn, but alternative views were also evident and one article referred to the 'exorbitant' claims of married women.[32] This paper, although privately owned, acted as a major channel of communication for cotton workers as union officials sent in material for publication.

The main unemployed organisation, the National Unemployed Workers' Movement (NUWM), was closely linked to the Communist Party and led by the Communist Wal Hannington. Hannington, an unemployed toolmaker, had views on women which were typical of many skilled men at this time and throughout the 1920s. Like the movement he led, he was largely indifferent to the concerns of unemployed women; typically, he was against the idea of women hunger marchers.[33] During 1929–30, however, as the number of women unemployed rose, not just in Lancashire but in Yorkshire and many other areas as well, there were signs of increased women's involvement in the NUWM. It was decided that the third National Hunger March in 1930 should for the first time include a women's contingent. Margaret McCarthy, who by this time was Burnley branch secretary of the NUWM, joined the 22-strong women's contingent which met up in Bradford with the Yorkshire women marchers. They marched separately from the main group of men, she recalled, to 'avoid scandalous gossip'. Setting off from Bradford on 20 April, they merged with the much larger men's contingent for a May Day rally in Hyde Park. The women, mainly Communists, carried banners declaring, 'Under-Fed, Under-Clad, Under the Labour Government' and were led by Rose Smith. They met with much goodwill and encouragement *en route*, although due to the NUWM's links with the CP and its sectarian policies, little help was offered from labour organisations. Consequently accommodation was a problem and on several occasions they had to resort to the workhouse. In accordance with NUWM policy they did so on their own terms and refused to be submitted to the degradation of 'casual treatment'. At Wakefield, McCarthy remembered, 'We reported ourselves at ten in the evening instead of eight; we refused to be searched, we agreed to bathe, but not in the presence of attendants, and we refused to get up at six, despite the insistence of the matron.'[34]

The changes in the benefit system in 1931 brought many more women into the NUWM, which fought against unequal benefit for women and the Anomalies Regulations for married women. Most of all the movement rallied against the new Means Test and this provided the main theme for the National Hunger March of October 1932. The women's contingent of 40 started from Burnley, led by Lily Webb and Maud Brown, who worked at NUWM head office with Hannington. 'We walked an average of twelve to fourteen miles a day in all weathers,' Webb wrote in her account of the march. 'Reception Committees awaited us in the towns we stayed for the night and often they marched out to meet us and carry our packs. Sometimes they came with bands and banners and always a great crowd awaited us.'[35] The reception committee were well organised and it appears that the marchers received much more assistance from labour organisations, particularly Labour and Co-op women, than they had in 1930. Even so, at times they still had to resort to the workhouse for accommodation. Again they did so only on condition that all the usual regulations were waived. Eventually the nine separate contingents merged and the hunger marchers did the last few miles to Hyde Park as a single group. An enormous crowd gathered in Hyde Park to greet them. Lily Webb spoke along with Pollitt and Hannington on the main platform.[36] Violence broke out between police and demonstrators and as a result 75 people were injured. Webb was one of the many arrested.

The cotton industry was not the only instance in this period of women's growing industrial militancy. The Yorkshire woollen workers also faced demands for wage reductions and here too the majority of the workforce were women. In Yorkshire, however, there was scarcely any union organisation amongst the women woollen workers, who worked for pitifully low wages. The strike of 100,000 woollen workers in 1930 was doomed from the start. The CP made frantic efforts to rally support but its ultra-left slogans and demands for a 'Revolutionary Workers' Government' did little to overcome the desperate isolation of the strikers. The 'new industries' also witnessed an upsurge in women's militancy. Employers often favoured women for low-paid, monotonous factory work in light engineering, synthetic fabrics and electronics. Demands for 'speed-up' and 'scientific management' were met with stiff resistance. During 1932 there were strikes of 10,000 women against the 'Bedaux' system at the Lucas motor accessory plant in Birmingham and 4,000 women in the hosiery factory owned by Wolsey in Leicester.[37]

During 1930 and 1931 the CP was at a low ebb with less than 1,500 members in employment.[38] Traditional areas of Communist strength such as mining and heavy industry were declining rapidly. Systematic victimisation by employers had also weeded out important activists. The 'new industries' were growing fast but their workforce, many of whom were women, showed little interest in the Communist Party. With its industrial base at an all-time low, it is not surprising that the party leadership expressed increasing anxiety about the need to recruit more industrial workers and focused specifically on the problem of women. Its eleventh congress in the autumn of 1929 demanded the 'utmost energy' in overcoming its previous neglect of this work. More women should be drawn into 'leading work in the Party' and 'special demands for women workers' formulated. 'The Party must make a radical change in its work among women,' the resolution continued. 'The Women's Department must be strengthened and its work, which must be based primarily on the women in the factories, must be supported by the Party as a whole.'[39]

By the beginning of 1932, after over a year of intense opposition to 'more looms' by the women weavers of Lancashire, the party had toughened up this line considerably. A detailed resolution on women was passed at the January 1932 Central Committee and subsequently reprinted in *Party Organiser*. The tendency to reduce 'women's work' to fund raising and social activities and to keep women on the margins of the party was roundly condemned: 'the idea that this area of work is solely the affair of women communists must be stamped out.'[40] At about this time the Women's Department at head office was dissolved, despite protests from Lily Webb at the national congress. Pollitt argued that a central women's department had no meaning if it had nothing to connect with and that a new base needed to be built from the bottom up, starting from women in local branches.[41] While a women's department undoubtedly added unnecessarily to the bureaucracy of a party shrunk to dismal proportions, the whole concept of 'women's work' as separate from party work generally was in question. If women's work was also 'mainstream' party work and a priority for all comrades, why have a separate department? Surely this work was too important to be relegated to a subsidiary party organ? Consequently the concept of a separate 'Women's Department' was abandoned and leading women cadres such as Lily Webb and Rose Smith were encouraged to work directly with the Central Committee.

Apart from organisational changes a much greater sensitivity to the needs of women was evident. Besides full support for the 'more loom' agitation and against the 'Bedaux' system in Birmingham support was given for 'equal pay for equal work'. A whole string of additional demands were raised, including dining-rooms and crèches, the latter to be paid for by the state and the employers. It was recognised that the Minority Movement had 'totally failed' to develop work amongst women. The exclusive, anti-women attitude of the engineering union was at last brought out into the open and challenged.[42] The party's work with women unemployed was declared to be 'totally inadequate' and had to be 'immediately improved', especially with regard to lower benefit for women and attempts to deny them benefit entirely. The YCL was instructed to make more effort to recruit girls. No stone was left unturned and every area of party activity was scrutinised for its failings in regard to women.

It does appear that during 1931 and 1932 at least, especially in the cotton industry, the CP made determined efforts to relate positively to the needs of women workers. There is little evidence however that these efforts were sustained. In 1936 the party issued a pamphlet by William Rust on *Communism and Cotton*. The five minimum demands he raised included the abolition of 'more looms', but nowhere were the needs of women mentioned. On the contrary the issue of the low wages of (male) piecers was revived – 'work for a boy's wage although many of them are married men with families'. Evidently the infusion of feminism into the Communist Party in 1931–2 did not come from any intrinsic commitment to women but arose out of particular industrial circumstances. From 1933, when the economy moved into an upturn, the party began to recruit male industrial workers again and inevitably traditional interests were asserted once more. Industrial policy reverted to its original male-oriented stance and women were once again marginalised. Eventually a central women's department did re-emerge and women's work once more took on a fairly separate existence, albeit on the rather different basis of the Popular Front. Now feminist organisations were no longer characterised as 'bourgeois' and Communist women involved themselves in a very broad range of activities with women's organisations in the attempt to build an anti-fascist alliance of 'all progressive forces'.[43]

Acknowledgement

The author is grateful to the editors of *Women's History Review,* in which a longer version of this chapter appeared, under the title 'Gender, Class and Party' (January 1993).

Notes

1. V.I. Lenin, *Lenin and the Emancipation of Women* (Progress Publishers, Moscow, 1965), pp. 69–70.
2. *Decisions of the Third Congress of the Communist International* (Moscow, 1921 edn), p. 100.
3. J. Liddington and J. Norris, *One Hand Tied Behind Us: The Rise of the Women's Suffrage Movement* (Virago, 1978).
4. Interview, 6 September 1977.
5. Mr Slynn, Trade Union Congress *Report*, 1932, p. 245.
6. S. Walby, *Patriarchy at Work* (Cambridge University Press, 1986). Appendix One lists only one woman organiser and no women on

the executive or local committees of any cotton trade unions before 1918.

7. J. Liddington and J. Norris, *One Hand Tied Behind Us*, p. 96.
8. M. Savage, *The Dynamics of Working-class Politics: The Labour Movement in Preston 1890–1940* (Cambridge University Press, 1987).
9. A. Fowler, 'Lancashire cotton trade unionism in the inter-war years', in J.A. Jowitt and A.J. McIvor (eds), *Employers and Labour in the English Textile Industries 1850–1939* (Routledge, 1988) p. 115.
10. J.H. Riley, 'The more looms system of industrial relations in Lancashire cotton manufacturing: 1928–35' (Manchester University, MA, 1981) p. 63.
11. J. Liddington, *Selina Cooper: The Life and Times of a Respectable Rebel* (Virago, 1984), p. 391.
12. M. Savage, 'Women and work in the Lancashire cotton industry: 1890–1939', in J.A. Jowitt and A.J. McIvor (eds), *Employers and Labour*, p. 216.
13. *Cotton Factory Times*, 22 January 1932; B. Dickinson, *James Rushton and His Times:1886–1956* (nd) (copy held by WCML), p. 28.
14. *Burnley News*, 3 September 1932.
15. *Burnley News*, 27 August 1932.
16. J. Liddington, *Selina Cooper*, p. 364.
17. H. Lee, 'The cotton lock-out', *LM*, September 1929, p. 553.
18. *Cotton Strike Leader*, 24 September 1932.
19. L. Webb, 'Some party history', autobiographical article, copy in CPA.
20. M. McCarthy, *Generation in Revolt* (Heinemann, 1953), ch. 8.
21. The Manchester Studies Archive, Manchester Metropolitan University, has a large collection of tapes, including a number of cotton workers. Some have been transcribed or partly transcribed. Unfortunately, the interviews were of a very general nature and give little insight into the cotton disputes of the inter-war period.
22. B. Dickinson, *James Rushton*, p. 22.
23. R. Leeson, *Strike: A Live History 1887–1971* (Allen & Unwin, 1971), pp. 124–5.
24. *Cotton Factory Times*, 5 April 1929.
25. Interview, 6 September 1977.
26. Interview, 6 September 1977.
27. M.A. Hamilton, *Margaret Bondfield* (Leonard Parsons, 1924), pp. 171–3.
28. M. McCarthy, *Generation in Revolt*, p. 151.

29. Louie Davis interview, 5 September 1977.
30. *Cotton Factory Times*, 26 December 1930.
31. *Cotton Factory Times*, 12 December 1930.
32. *Cotton Factory Times*, 18 September 1931.
33. According to M. Henery, a Scottish hunger marcher, in I. MacDougall, *Voices from the Hunger Marches*, vol. 1 (Polygon, Edinburgh, 1990), p. 4. Interviewees who worked with Hannington confirmed that he was indifferent to women's interests.
34. M. McCarthy, *Generation in Revolt*, pp. 152–3.
35. L. Webb, 'Some party history'.
36. *The Times*, 2 November 1932; *DW*, 1 November 1932.
37. N. Branson and M. Heinemann, *Britain in the Nineteen Thirties* (Granada, 1973 edn), p. 127; *DW*, 23 January 1931.
38. About half the membership of 2,756 in June 1931 were unemployed. See H. Pollitt, *The Road to Victory* (CPGB, 1932), p. 50.
39. *Resolutions* of CPGB 11th congress, 1929, pp. 48, 27, 18.
40. 'CC resolution and work among women', *Party Organiser*, May 1932, p. 27, and June 1932, p. 16.
41. H. Pollitt, *The Road to Victory*, p. 86.
42. 'CC resolution', p. 17; 'Resolution on work among women (continued)', *Party Organiser*, July/August 1932, p. 30.
43. See S. Bruley, 'Women against war and fascism', in J. Fyrth (ed.), *Britain, Fascism and the Popular Front* (Lawrence & Wishart, 1985).

Further Reading

The fullest account of women and the CP remains my 1980 University of London PhD thesis 'Socialism and feminism in the Communist Party of Great Britain, 1920–1939'. This was later published as *Leninism, Stalinism and the Women's Movement in Britain, 1920-1939* (Garland Press, New York, 1986). Important works on politics and trade unionism in the cotton districts include A. Bullen, *The Lancashire Weavers' Union* (Amalgamated Textile Workers' Union, 1984); A. and L. Fowler, *A History of the Nelson Weavers' Association* (Burnley, Nelson, Rossendale and District Textile Workers' Union, 1984); M. Jenkins, 'Cotton struggles 1929–32', *Marxism Today*, February 1969; J.A. Jowitt and A.M. McIvor, *Employers and Labour in the English Textile Industries 1850–1939* (Routledge, 1988).

5 Authors Take Sides: Writers and the Communist Party 1920–56

Andy Croft

> Those who come after,
> Who are riding the wave when it breaks at last and the foam
> Dazzles with rainbow colours of the days of hope,
> They will not remember who you were, far back
> In the broil of ocean and out of sight of the shore
> Who kept your course though the tide ran out against you.[1]

No political organisation in Britain ever attracted so many distinguished artists, generated so much cultural energy, so many plays, novels, poems, paintings, songs and films as the Communist Party did. It may have been tiny, but its impact on British literary culture, like so much else, was profound. To some extent this was part of an international phenomenon in the middle years of the century. Communism may have become a prison for some artists and a barracks for many more, but it was for some a refuge, and the distant shining city of the future for many others. Aragon, Anand, Becher, Bierman, Brecht, Breton, Calvino, Ehrenberg, Eisler, Eluard, Fast, Gorki, Guillen, Guthrie, Hughes, Hikmet, Kastner, Koestler, Leger, Lukacs, Mayakovsky, Neruda, Picasso, Pritchard, Reed, Rivera, Robeson, Sartre, Seghers, Shostakovitch, Sholokov, Silone, Tikhonov, Tzara, Wolf, Wright, Yevtushenko – despite its own instinctive suspicion of the world of the imagination, the international Communist movement enjoyed, however briefly, the energy and commitment of most major European and American twentieth-century writers and artists.

Even the British party was able to attract poets like Hugh MacDiarmid, Hamish Henderson, Stephen Spender, Roger Woddis, Edgell Rickword and Cecil Day Lewis; novelists like Patrick Hamilton, Sylvia Townsend Warner, Lewis Grassic Gibbon, Doris Lessing and Olivia Manning; playwrights like Sean O'Casey, Brendan Behan, Robert Bolt, Joan Littlewood and Ewan McColl. Arnold Wesker was a member of the Young Communist League; Dylan Thomas used to claim that he had been a party member in Swansea before the war; Graham Greene briefly joined the party when he was a student; Hugh MacDiarmid had the distinction of being expelled from the SNP for his Communism and from the party for his Scottish nationalism, characteristically rejoining the party only in 1956, just as most of the other writers were leaving.

Thereafter, though the party never again enjoyed the allegiance of so many writers, its long-term cultural influence may still be seen through some of the doors it held open for so long. The Edinburgh Festival fringe began in 1951 when the cultural committee of the Communist Party in Glasgow organised a people's festival in opposition to the 'high art' of Rudolf Bing's Edinburgh Festival. The story of post-war British radio would have been very different without the innovations of Ewan McColl, Charles Parker and Reggie Smith; the British folk revival may not have happened without the work of Hamish Henderson, Alan Lomax, Karl Dallas, Ewan McColl or A.L. Lloyd; or the Notting Hill carnival without the efforts of Caribbean Communists like Claudia Jones. The early years of British TV drama were profoundly shaped by writers who had learned their trade with Unity Theatre. Even British TV soap may be said to derive some of its distinctive features from a kind of anglicised socialist romantic realism influenced by Unity and the later work of Ted Willis. While American and Australian TV soaps are constructed around desire – upward social mobility, money, power and sex – British TV soaps remain determinedly located in nostalgia, in the idealised working-class communities of the past. From 'Magnolia Street' to 'Coronation Street', these are organic and closed communities, inhabited by historically 'typical' characters, cheerfully resolving problems in the narrative that remain unresolved in society – from Cable Street through Dock Green to Albert Square. The legacy of Buzz Goodbody's productions at the RSC can still be seen in the work of Trevor Nunn; the poet Jackie Kay published her first, adolescent poems in the *Morning Star*; Derek Jarman's favourite actress, Tilda Swinton, was inspired to join the party by Margot Heinemann, whom John Cornford had called, 50 years earlier, the 'heart of a heartless world'.

Heinemann herself was one of a number of novelists who once enlivened English fiction at its edges, and who published their best work while they were Communists, like John Sommerfield, James Barke, Ralph Bates, Maurice Richardson, Jim Phelan, John St. John, Charles Ashleigh, Iris Morley, Robert Briffault, Philip Toynbee, Geoffrey Trease, Edward Upward, Alexander Baron, Sylvia Townsend Warner and Jack Lindsay. Similarly, English poetry was undoubtedly enriched by the verse of many Communists, notably Randall Swingler, Jack

Beeching, Montagu Slater, John Cornford, Arnold Rattenbury, Geoffrey Matthews, Nancy Cunard, Sylvia Townsend Warner, Maurice Carpenter, Hugh Sykes-Davies, Roger Roughton and Valentine Ackland.

And though their work is now very largely forgotten most once enjoyed both critical and commercial success. Hamish Henderson's *Elegies for the Dead in Cyrenaica* won the Somerset Maugham Prize; Ralph Bates – a Swindon railway worker whose novel *Lean Men* was one of the first Penguins – was *routinely* compared to Malraux and Tolstoy; after the War the Clydeside shipyard worker James Barke ('The Scottish Zola') wrote a best-selling sequence of novels about Robert Burns and Jean Armor; Jack Lindsay's poem 'On Guard for Spain' played at meetings all over Britain in the late 1930s. including a performance to a packed Trafalgar Square rally; Montagu Slater wrote several libretti for Benjamin Britten, including his most important opera, *Peter Grimes*; in 1939 Randall Swingler (who wrote the words with Auden for Britten's 'Ballad of Heroes') filled the Albert Hall with a historical pageant set to music by – among others – Vaughan Williams, Alan Rawsthorne, Elizabeth Lutyens and Alan Bush; and few playwrights of his generation can have enjoyed greater popularity (or made more money) than Patrick Hamilton.

It is of course easy to overestimate this kind of success. If the London literary world was, for a short period, excited by the impact of Communism, only a very few Communist Party writers had any real purchase on the imaginations of the wider book-buying and library-using public. Nevertheless, such was the apparent success of the Communist Party's literary culture between 1933 and 1948 that George Orwell constructed his writing career in opposition to it, and defined his ideas about literature through a series of polemics against the Communist 'orthodoxies' of the London literary scene, when he warned that 'the central stream of English literature was more or less directly under Communist control'.[2]

A Bit Ambitious, Perhaps

Most writing about Communist literary history has started here in the 1930s, following Orwell, when British writers were supposedly attracted to 'the most violent system on earth because they knew it was that'. Communist writers are generally obliged to bear a special responsibility for the crimes and disappointments of Communism, their writings given a special place in the horrified culture of anti-Communism, the point where individual creativity was exchanged for ideology and an uncreative collectivity. As writers they had a special duty to see and to tell the truth; either fools or knaves, they abdicated that responsibility. According to this view, writers were especially attracted to Communism because they were politically naive, innocents in the hands of cynics, neurotic refugees in revolt against their education and background, or because they were inhuman intellectuals motivated by abstract systems of thought, Nietzchean power seekers, the *jeunesse dorée* eager to belong to a new elite.[3]

There were perhaps other, more immediate reasons for joining the European Communist parties after 1933, some rather more local explanations of why so many distinguished writers joined, say the German Communist Party in the 1920s, the French party in the 1930s, the Italian party in the 1940s, even the American party in the 1950s. Membership of so unlikely an organisation as the tiny British Communist Party was never likely to further any writer's career; on the contrary, British literary culture has always been uneasy in the presence of political ideas. The British party never had the resources to create a literary culture of its own that was strong enough to engage with the dominant literary culture or to compensate Communist writers who found themselves excluded from its rewards. The party did not possess a literary magazine before 1933 or after 1952; Martin Lawrence published no native imaginative literature before the middle 1930s, Lawrence & Wishart after the early 1960s; there was no real attempt to coordinate the party's cultural work before 1945. Negotiating between the hostility of London publishers and editors and – at best – the indifference of King Street left little time that was not absorbed by meetings, committees, drafting, editing and speaking and all the endless claims of party life. And while at times the party made considerable efforts to engage with contemporary literary culture, and to work with writers and intellectuals, at others it seems to have gone out of its way to appear as unattractive as possible to everyone; there were long periods when intellectuals were expected to sublimate their professional identities within a self-lacerating Communist one. The British Communist Party changed a great deal over 70 years, and the likely reasons for anyone joining in 1926 would have been rather different to those for someone joining in say, 1936, 1946 or 1956.

There is no evidence to suggest that writers did not join the CPGB for much the same mixture of confused and complicated *political* reasons as anyone else, most of them honourable, not all of them either conscious or explicable. Anyway, few published writers actually *joined* the British party or stayed members for very long. Most Communist poets, playwrights and novelists joined the party long before they started writing, emerging rather from *within* the party, becoming writers as a result of the party's characteristic internal culture. The issue then is not why so many writers were so attracted to Communism, but *why Communism produced so many writers*.

The party was never less than an extraordinary educational opportunity, opening the gates of cultural access to all its members. It encouraged serious, sustained reading through branch education programmes, summer schools and district schools, courses at Marx House before the war and the big cultural conferences of the early 1950s. Routine branch activity gave members experience of writing, speaking, editing, singing and acting through branch publications, film societies, choirs, street theatre, provincial unity groups, and of course Glasgow and London Unity Theatres:

> People were sitting on top of each other. The play was *Waiting for Lefty* by Clifford Odets. I had never had such an experience. People were literally jumping up and down with excitement at the end. I said, 'I've got to join this, I've got to join.' So I started when I was nineteen, acting, and then I started writing. And once you got involved with it nothing else in the world seemed to matter. We didn't regard writing as something up in the air, or terribly cultured, it was a job to do, and my God, you learned to write quickly.[4]

Through its extraordinary publishing network the party provided opportunities for young, amateur and working-class writers to write about their own experiences and to publish their work, often alongside distinguished British and European writers. Several – notably Arnold Wesker, Ted Willis and Roger Woddis – went on to enjoy very considerable success as professional writers after they left the party. The party also introduced the pleasures of reading and writing to many young, working-class members, a number of whom later published full-length work – Lewis Jones (*Cwmardy, We Live*), George Chandler (*Revolt*), Billy Holt (*Backwaters, I Haven't Unpacked*), Julius Lipton (*Poems of Strife*), Harry Heslop (*The Gate of a Strange Field, Last Cage Down*), Simon Blumenfeld (*Jew Boy, Phineas Khan, They Won't Let You Live*), Willy Goldman (*East End My Cradle*), Alexander Baron (*From the City, From the Plough, There's No Home*), Fred Ball (*A Grotto for Miss Maynier, A Breath of Fresh Air*) and Max Cohen (*I Was One of the Unemployed*). Like many London cab drivers, Charles Poulsen served as a fireman during the Blitz; one day, waiting to be called out, he found himself in an argument about English history:

> There was this bloke in our station who slept in the next bunk to me, and he maintained that Britain by virtue of the pacific nature of its people and their willingness to compromise had escaped the long series of violent revolutions that most continental countries had been through, and through reason and law and constitutional practices had evolved through history to the fine state of popular representative democracy that we enjoy in England today. And so we argued for a bit, and then I thought I'd write a book about this, make it a novel. A bit ambitious, perhaps.[5]

He began writing a historical novel about the Peasants' Revolt, finished on service overseas on sheets of toilet paper stolen from the Mess. Eventually published after the war, *English Episode* was translated into Polish and Russian and dramatised by Unity Theatre. Ambitious indeed.

This was clearly a political culture at ease with the impulse to write. Ralph Bates, who served as a political commissar with the International Brigades in Spain, also wrote a biography of Schubert; Fred Ball wrote two pioneering biographies of Robert Tressell; Willie Gallacher wrote a detective novel; Harry Pollitt reviewed children's fiction for the *Daily Worker*. Even in the late 1950s and early 1960s, arguably the party's most anti-intellectual period, Lawrence & Wishart launched an ambitious series of novels by working-class party members – several of whom had published their first work in the party's literary magazine *Daylight* - Len Doherty (*The Man Beneath, A Miner's Sons*), Herbert Smith (*A Field of Folk, A Morning to Remember*), Dave Wallis (*A Tramp Stop by the Nile, Paved with Gold*), Brian Almond (*Gild the Brass Farthing*), Dave Lambert (*He Must So Live, No Time for Sleeping*), Frederick Harper (*Tilewright's Acre, Joseph Capper*) and Robert Bonnar (*Stewartie*).

It was a unique kind of cultural patronage, one which Lewis Jones acknowledged when he thanked Douglas Garman for editing the manuscript of his first novel *Cwmardy*, calling it 'our book'. Writing to Garman about the draft of 'their' sequel, *We Live*, he felt it was

> misleading to name myself as the author because yourself and the other comrade have at least as much responsibility for it ... I want you to know how much I appreciate your efforts that made an idea into a fact, that made reminiscences and emotions into a book [which] helps to prove that communists are essentially regenerative and creative. It gives our party in SW a new intellectual status in the eyes of the masses

here, precisely because I have been regarded as a leader of the party,
a good chap and all that, but necessarily limited. We have not taught
the workers that ... communists are concerned with and understand
every phase of human existence, and all its 'cultural' aspects as well as
the political. In other words we have not shown that communism is
not a creed but that it is *life*. The very fact that I am supposed to have
written the book raised the prestige of the party in the eyes of the
workers and the middle class ... [it is] a *party* achievement ... because
it was born in the party and belongs to it.[6]

A Weapon in the Fight for Culture

We Live was very much a party novel, about the work of Communists
in South Wales, in the National Unemployed Workers' Movement
(NUWM), the South Wales Miners' Federation and in Spain. In this
respect it was unusual; few Communist novelists wrote about the party
itself, or only about Communist characters. But then the party in the
Rhondda was unusual, and so was Lewis Jones – Glamorgan county
councillor and delegate to the historic seventh congress of the Comintern,
where he distinguished himself by refusing to stand for Stalin. But for
most Communists, choosing to write about the party would have been
to disfigure any claims to realism, or to turn away from the reality of
British society and make a literature out of an experience which was
not shared by most people. No writer hoping to find a publisher could
afford to do that, and most Communists were too aware of the party's
isolation, too conscious of accusations of alienness, to want to try. 'It
is vital now that we pass out of the "party" into the "national" view of
life, almost from the "class" to the "human" viewpoint', wrote Randall
Swingler, after making contact with the Yugoslav partisans in 1945:

> We have left far behind now, the time when the existence of the
> Communist party had to be constantly asserted, defined, consolidated,
> defended ... we take a great stride forward, out of specific 'class war'
> or even people's war, to a total human viewpoint, the reconstruc-
> tion on a socialist basis of all human life ... We must feel ourselves
> as wielders of the *whole* body of human thought and organisation and
> culture ... there are quite a number of scientists, writers etc. in
> Britain struggling their own way towards Communism by their own
> efforts and thinking much along the same lines as us but who have
> been repelled by this constant threat that they must know what
> Marx said about everything, in order to qualify.[7]

The high hopes of 1945 did not of course last very long, though the hopes for a generous, outgoing, humanist literary culture that did not march behind banners of difference were to last rather longer. Even during periods of self-imposed and sectarian isolation the party always hoped that its cultural efforts would establish a bridgehead for its ideas on the mainland of British politics. At the beginning of the war, for example, when the Comintern thesis of 'imperialist war' threw a *cordon sanitaire* between the party and the rest of British society, with the *Daily Worker* banned and the party preparing to go underground it was left to *Poetry and the People* and the People's Convention to defend the party's identity, eliding opposition to the war with arguments for cultural access and opportunity which attracted the signatures of several distinguished non-Communist figures like James Hanley, Henry Moore and Walter Greenwood. Even in the late 1940s and early 1950s the party's uncritical support for Zhdanovism in the Soviet Union may be seen paradoxically as part of an attempt to demonstrate the party's 'Englishness', invoking Dickens as a precursor of socialist realism, and looking back to Milton, Shelley, Blake and Morris to define a radical national cultural tradition against the 'penetration' of American culture. Despite the obvious Soviet provenance of these ideas, Communist novelists went to considerable trouble to anglicise them, characteristically turning to historical fiction, notably Sommerfield's *The Adversaries*, Slater's *Englishmen with Swords*, Lindsay's *Men of 48* and *Fires in Smithfield*, Townsend Warner's *The Corner that Held Them*, Heslop's *The Earth Beneath* and Barke's *The Wind that Shakes the Barley* and *The Well of the Silent Harp*. If there is a body of imaginative writing identifiable as a Communist literary tradition in Britain, it may be defined by this sense of the past: historical novels more common than novels about contemporary Britain, dystopias rather than utopias, realist rather than idealising, critical rather than sentimental. It was rarely about the Communist Party, and certainly not about 'socialism', or the Soviet Union. If there was a utopian vision always present in the party, it ran rather deeper than 'actually existing socialism', as even so apparently a loyal writer as Alick West argued at a weekend school on the theme 'Culture is a weapon in the fight for socialism':

> I felt that the theme stated no more than a half truth … culture, as Caudwell had written of poetry in *Illusion and Reality*, heightens our consciousness of the world we want to win and our energy to win it. In this sense it was true that culture is a weapon in the fight for

socialism. But the truth depended on recognition of the greater truth that socialism is a weapon in the fight for culture.[8]

The Centre of Contradiction

Curiously, Communist Party history has generally disregarded the party's cultural record, although it may prove to be one of its most enduring contributions to British life. This is unfortunate because it renders so much literary history simply inexplicable, not to say unexciting. But it also severely limits a full assessment of the party's achievements and disappointments. We should not be surprised if the party is generally restricted to a few footnotes to British social history – the big public set pieces of the NUWM and the hunger marches, Cable Street, Spain, the campaign for a Second Front, 1956 – exotic and unproblematic tableaux, in front of which historians pause before reaching for caricatures about Moscow's puppets.

And yet it is clear the party's cultural life was far less damaged by its international obligations than by most other parts of its work. None of the literary magazines commonly regarded as party publications – *Left Review*, *Left News*, *New Writing*, *Poetry and the People*, *Our Time*, *Seven*, *Theatre Today*, *New Theatre*, *Arena*, *Circus* – were in fact owned or controlled by the party. Consequently, when the leadership did wish to use these magazines to enunciate its immediate political objectives, it had to negotiate a minefield of complex personal and cultural politics.

In fact, the party's attitude to literary culture was never settled, always a point of fierce internal engagement. There was a continual tension between the instincts of the apparatus and the needs of writers who had to take their writing, their concerns, anger and imagination way beyond the party and into the crowded market-place of the imagination. For much of the party's history this was a creative tension – *to be at the same time both a part of British society and apart from it*, a place of retreat from the world and a route back into it, inspiring a counter-cultural literature of both witness and prophecy, swinging between repudiation and engagement, dissent and social protest, revolt and revolution. It was often a contradiction within the party, and frequently a tension within individuals. For many writers the tension became unbearably painful, torn between loyalty to their own creative work and to a party which never made up its mind whether literary culture was something to be enjoyed or endured, an unpredictable source of pleasure and wonder or a political weapon. Compare, for example, the following congress resolutions:

... this Congress is concerned at the slow growth of our Party and attributes some part of the responsibility for this to the sectarian outlook still prevailing in some sections of our Party. To change this, it is essential that our members take a lively interest in all questions in which the people are interested, including social, art, music, literature, entertainment and sport. We must strive to end the feeling, which undoubtedly exists, that members of the Communist Party should be interested only in political activity ...

... this Congress calls on all Party organisations to develop the cultural struggle as part of the political struggle ... to increase activity against the Americanisation of Britain's cultural life, against reactionary film and lurid and debased literature and comics ... to help our members working in this field to bring their work closer to the needs of the Party's fight for peace, independence and Socialism; and to strengthen their Marxist–Leninist approach in the fight against capitalist and social-democratic ideas and propaganda.

The first was agreed at the 1945 congress, the second at the 1952 congress; between the two lie seven years of cold war, the Cominform's 'battle of ideas' and the party's retreat from being a part of the post-war consensus to being apart from it. Where in 1945 the leadership was happy to use the party's writers as a lever against sectarianism inside the party, by 1952 it needed all the resources of sectarianism to wage war on its own writers.

The years when the party played its most significant role in British cultural life were those when the two impulses were not in contradiction, when the party apparatus was pleased simply to share in the success of its writers, and when Communists wanted to write on behalf of the party, as Communists. These were the periods when the party succeeded in mobilising writers well beyond the traditional left around specific issues: fascism, Spain, the war, peace. When it took writers seriously, as it did between 1934 and 1948, the party was able to draw many distinguished writers towards a progressive political agenda, to play a part in contemporary cultural life, taking politics into literature, and bringing literature into politics. When the party dismissed contemporary literary culture as 'bourgeois' – as it did in the early 1930s and again in the 1950s – it remained isolated, *apart*, talking only to itself.

The strategy of a popular front against fascism, which saw the party move rapidly in the late 1930s from isolation to engagement, was crucially defined by cultural considerations – nationality, tradition, democracy, intellectual liberty and the arts. The party's cultural work was therefore central to its success in these years. Edited by poets like Randall Swingler and Edgell Rickword, *Left Review* was soon one of the best-selling literary magazines of the day, helping to construct a remarkable intellectual and artistic alliance against fascism and the National government, and drawing towards it many influential non-Communist writers. Ralph Fox helped John Lehmann launch *New Writing*, one of the key literary projects of the decade, Lawrence & Wishart began publishing new fiction, the party helped Gollancz launch the phenomenally successful Left Book Club, Virginia Woolf wrote for the *Daily Worker* and E.M. Forster announced that if he were younger he should join the party, for in Communism he saw 'hope'.

In these years, Communist novelists helped invigorate the native British realist tradition with working-class *Bildungsroman*, novels about unemployment, work, housing and educational disappointment written out of direct experience. Communists like Cecil Day Lewis (as 'Nicholas Blake') and fellow-travellers in the Popular Front like Eric Ambler, Graham Greene and Bruce Hamilton breathed new life into a dying form by writing popular anti-fascist thrillers. And at a time when West End theatre was in desperate need of new ideas, Unity Theatre introduced new theatrical forms to Britain, like living newspapers, political cabaret, mass declamations.

As the party expanded dramatically after 1941, so did its literary culture. *Our Time* was the most popular literary magazine the party ever produced, successfully identifying with the new mass readership created by the war, in uniform, on railway platforms and troop ships, publishing a new generation of radical artists and critics like Edward Thompson, Hamish Henderson, Paul Hogarth and Roy Fuller. At the same time Communist writers overlapped with Fitzrovia and with the cultural institutions of the war like the Army Bureau of Current Affairs, the Council for the Encouragement of Music and the Arts and the Ministry of Information. For a while it seemed as if this radical 'cultural upsurge', like the party's rapid expansion during the war, could be maintained in peacetime. Unity launched a professional theatre company in 1946; *Our Time* began an ambitious series of sister publications; the Scala Theatre ran a trades-union sponsored theatre festival with plays by Lindsay and Slater; J.B. Priestley, then at the height of his fame, threw himself into the work of the Society for Cultural Relations. Many Communist writers published their best work in this period. Indeed, the contribution of Communists to the soldiers' literature of the war may be regarded as the party's most distinctive contribution to British literary history, achieving (more successfully perhaps than in the Spanish Civil

War) a sensibility that was neither simply pacifist nor triumphalist. In particular, fiction by Sommerfield, Baron and Dan Billany (*The Trap, The Cage*) and poetry by Henderson, Swingler, Geoffrey Matthews and Maurice Carpenter, successfully asserted both the horror and the necessity of fighting the war, looking back to Edward Thomas rather than Sassoon or Owen:

> No, it will never be worth it, nor the loss redeemed.
> The dead lie hideously and there is no honour.
> The blood that runs out in the sand can only embitter
> The violence of a fate that is still unmastered.
>
> Even though some should slip through the net of flame
> And life emerge loaded with secret knowledge,
> Won't they be dumb, sealed off by the awful vision?
> Or should they speak, would anyone believe?
>
> Only this price we have, both now and after,
> Because we have grasped the fate ourselves created,
> And to have been the centre of contradiction
> And not to have failed, and still to have found it hateful.[9]

Responding creatively to the challenge of modernity, addressing the role of the artist in mass society, specifically the responsibility of the writer in a world of ideological and armed conflict, the party developed a cultural identity which was neither modernist nor anti-modernist. In particular, the party opened a critical space between the conservatism of the *London Mercury* and the formal experiments of Bloomsbury, later between *Horizon* and Eliot's *Criterion*. The generation of writers and critics who in the 1920s and early 1930s had gathered round the *Calendar of Modern Letters*, the *London Aphrodite*, *Twentieth Century* and the early *Scrutiny* (Garman, Rickword, Lindsay, Morton, Swingler and Wishart) were to be the core of the party's literary intelligentsia for a quarter of a century. They sought to root an internationalist literary culture in an otherwise insular, metropolitan one, introducing a number of writers hitherto unknown in Britain like Brecht, Sartre, Mickiewicz, Aragon, McGrath, Adamov, Neruda and Hikmet. They took a kind of left-Leavisism into the party, where it was sharpened by a sense of class and given a historical basis. There they developed an influential school of native, popular, Marxist cultural criticism – notably work by Morton, Fox, Jackson, Caudwell, Thomson, West, Rickword, Lindsay and Lloyd; later Hill, Williams, Thompson and Kettle – which was relatively untouched by the destructive conflicts elsewhere in Marxists aesthetics.

Committed to cultural experiment, to the new, and deeply respectful of literary tradition – they helped mitigate and delay the effects of Soviet literary politics on the British party. For all that its cultural work was embattled and often self-defeating, the party earned itself in these years a place in British cultural life, enjoying a kind of recognition and respect which neither the Labour Party nor any ultra-left sect ever had. In the often anti-intellectual world of the British Labour movement the party's cultural work, even during its most sectarian phases, always marked it out as different. In the deeply anti-political world of British literary culture Communist writers tried to challenge the narrow range of experience upon which so much of 'Eng. Lit.' is built, insisted on the wider ownership of books, of ideas and the imagination, of the future.

All your Answers Questioned

But the literary life of the Communist Party always had another face. It was always as much a narrative of conflict within the party as it was a measure of the success of its politics without. The history of the party's relationship with its own writers is a good measure of its fortunes – of the relationships between the centre and the membership, and of the party's wider relationship with the rest of British society. While the party was able to move forward, at ease with itself and with its neighbours, Communist writers and their work prospered; as long as their work was published and read and emulated, the party was less isolated, seemed a more natural part of British life and had a way of talking to people in a vocabulary that was not only political. When Communist writers were frustrated artistically, there was always the temptation to blame the party; when the party was in retreat, it often internalised its disappointments by waging war on its own literary intellectuals.

Despite – because of – the relative autonomy of the party's cultural apparatus, internal organisational and ideological debates were often mediated through cultural debates. Literary criticism, fiction, poetry and drama were a means of saying the unsayable in a movement which was always deeply respectful of the world of books. As early as 1923, for example, Dutt used the pages of the *Workers' Weekly* to publish a thinly disguised story satirising the party's first leadership.

During the late 1920s the popular arts pages of the *Sunday Worker* were marked by a series of fierce and coded literary controversies around D.H. Lawrence, the Workers' Theatre Movement and Shakespeare ('I cannot imagine a South Wales miner nor yet a cotton operative going into ecstasies over Shakespeare ... if it was "Das Capital" I could understand ... but Shakespeare!').[10] Some readers objected to the paper carrying any arts coverage at all, and in a way that left no one in any doubt that the debates was 'really' about the relationship of the party to its allies in the National Left-wing Movement and to the rest of British society. The editors – William Paul, Walter Holmes, T.A. Jackson and Ralph Fox – resisted these increasingly strident Proletcult claims and instead opened the paper to reviews of BBC radio and West End theatre (as well as Soviet literature) and a long series of articles popularising the English literary tradition. It was a popular page, attracting contributors like Epstein, Toller, Barbusse and the Scottish playwright Joe Corrie as well as the party's first generation of writers like Charles Ashleigh, Dick Beech, Frederick le Gros Clarke and Tom Wintringham.

But by the end of 1929 the debate was over, as the party began to lurch after the Comintern towards the anti-intellectual politics of the Third Period. When Jackson and Fox ridiculed the sectarian language of 'Class Against Class', the Executive Committee of Communist International took the opportunity to overhaul the British party leadership; the Left-wing Movement was liquidated and the *Sunday Worker* closed down. The new *Daily Worker* did not have an arts page at all, reflecting (and helping to reproduce) the self-imposed and anti-intellectual isolation of the Third Period. When the paper did review new books, it was only to denounce them; even a party novelist like Heslop now found his work out of favour. During these sectarian years the party almost collapsed, and it was hardly surprising that the unexpected tilt in these years of a group of Oxbridge poets towards the party was only noticed with a sneer.

And yet two years before the seventh congress the beginnings of an articulate opposition to 'Class Against Class' could be heard, mediated again through literary debate. First at the founding of the British section of the Writers' International in early 1934 (by Fox, Wintringham and Rickword), appealing to all writers to defend 'the best achievements of human culture' against fascism; later that year at the Soviet Writers' Congress when the Proletcult excesses of the Third Period were rejected in recognition of the need for the widest possible intellectual alliance against fascism; at the launch of *Left Review* where British advocates of the Proletcult were defeated by Wintringham, Slater and Garman; and in the decision to replace the Workers' Theatre Movement with the more ambitious Unity Theatre. The decisions of the seventh congress may be seen as simply the political application of the accelerating arguments among Communist writers ever since Hitler came to power.

On the other hand, after 1935 there were clearly elements in the party leadership acting as a brake on the terrific cultural energy they had unleashed, anxious about the risks of 'diluting' the party in the broader activities of the popular front. Palme Dutt, for example, used Alick West as his instrument inside *Left Review* against 'bourgeois baggage'; after Ralph Fox was killed in Spain, Lawrence & Wishart suddenly withdrew their support for *New Writing*; by 1938 Swingler was looking for a commercial publisher for *Left Review* because (he later said) the party was trying to reassert control over the journal; meanwhile, Palme Dutt and Emile Burns ensured that the debates generated inside the Left Book Club took place within certain limits. All this was to prove counterproductive in 1939, when the party's interest in culture suddenly looked as cynical and manipulative as its anti-fascism seemed shallow, and by the end of the decade the party was as isolated as it had been at the beginning.

And though the National Cultural Committee (NCC) was created in 1947 in recognition of the party's cultural successes during and immediately following the war, it may also be seen as an attempt by the centre to assert control over the influx of intellectuals during the war, especially over Communist writers returning from overseas, changed by what they had seen and rather less patient of the leadership. The Wroclaw and Paris conferences in 1948 and 1949 and the Authors' World Peace Appeal demonstrated that the party no longer commanded even the qualified support around specific issues which it had come to expect among writers and artists. Meanwhile, the enemy had already chosen the literary high ground where much of the Cold War was to be fought in Britain; when a group of famous anti-fascist, ex-Communist writers came together in *The God That Failed*, they significantly identified the evils of Communism with questions of aesthetics and artistic freedom.

As the international situation deteriorated the party expected its writers to play their part in the 'battle of ideas'. But the sales of *Our Time* were collapsing as its wartime readership was demobilised; in the rapidly worsening political climate the decision to turn the magazine 'left' and to replace Rickword as editor with an 'editorial commission' only left the magazine looking sectarian and isolated. Swingler returned as editor to find himself engaged in a series of debilitating battles with Emile Burns and the NCC over Lysenko and Zhdanov; as a result the magazine was not always published on time and W.H. Smith refused to handle the distribution. Again Swingler looked outside the party for commercial backing, again he was unsuccessful and the magazine folded in 1949, too political for London literary culture and too literary for the party, caught in the cross-fire of the Cold War.

Literature was rapidly becoming a crucial site of conflict both between and within the blocs. When Swingler's own small publishing house, Fore Publications, launched a series of poetry pamphlets in 1950 (including George Barker and Edith Sitwell) they found themselves arraigned at a meeting at Marx House and their poetry denounced as 'bourgeois'. Fore also published *Arena*, a quarterly magazine edited by Lindsay, Swingler and John Davenport, and which attracted a dazzling list of European writers – Eluard, Tzara, Neruda, Aragon, Hikmet, Pasternak and Camus – as well as Dylan Thomas, Angus Wilson and Malcolm Lowry. *Arena*, they declared:

> neither seeks to label our culture as 'decadent' nor to acclaim it as securely progressive. We believe that the culture of our world is rent by intense conflicts, and for that very reason is full of the most violent potentialities for good and evil, for integration and disinte-gration ... The work in which *Arena* is interested is the sorting-out of these confused and often vital trends of resistance ... This work involves a give-and-take between Marxism in its critical aspects and the free play of the creative elements in our culture.[11]

But dialogue between Communist and other writers was by 1949 a heresy on both sides. The NCC instructed Lindsay to turn *Arena* into a 'fighting journal' of socialist realism, and by 1952 it had effectively folded. If Communists had nowhere to publish inside the party, they found it increasingly difficult to publish elsewhere in the climate of the Cold War. Swingler, Davenport and Paul Hogarth made a last attempt in 1950 to launch a new journal, outside the party. *Circus* opened with a fanfare of publicity, the implications of which cannot have been lost on the NCC:

> Circus is the magazine which Britain has always declared she wanted, and has never yet had. Wit, wisdom, sanity and enjoyment of life, without pomposity, exclusiveness or wailing self-pity will be the ingre-dients of this medicine for the public conscience. 'Health-giving and pleasant to take!' Why not?
>
> We believe in life, and in man's capacity to extend his control and his appreciation of it. We believe in literature and the arts as the widest and readiest means towards that extension. We do not believe in appealing to any clique of the Best People, or in making dark ways even darker. To us the current culture of despair has become one of the funniest jokes in the West.[12]

The list of contributors included Jocelyn Brooke, Joyce Cary, Dan Davin, Constantine Fitzgibbon, Constant Lambert, Louis MacNeice and Dylan Thomas. It was the kind of line-up that no party publication could have attracted, and *Circus* was an instant success; Hulton first wanted to buy the magazine, then to sue them for producing so successfully what the *TLS* called 'a left-wing Lilliput'. But with only three issues published, their backer discovered that his magazines was being run by Communists, and with another six issues ready for publications the bank account was closed down and *Circus* was over.

By the early 1950s the party's literary culture had become a largely internal one, increasingly only a site for coded conflict about the role of the party in the Cold War. The Caudwell controversy of 1950–1 may be seen as an attempt to limit the influence of the party's most original critic and theorist (and his use of 'bourgeois psychology') as well as an exercise in acquainting the party's writers with a kind of second-hand Zhdanovism. In 1950 the troublesome writers' group was replaced by a smaller group, restricted to those party members who were eligible for membership of the Society of Authors. The new group embarked on a collection of essays on contemporary fiction called 'The Literature of the Graveyard'. The best that could be said for this kind of defensive, internalised cultural life was that it strengthened a sense of unity in isolation, expressed in the workerist clichés of the Party's last – and short-lived – literary magazine, *Daylight*. At its worst it was a negative and uncreative culture, confirming the party's isolation (as for example during the campaign against American comics). Moreover, this kind of activity was increasingly a substitute for creativity; no amount of shrill exhortation could compensate for the growing gloom and silence among the party's writers, locked in conflict with what E.P. Thompson called 'Emilism', a conflict which was not finally settled until 1956.

Even then the crisis in the British party was again partly played out through a series of struggles between the leadership and the party's writers, and not only those around the *New Reasoner*. A few weeks after the Soviet invasion of Hungary, Unity played *World On Edge* ('All Your Answers Questioned') to packed houses about the events in Suez and Hungary. Although several party members were involved, the leadership made its disapproval clear. By then they certainly did not want their answers questioned, and the party's relationship with Unity was never the same again. The two opposing impulses in the party's history, centripetal and centrifugal, could not be contained in one organisation any longer. Within a few months most of the party's most distinguished writers had left – Lessing, Thompson, Swingler, Rickword, Beeching,

Doherty and Sommerfield. Yet still, in this moment of disarray and collapse, the party left its mark on literary history, as over the next few years many of those who left (and some who stayed) began of course to work the crisis of 1956 into novels, plays and poems:

It has happened all before, and yet
it has all to happen. So it seems.
Darker grows the maniac threat
and richer swell the answering dreams.
Just past our straining fingertips
It lies. And that's the very thing
they said two thousand years ago,
broken with hope unslackening.
At every gain, away it slips.
In struggle, entire and strong it grows;
the bonds of brotherhood hold fast.
Someday the treacherous gap will close
and we'll possess the earth at last.[13]

Acknowledgements

This essay began life as a documentary for BBC Radio Four, 'Damn, damn, damn, the Commmunist Party man', first broadcast on 29 December 1991. I wish to thank Arnold Rattenbury, Jack Beeching, Paul Hogarth and Dave Sheasby for their comments on earlier versions, and Judy Williams for permission to quote from her father's papers.

Notes

1. R. Swingler, 'In praise of the anonymous', *The Years of Anger* (Meridian Books, 1946).
2. G. Orwell, *Inside the Whale* (Gollancz, 1940), reprinted in G. Orwell, *Collected Essays, Journalism and Letters* (Penguin edn, 1970), p. 562.
3. G. Watson, *Politics and Literature in Modern Britain* (Macmillan, 1977), p. 70.
4. Roger Woddis interview, 23 October 1991.
5. Charles Poulsen interview, 23 October 1991.

6. Lewis Jones to Douglas Garman, 7 February 1938 (Garman papers, University of Nottingham; DG 6/4)
7. Randall Swingler to Geraldine Swingler, 9 October 1945 (papers in private possession).
8. A. West, *One Man In His Time* (Allen & Unwin, 1969), p. 190.
9. R. Swingler, 'Briefing for invasion', *The Years of Anger*.
10. *Sunday Worker*, 11 August 1929.
11. *Arena*, 1, 1949.
12. *Circus* publicity flyer, 1950.
13. J. Lindsay, 'It has happened', *Collected Poems* (Chiron Press, Illinois, 1981).

Further Reading

For reasons of space, I have restricted the footnotes to this essay to the sources of quotations. Readers wishing to pursue further what must appear to be a series of unsupported assertions are referred to my book *Red Letter Days* (Lawrence & Wishart, 1990), and to 'Betrayed spring: the 1945 Labour government and British literary culture' in J. Fyrth (ed.), *Culture and Society in Labour Britain 1945–51* (Lawrence & Wishart, 1995); 'Writers, the Communist Party and the battle of ideas, 1945–50', *Socialist History*, no. 5 (1994); 'The end of socialist realism: Margot Heinemann's The Adventurers' in D. Margolies and M. Joannou (eds), *Heart of a Heartless World: Essays in Cultural Resistance in Honour of Margot Heinemann* (Pluto, 1995). Three critical overviews provide further context: C. Chambers, *The Story of Unity Theatre* (Lawrence & Wishart, 1989); J. Lucas (ed.), *The Thirties: A Challenge to Orthodoxy* (Harvester, 1978); G. Klaus (ed.), *Tramps, Workmates and Revolutionaries: Working-class Stories of the 1920s* (Journeyman, 1993). Two excellent biographical studies also provide a good deal of background information: C. Hobday, *Edgell Rickword: A Poet at War* (Carcanet, 1989); W. Mulford, *This Narrow Place: Sylvia Townsend and Valentine Ackland, Letters and Politics, 1930–1951* (Pandora, 1988). Most of the period's literature has still to be sought out in contemporary editions and periodicals, although in the 1980s Lawrence & Wishart did reprint a number of 1930s novels, including Harold Heslop's *Last Cage Down*, Simon Blumefeld's *Jew Boy*, John Sommerfield's *May Day* and Lewis Jones's *Cwmardy* and *We Live*.

6 No Home but the Trade Union Movement: Communist Activists and 'Reformist' Leaders 1926–56

Nina Fishman

Conventional British historians have assigned Communist activists a minor role in trade union events between 1926 and 1956. Official party historians, and some other Marxist historians,[1] arrived at the opposite conclusion: that Communist activists were significant participants, indeed prominent leaders, of 'rank-and-file' union members.

It is notable that conventional and 'left' historians based their opposing conclusions on the same narrow band of evidence. The conventional historians' line of vision has apparently been directed by the strong anti-Communist prejudice of inter-war trade union leaders like Walter Citrine, the general secretary of the TUC, his able young subaltern Victor Feather and Ernest Bevin, architect and general secretary of the Transport and General Workers' Union (TGWU). The denunciations were intensified and codified during the late 1940s by Bevin's successor Arthur Deakin and Feather, who orchestrated the TUC's anti-Communist offensive.

Following this trail, conventional historians have investigated Communists' activities only when they led protracted and/or contentious strikes. They find that Communists seized the leadership of normally level-headed men and women on the shopfloor and turned their heads towards militancy. But they are unable to explain why revolutionaries were suddenly able to usurp power inside lay union institutions and factory works committees.

'Left' labour history has concentrated on the same peaks of industrial conflict – the General Strike, the staydown strikes in South Wales pits against the 'scab union' in 1934–5, the 1937 London bus strike, the 1949 docks strike. Their choice stems from the assumption that these episodes were most likely to precipitate revolution.

Historians of all kinds have remained stubbornly incurious about what Communists did in the troughs and lulls. The historiographical problem with investigating only the peaks of industrial conflict is that occurrences of militant 'economic struggle' were comparatively few. Yet Communists were continuously active inside trade unions and factories throughout the period. They routinely performed copious amounts of bureaucratic labour inside union lay institutions and in workplace collective bargaining committees during the long stretches of calm.

The years between 1926 and 1956 include the General Strike and the Second World War, both of which had a crucial impact on the course of British political and trade union history. They are marked by the continuation of the upward if somewhat bumpy trend in trade union fortunes discernible from 1889. Unions' recovery from the débâcle of the General Strike began slowly and suffered a set-back with the 1931 economic crisis. However, union membership and influence resumed their upward climb from 1933, silently aided and abetted by large, successful and corporate-minded companies and the Baldwin government's paternalism. Rearmament greatly reinforced these conciliatory tendencies. The onset of war re-created the circumstances of 1914–18 in which unions had increased their power dramatically.

The sustained post-war economic boom enabled unions to extend their positions in factories where a union presence and collective bargaining would previously have been unthinkable, notably Ford's enormous plant at Dagenham, Essex, Morris Motors in Oxford and Austin's in Longbridge, Birmingham. By 1956 union membership was a mass phenomenon and trade union leaders were an accepted part of the political establishment, playing their assigned role in promoting industrial peace and voicing the legitimate concerns of British working people in the corridors of power.

Between 1926 and the mid-1940s CPGB trade union activists were almost unique in having intimate links with three discrete worlds: the largely apolitical world of the shopfloor and pit with its myriad of local specificities in which the trade union presence was far from all pervasive; the trade union world whose rich culture of union loyalism, rank-and-filism and activism was usually impermeable to outsiders, including mere 'card-carrying' union members; and the third, political, world, which comprised not only King Street (the CPGB's headquarters), the Third International and other domestic left-wing activists, but also the Westminster political establishment – the government, Parliament and the parliamentary Labour Party.

There were only a few occasions when the trade union activists had to deal with a situation in which all three of their worlds intersected *and* the CPGB's political position was determined mainly by the Comintern's priorities: the delayed incidence of the extreme Third Period line on the British party in 1929–30, the CPGB's first policy change on the war against Germany in October 1939, 1948–9 when the full impact of the Cold War on trade unions was finally felt and the upheavals of 1956, the 20th congress revelations of Khrushchev about Stalin and the crushing of the Hungarian revolution. These points presented critical problems for party union activists which have been insufficiently considered by historians.

Most, though by no means all trade union leaders during this period shared a strong political commitment with their party counterparts. Many, including Bevin, Julia Varley (one of the TGWU's full-time officers in Birmingham in the mid-1930s), Jack Little (the Amalgamated Engineering Union (AEU) president from 1933–9), and his successor to 1956, Jack Tanner, had a similar political socialisation to the cohort of foundation party members: active pre-1914 membership in the Marxist Social Democratic Federation (SDF), experience in militant trade union activity and either radical rank-and-file movements or militant trade union organisation.[2]

The two worlds of trade union and politics intersected for this top layer of the trade union establishment. However, these men and women operated at one remove from the shopfloor; moreover, throughout these three decades many of them tried but always failed to establish their own reliable channels of communication with the shopfloor world. They recognised, often reluctantly, that Communists were the most effective trade union NCOs (to use the Webbs' evocative term) – the shop stewards, branch secretaries and chairmen and other lay activists. British trade union fortunes depended on the continuing commitment of Communists. It is for this reason that party activists were so strategically important during the Second World War. They were an organised force within the shopfloor when war production was crucial to the very survival of the state.

A second inaccurate assumption shared by conventional and Marxist historians is that CPGB union activists were unquestioning enthusiastic followers of Comintern/Soviet/Cominform diktat. They conclude that even if there were dissenters, the party leadership was committed to ensuring a uniform application of the 'party line' and pressurised their membership into obedience.

The conclusions of the two serious historians of early British Communism, L.J. Macfarlane and Roderick Martin, render the line-following assumption about King Street highly questionable. Their evidence shows a group in the British party leadership, led by Harry

Pollitt and Johnny Campbell, who tempered the Comintern line while consistently gaining Comintern support.[3] They remained within the Third Period's parameters, and yet sought solid results in union activity.

It is clear that historians need to investigate how the British party centre interpreted the pronouncements of the Comintern. It is then essential to discover first what Communist union activists were saying and second what they were actually doing. It should not be assumed there was a simple assembly-line transmission belt conveying instructions from the Kremlin through King Street down to the shopfloor and pit.

In 1930 the Comintern endorsed Pollitt's and Campbell's early adaptation of 'Class Against Class', 'the fighting united front of the rank and file'. The extreme left wing inside King Street were marginalised. The zealots at the party centre – including Young Communist League (YCL) activists Bill Rust, Wally Tapsell and Johnny Mahon – had confidently predicted revolution in Britain and believed that the proletariat's exodus from 'reformist' to red unions was imminent if party union activists would provide a clear lead. However, their 18 months at the helm of the CPGB was marked by a drastic decline in party membership and the party's increased isolation from the 'labour movement'.

Pollitt and Campbell used their trimming dexterity and trade union loyalist reflexes to guide the British party back to relevance inside the working class. With Comintern approval, they launched a domestic offensive exhorting activists to anchor themselves inside trade unions in order to promote a rank-and-filist policy. Communists resumed leading roles in industrial conflict and cooperated with 'social fascist' union officials. During 1931 Arthur Horner was rescued by the Comintern from the accusations of Rust and Tapsell in a final attempt to enforce the extreme left version of the Third Period line. His unconditional pardon from Moscow for a venal error (when he had actually been guilty of a mortal sin under Class Against Class canon) showed that the Comintern was more interested in practical gains than ideological purity.

Horner was not alone in his refusal to repudiate his reformist union. His actions were merely the most public. Many other party members had also ignored Rust's and Mahon's exhortations and continued rank-and-filist activities inside their unions. They included close colleagues of Pollitt and Campbell, such as the West London toolmakers, Claude Berridge, Joe Scott, Wally Hannington and Bob Lovell, as well as the Paisley coppersmith Willie Gallacher. They had all been formed by the same dense British trade union culture and responded to predictions of mass desertions from social fascist unions with the same jaundiced eye.

However, the extreme Third Period rejection of social fascist unions tallied with the recent experience of many other foundation party members. With the demoralisation of union members after the TUC's hasty retreat in the General Strike, they had ceased to take unions seriously. Nevertheless few were inspired to organise alternative revolutionary activity and red unions. The predominant feeling amongst Communists in 1930 was disillusion. It required all Pollitt's and Campbell's energy to shift official party institutions and the rump of members out of self-imposed isolation and pessimism.[4]

But after their victory over the pure revolutionaries at the twelfth Congress in December 1932, Pollitt and Campbell presided over the highly successful expansion of the CPGB's activities inside unions and on the shopfloor. Communist participation yielded increased union membership, the rehabilitation of workplace organisation where in disuse and the extension of collective bargaining to new workplaces.

A division of labour emerged inside the party. Pollitt and Campbell provided the general orientation to the economic struggle, an inspired development of their early political and trade union socialisation, which I have called revolutionary pragmatism. Its four elements were trade union loyalism, rank-and-filism, the pursuit of the Real United Front for the Labour movement and the absolute certainty of an eventual revolutionary situation. Employing the Comintern's rhetoric, I have described this faith in revolution as Life Itself.[5]

Communist pragmatism was visible in episodes of conflict. Activists combined militant rhetoric with capable leadership of strikes and the acceptance of negotiated compromises. The evidence reveals a wide range of responses which is explained only partially by the variety of temperaments, different local trade union cultures and contrasting individual styles of dealing with people. A large area remains which could be broadly but imperfectly described as force of circumstance.

The trade union establishment had embarked on an enthusiastic scapegoating of Communists in the aftermath of the General Strike. But full-time union officials appreciated Communist successes in gaining union recognition and recruiting union members. By 1934 union officials were ready to judge Communists primarily by their actions, and to discount Comintern pronouncements and even *Daily Worker* editorials.

In March 1934 Pollitt anticipated the Comintern's public turn from the Third Period by writing to Walter Citrine to suggest a formal united front between the CPGB and the TUC. Citrine responded with an attempt to re-activate an anti-Communist crusade inside the trade unions, dubbed 'Black Circulars' by party activists. Most union leaders were distinctly chary of implementing the suggested bans on Communists holding union office.

The circulars received the formal approval of Congress, but only after substantial opposition had been registered. Will Lawther spoke at the 1935 TUC on behalf of the Miners' Federation of Great Britain (MFGB). He declared that the real disruptors in the Labour movement were not 'what are presumed to be our enemies of the Left'. He continued: 'We do know that there are disruptive elements within our organisation ... We find them in the people who went with MacDonald at the last [1931] General Election.'[6]

Bevin spoke in support of Citrine, but went to considerable lengths to distance himself from the circulars. 'If there is one thing I would regret it would be the introduction of a political or religious test in this Movement.'[7] He knew that without the efforts of Communists his own union would have fewer members and far less lay enthusiasm.

Pollitt and Campbell expected union activists to *think for themselves*. Union activists met with and worked in a democratic centralist fashion with other party activists (*and* trusted left-wingers) in their own factory/pit/office/union branch, but they habitually made up their own minds about their local economic struggle according to the disposition of forces on their ground.

The veteran foundation members who led the shop stewards committee at Napier's aero-engine factory in West London from 1936 taught their young and enthusiastic shop stewards who became Communists a healthy contempt for 'line followers'. Napier's was one of the party's foremost strongholds and its stewards' independence was by no means atypical. Communist union activists accepted an internal political hierarchy, not merely because they knew the party centre was in intimate touch with the Comintern and the Soviet Communist Party. They expected to *receive* guidance and illumination from their party leaders about political issues for the same reasons that they expected to *give* a strong lead to their own shopfloor and trade union rank and file about what to do in an industrial dispute.

Palme Dutt, Harry Pollitt and Johnny Campbell communicated the essentials of the party's position on fascism, Spain and the Popular Front through *Labour Monthly*, the editorials in the *Daily Worker*, speeches during party campaigns and internal party meetings and communications. However, Communist union activists could not simply repeat a litany. The rhetoric from their political world did not directly translate into their other two spheres of operation. Union activists who employed party political propaganda indiscriminately made no impact on the shopfloor or in the union branch. Party union activists had to develop their own voices to enthuse their workmates.

The principal challenge before the Cold War to Communist activity inside trade unions gathered force in the spring of 1937. Its origin was not the venom of reformist union leaders, but the inherent contradiction in revolutionary pragmatism between trade union loyalism and rank-and-filism. The party centre had maintained a public even-handedness towards these two, and declined to acknowledge that there might be situations when party activists might have to choose between them. In practice party activists had been regularly faced with such choices. Some had chosen union loyalism, others rank-and-filism.

During the spring of 1937 the gathering pace of economic recovery and rearmament produced an upsurge in militancy unprecedented since the General Strike. The party leadership caught the momentum and issued a special statement on 2 April which anticipated a national struggle of epic dimensions. 'The trade unionists in Britain, in line with their comrades in France, Spain, America and India, are now moving into action. All the threats and restrictions of employers, National Government and trade union leaders are being swept away.'[8]

Fleet Street responded with barely repressed hysteria. On 6 April, the *Daily Worker* replied:

> A great popular movement in support of claims for increased wages ... is sweeping through the trade unions ... Here is no 'plot' but a determined mass movement of British trade unionists to secure a little more food, a little more leisure, and a little better life for themselves, their wives and their children.

> On 13 April the *Daily Worker*'s expectations were even higher: 'The whole trade union movement is pulsating with life and the will to fight. With a militant leadership at the top, such an army would prove unconquerable ... Increase the pressure on leadership. Victory can be won.'

On 1 May the TGWU London Central Bus Committee (CBC) duly led their members out on official strike. Compelled by strong pressure from its London bus branches, the TGWU executive delegated responsibility for the strike to the CBC, but only reluctantly because the CBC leaders were prominent in the Busmen's Rank-and-File movement whose loyalty to the union had been regularly questioned by Bevin. The aircraft rank-and-file movement, the Aircraft Shop Stewards' National Council, was so inspired that they decided on 2 May to call an unofficial national aircraft strike.

Almost simultaneously, the protracted strike against the Nottinghamshire scab miners union at Harworth colliery became a national issue. (The Harworth branch of the Nottinghamshire Miners' Association (NMA) was ably led by the veteran Communist activist Mick Kane.) The MFGB executive had won an overwhelming endorsement in a national members' ballot for a strike in support of the Harworth men and their fight to belong to a free and democratic trade union. On 30 April an MFGB delegate conference had agreed that miners should hand in their notices on 7 May and prepare for a national strike on 22 May.

However, industrial peace had broken out with a vengeance by the time the 14th party congress convened in late May. Party AEU activists had taken steps to pre-empt the unofficial aircraft strike and they had been backed by Pollitt and Campbell. On 26 May the TGWU executive revoked the CBC's authority and settled the strike with London Transport on the favourable terms recommended by the Ministry of Labour Inquiry. The busmen's return to work was marred by a serious rift in the rank-and-file movement – one faction preached loyalty to the TGWU and the other argued for a new, red-blooded rank-and-file union.

There had been no national miners' strike. The Harworth strike was settled by a merger between the NMA and the scab union. The MFGB accepted the employers' word that the strikers would be taken back when 'suitable openings' occurred. The unspoken expectation was that most strikers would never get back. (The leaders, notably Mick Kane, never worked in Nottinghamshire pits again.) Arthur Horner, President of the South Wales Miners' Federation (SWMF) since 1936, had publicly supported the MFGB officials' attempts at accommodation with the scab union from the beginning. The *Daily Worker* had argued against compromise and for a national strike.[9]

Pollitt and Campbell referred obliquely to the failure of events to live up to their earlier militant promise, but then concluded the 14th party congress on an upbeat note. Campbell acknowledged that Communists were accused of not being interested in better wages but only revolution. He rejoined that the question was like being asked whether he wanted jam or marmalade, and that he wanted jam first:

> It is because we are the irreconcilable partisans of the proletarian revolution that we are the most consistent fighters for increased wages as the way to mobilise the working class and lead them towards the conquest of power …

Our main task is not to ensure that the working class will fight, but to ensure that when the working class does fight it will fight in a powerful and united movement that will enable it to gain victory comparatively quickly and painlessly. There are obstacles in the working class itself, but these obstacles would be trivial if they were not reinforced by the whole class collaboration policy of the leadership.[10]

The *Daily Worker* refrained from condemning the MFGB leadership over its compromise on Harworth. Without drawing any conclusions from the fact that Horner's persuasive arguments for compromise had been vindicated, the party leadership drew the veil of ideology over the uncomfortable turn which events had taken. When Mick Kane attended the 14th party congress he was given a hero's welcome and elected to the party executive. He proudly declared: 'Today in Harworth the Communist Party and the *Daily Worker* are looked on as the leadership of the working-class movement.'[11]

Pollitt and Campbell took care to maintain the appearance of revolutionary pragmatism's seamless garment. Union loyalism and rank-and-filism remained formally equal. However, whenever a conflict between the two occurred, the party centre came down on the side of union loyalism. The party leadership argued passionately that union activists on the London buses should stay in the TGWU and fight against the executive's summary sentences of prohibition on holding union office and the expulsions of Rank-and-File leaders.

Nevertheless, a serious breakaway union emerged, led by a rump of disillusioned Rank-and-Filers. Most activists followed the exemplary lead of the remaining expelled and proscribed rank and filers who received strong support from the party leadership. By early 1938 Bevin recognised that the union would indeed be in jeopardy unless they sued for peace and pardoned the loyal Rank-and-File leaders.

Most party union activists had been practically unaffected by the momentum of the spring strikes. Their immediate sphere of operation in the daily economic struggle had remained remarkably insulated from the trials of the London busmen and the Harworth miners. From their vantage point of their other two worlds, the trade union and the political, Communist activists were keenly sympathetic and intimately interested in the strikes. However, they saw no reason to modify day-to-day strategies in their particular factory or pit.

The unions' rising national fortunes were actually reinforced by the skilful compromises of the MFGB and TGWU. The Westminster establishment and employers were more inclined to do business with a trade union leadership in control of its more unruly rank and file. Consequently, Communist activists expanded their local militancy to gain concessions from employers.

The *de facto* cooperation between party activists and reformist trade union leaders was not disrupted by the events of May 1937. The party leadership had publicly supported more radical positions than the reformist officials, but the party centre had also argued against militants' impulse to repudiate the sell-outs and leave the unions. The reformists in the union establishment recognised that the common interests shared with Communist activists were more important than the areas of conflict. To the outside world, including the Westminster political establishment, the British trade union movement continued to be the real united front over which Bevin and Citrine proudly boasted they presided. The *modus vivendi* was uninterrupted even by the escalation of political hostilities when the CPGB opposed the war against Germany.

The change of party line in October 1939 from pro- to anti-war is often seen as King Street imposing a position on an unwilling membership. Though clearly surprised, most union activists accepted it in the same spirit as they had adapted to the previous change of Comintern line in August 1935 after the seventh World Congress. The example of both Pollitt and Campbell taking their democratic centralist medicine in an exemplary fashion was undoubtedly important to men and women who had placed trust and faith in these two men, so like themselves. Morever, party activists soon realised that the new party leadership did not expect them to make any significant alteration in their conduct on the shopfloor and inside their union.[12]

There is a rich if unappreciated irony in the party's formal *volte-face* on the war being accompanied by the resounding continuation of the *status quo ante* in the economic struggle. The Comintern's calculated unconcern with its British affiliate's palpable failure to undertake Leninist activities on the shopfloor is explained by the Soviet Union's *raison d'état*. The Comintern was keen that Britain should continue its imperialist war against Germany[13] and therefore had no reason to encourage revolutionary sabotage or incitement to treason amongst the troops.

However, the newly installed party secretariat, Bill Rust and Palme Dutt, were initially determined to implement the anti-war line with its full revolutionary implications in factories and pits. The two men had opposed the Pollitt–Campbell pragmatic offensive in 1930–2 and argued for keeping a pure revolutionary policy. In 1939 they viewed the war as a fresh opportunity. Nevertheless it was only a matter of weeks before they executed a headlong retreat to the 'war on two fronts' position enunciated by Pollitt and Campbell in early September 1939. The famous Comintern instructions to denounce the war issued later in the month evidently did not include organising serious anti-war activity.

Bill Rust spoke to the central committee in late December 1939 about the problems of developing a 'broad political movement of opposition to the war on a common platform'.[14] In January 1940 delegates at the London District Congress criticised the party centre's tendency to soft-pedal the anti-war line. Dutt parried with a strong dose of reductive logic: 'to fight for the needs of the people means at the same time to fight for the end of the war.'[15]

Rust's and Dutt's trimming was the triumph of enlightened self-interest. Having no wish to marginalise the party or sacrifice the considerable position of importance and influence which activists had established in the trade union movement, they resorted to the same expedients which Pollitt and Campbell had used in 1930–2 to underpin their bending of Class Against Class.

British workers responded to Chamberlain's declaration of war with neither wild enthusiasm nor rebellious refusal to fight. For the most part there was a resigned acceptance. The trade union leadership were determined to cooperate with the war effort, but not at the expense of trade union principles. Men and women on the shopfloor and in the pits were digging in, intending to deal with Jerry once and for all. The unexpected appearance of this anti-German phlegm explains why Rust and Dutt rowed so quickly back to the safe haven of war on two fronts.

As developed by Campbell, war on two fronts stressed the vital importance of defeating German fascism and the need to expose the narrow class motives of the Chamberlain government and any anti-union measures it might attempt. Dutt and Rust effected a slight adjustment in November 1939. The war effort against Germany was taken as given and not discussed, though workers' opposition to fascism *in the abstract* was acknowledged. The second front – the domestic class struggle – was emphasised, so allowing activists to concentrate on that fight without repudiating the war.

The importance of increasing war production was not questioned, but attention was focused on upholding democratic trade union rights on the home front against any 'fascist' tendencies of the government. The other essential was unions' demand for reasonable wages and conditions; the rich must not be allowed to make shameless profits from this war as they had in 1914–18. This revisionist position coincided with the priorities which Communist trade unionists had already arrived at for themselves. Moreover, it also coincided with the response of the reformist trade union leadership.

The foundation cohort of party activists had been shop stewards in 1914–18; they were now typically full-time or lay trade union officials actively cooperating with the Second World War effort. Their reformist colleagues in the union leadership had been stewards in 1914–18 who had also rebelled against the enthusiastic patriotism of the full-time officials. They had *all* learned from this experience and now concentrated on the defence of trade unionism and the pursuit of 'fair' wages and conditions in wartime. Their outlook was eloquently stated by Jack Tanner in his first address to the AEU national committee as president in 1940:

> There is need to think deeply and clearly, free from narrowness and prejudice, and to act decisively in the interests of the Union, its members and the whole working class ...
>
> As engineering workers, we are in many respects better placed than we were in the last war ...
>
> In the last war we had no agreements recognising shop stewards. The needs of the situation during that time brought into being the Shop Stewards Movement. To-day we have shop stewards as an integral part of the organisation able to perform their duties freely and fully, backed by the strength of the Union ...
>
> During the last war there were no agreements on dilution. To-day we have such agreements, and providing we win this war, we will be in a position to see that they are implemented after; if we do not win this war, then no one present here will be concerned at all about agreements, the restoration of custom and practice, many will not be interested whether the sun rises or sets.[16]

As president of the SWMF, Arthur Horner played an important part in quasi-governmental institutions to promote the war effort. The tacit resumption of the war on two fronts for the economic struggle eased his position considerably. Nevertheless, he discharged his official duties with such undisguised enthusiasm for the war that the South Walian mining MPs, Aneurin Bevan, Jim Griffiths and Bill Mainwaring, threw down their political gauntlet. They felt threatened by his dexterity in juggling his passionate anti-fascism, the union's commitment to the war effort and the party's anti-war line. They were evidently determined to force him to choose between the party and the union presidency.

The substantial knot of South Walian Communists who found Horner's conduct unacceptable also moved against him. They promoted a strong anti-war motion inside the union and pressurised Horner to fall in behind the party's line. Horner, however, was not to be caught in a pincer movement. He presided with olympian impartiality over a prolonged and public debate between the MPs' war on two fronts motion, which stressed the fight for socialism at home, and the anti-war motion. When the latter was eventually defeated at the second coalfield conference, Horner encouraged the war effort with renewed zeal.[17]

The illegal strike at Swift Scales in north-west London in March 1941 is often cited as a case of Communists challenging the state. However, the aim of the strike, publicly proclaimed by its youthful leader Reg Birch, was *productionist*. Birch, a protégé of Wally Hannington, never deviated from his insistence that the strikers were helping the war effort by exposing managerial incompetence.

Fate intervened to let the government and Birch off the hook. The Swift's case was heard in court just over a week after Hitler invaded the Soviet Union, and the recorder merely bound the stewards over. However, even if they had been fined (it is extremely unlikely that a canny Ministry of Labour would have allowed their imprisonment), it is improbable that party activists would have used their 'martyrdom' as the occasion for escalating conflict.[18] Neither the party leadership nor union activists were interested in exploiting the potential for upheaval inherent in the wartime emergency. The party leadership had already declined to transform the popular People's Convention into an anti-government crusade.[19] Union activists were more interested in using the situation to make tangible gains in wages and conditions.

The only party members who adopted a principled Leninist position on the war were YCL activists in Glasgow. They had been well grounded in Marxism–Leninism by the Scottish party, but had little experience of either employment or trade union activity. They found work in engineering factories and bypassed Scottish trade unionism which they viewed as craft oriented and conservative. However, their efforts to resurrect the revolutionary spirit of the Clyde shop stewards were firmly checked at the first opportunity by senior party union activists.[20]

Most party union activists were relieved when Hitler invaded the Soviet Union. They were now able to give full vent to their anti-fascism. For British Communists, the anti-fascist position nurtured by the Comintern from 1935 was not merely a pro-Soviet response. Along with Aneurin Bevan, Clement Attlee and Ernest Bevin, they were repelled by fascism for the same reasons as Stanley Baldwin and Lord Halifax. Fascism conflicted directly with the individualistic, liberal underpinnings of British political culture.

The British party leadership's priorities altered dramatically and the defence of the Soviet Socialist Fatherland became the highest priority. King Street, including the newly reinstated General Secretary Harry Pollitt, exhorted party union activists to put parochial industrial conflict into perspective. Domestic class interests remained important, but were strictly subordinate to the historic mission which life itself presented to ensure the survival of Soviet socialism.

Party union activists remained sceptical if not downright hostile to notions of sacrificing trade union principles on the altar of defending the USSR. It is notable that most CPGB union activists made no attempt to form Shock Brigades or promote in their workplaces the Self-Denial Weeks which party officials recommended so that the British working class could fulfil its duty to defend the Soviet Union.

The party centre joined the Minister of Labour and trade union leaders, particularly Jack Tanner, in promoting Joint Production Committees (JPCs) to help the war effort. Bevin, Tanner and Pollitt shared a Marxist background. Their common conviction that the working class played a pivotal role in industrial production was reinforced by their experiences as trade union activists in 1914–18. Though Bevin became a staunch social democrat, he retained the SDF view of the working class as the essential bedrock of society. They expected increased war production through union representatives' democratic involvement in workplace decisions on JPCs where they sat as equals around the table with management.

The fruit of their separate but complementary efforts was that a large number of engineering factories had operational JPCs by 1943. Encouraged by the persuasive productionist propaganda, Communist and other 'left-wing' shop stewards took the first steps to form their JPCs with little more than than vague enthusiasm for the war effort and determination not to be left behind.

However, the JPCs brought no qualitative shifts in workers' attitudes towards production. Most union JPC representatives did not attempt seriously to influence production decisions; nor did they urge their shopfloor colleagues to redouble their efforts because they had become enfranchised, industrial citizens with responsibilities for production. Productivity in engineering factories was certainly higher during the war. But shopfloor workers were not moved principally by a belief that their union representatives had finally assumed their rightful role in production, rather by the increased piece-rates which shop stewards were winning, the realisation that their self-preservation depended on their production efforts and the boost to productivity provided by American machine tools and Fordist methods.[21]

Nevertheless, JPCs did help provide strong foundations for workplace union representation in peacetime.[22] Union activists, who exploited the advantages of the wartime emergency, now adapted JPCs to complement the existing efforts of shop stewards' committees to extend union prerogatives through collective bargaining. In many factories where union activists had been unable to pressurise management into conceding union recognition, they demanded JPCs to be able to play their part in the wartime production efforts, and then deployed the morally coercive powers of Ministry of Labour officials and mobilised shopfloor and public opinion. The *de facto* union recognition was typically transformed into routine collective bargaining after the war.

In the shipyards and coalmining, parallel attempts to form Yard Production Committees and Pit Production Committees misfired. The economic slump in the inter-war period had produced a trench warfare mentality on both sides of industrial relations. There had been too long and bitter a history of conflict and unemployment to convince either management or unions to put national interests before their respective self-interests. Compared to their engineering counterparts, managements were notably unwilling to invest time or energy in changes to production technique. Few shop stewards and lay union representatives took democratic productionism at face value. It is hardly surprising that union activists saw no prospects in utilising production committees as an auxiliary to collective bargaining.[23]

In 1945 the Communist Party's total membership stood at 45,435, compared to 18,000 in 1939.[24] CPGB membership in engineering factories had been increasing steadily since 1934. Many of the new members joining in 1939–45 were engineering workers who were typically shop stewards and also held office inside their unions' lay institutions. The period of the party's formal opposition to the war had no negative effect on this upward trend. The 18-month period after Soviet entry did, however, produce an extraordinary acceleration. After this, the pace of recruitment declined, though not immediately, to its pre-war level. There was no parallel rate of increase in either the shipyards or coalmining. There was evidently a strong link between Communist activism and trade union advance.

The election of the 1945 Labour Government with an enormous majority rendered even more crucial the position of Communist union activists in straddling the three worlds of politics, trade unions and shopfloor. The CPGB leadership, particularly Pollitt and Campbell, believed Communists should play a crucial part in ensuring the government fulfilled its manifesto promises and begin to build socialism through nationalising the basic industries. Their vision of how British socialism would function was strongly influenced by the wartime productionism which they had played so conspicuous a part in encouraging.

The potential which Bevin, Tanner and Pollitt had seen in JPCs could now be permanently institutionalised and deployed to deal with the structural economic problems which Campbell, the party's leading practical economist, recognised as serious and possibly fatal. Whilst the Labour leadership took great care to sabotage the CPGB's application for affiliation to the Labour Party, there could be no question of curbing the CPGB inside the trade union movement. The increased party membership on the shopfloor was reflected in increased numbers of party members elected to full-time and lay union office. Far from pursuing extremist policies, they were operating as enthusiastic union loyalists eager to support the new government.

This exemplary behaviour was especially visible in coalmining. Arthur Horner was elected General Secretary of the newly unified National Union of Mineworkers (NUM) in 1946. Communists occupied important full-time and lay offices in the new NUM areas of South Wales and Yorkshire. The Scottish area was almost completely dominated by Communists who had led the inter-war breakaway revolutionary union, the United Mineworkers of Scotland.

Many party activists were sceptical about the ability of the unions to combine productionism with standing up for the interests of the rank and file. But their views were disregarded until well into 1948 by Pollitt and Campbell who remained committed to the rosy future in store for British socialism under a Labour Government. Even after the Cold War had compelled the party centre to polarise relations elsewhere, they continued to enforce a productionist view in coalmining. Party coalmining activists followed Arthur Horner's lead in maintaining the industrial relations system on two levels: a formal adversarial structure was underpinned by strong informal cooperation.[25]

Received wisdom focuses on the disruption and conflict precipitated inside British trade unions by the Cold War. The trade union establishment became convinced that party union activists would use their new positions to sabotage the very fabric of British society. It is unlikely that this grim prophecy of subversion was accurate. There is no evidence that Pollitt and Campbell changed their preference for union loyalism over the illusory potential of militant rank-and-filism.

If there was any basis for Deakin's and Tanner's increasingly shrill anti-Communism, it lay rather in their fears that party activists would successfully execute a take-over of the official institutions, a *coup d'état*, equivalent to the take-over of the Czech state in 1948. By late 1948 the CPGB faced a simultaneous attack from Westminster and Transport House waged with a determination not seen since 1926–8. Deakin's resort in 1949 to a ban on Communists holding any office in the TGWU was an act of desperation from a general secretary increasingly unable to promote 'his own' men and women inside 'his' union.

Deakin took the lead in pressing the TUC General Council to come out against the Communist threat. Two stridently anti-Communist statements appeared in October and November 1948.[26] However, the General Council doggedly declined to organise an anti-Communist campaign amongst the rank and file. Unlike its American counterparts, the British trade union leadership left Communists *in situ* – even inside the Electrical Trades Union (ETU) where the party's domination was notorious. Evidence of ballot rigging by Communists was sent to the TUC by angry activists, but it gathered dust in the files.

Moreover, the ban on Communists holding office inside the TGWU was neither strictly policed nor enforced. The union's lay activists had probably never sympathised with its intentions and it quickly proved unworkable to operate a proscription which went directly against the grain of the 'united front in action' forged in the aftermath of the London bus strike. Certainly when Frank Cousins bowed to rank-and-file pressure in 1959 and sanctioned an official London bus strike-party activists were conspicuous by their discreet but unmistakable presence.

Serious anti-Communist campaigning was confined to a small ideologically motivated minority of right-wing Labour and Catholic trade union activists, like Woodrow Wyatt. Joan Keating has shown that many Catholic trade unionists, including the AEU President William Carron, refused to associate themselves with this vociferous minority – probably for tactical reasons – for fear of offending against the dominant united frontism of trade union culture.[27]

Keating also casts doubt about the effectiveness of these crusades. It required the inspired determination of a left-wing socialist to expose the party machine inside the ETU. Les Cannon, an idealistic Communist activist in the ETU and Harry Pollitt's protégé, was shaken not only by the evidence he uncovered of ballot rigging but also by the creeping disillusion with Soviet socialism he detected amongst those Communists he respected, including Pollitt.[28]

The year 1956 was an important watershed in Communist participation in British trade unions. The effect of Khrushchev's 'revelations' about Stalinism to the 20th Congress of the Soviet Communist Party undermined all the party activists' preconceptions about how socialism might function in Britain. Most found themselves unable to argue on the shopfloor that socialism was superior to capitalism. They retreated into the narrow cocoon of union activism and began to lose touch with that vital third world of the shopfloor.

For party union activists, the impact of the Soviet invasion of Hungary was less important than Khrushchev's speech. For other left-wingers, however, the repression of the Hungarian revolution was crucial. Jack Tanner became a dedicated anti-Communist as a result, and his influence was probably responsible for subsequent failures of Communists to win elected office in the AEU.

Party shop stewards curtailed their sphere of operation increasingly to the two smaller worlds of politics and trade union institutions. It is hardly surprising that the second generation of CPGB activists – typified by Les Ambrose, Dick Etheridge and Will Paynter – were unable to reach out and involve a critical mass of uninitiated but potentially gifted young workers. There were isolated individual exceptions, like Jimmy Reid and Jack Adams. However, many other young militants either joined briefly and left disappointed, like Lawrence Daly, or joined a Trotskyist grouping instead. It was the failure of a third generation of union activists to appear by the late 1950s which set the seal on the party's (and arguably the trade union movement's) demoralisation and ultimate demise.

It is an interesting exercise in counter-factual speculation to wonder what CPGB activists might have done had they continued their spectacular run of election victories inside all unions in the immediate post-war period. The political line of the newly established Cominform had contradictory implications for Britain. On the one hand, it insisted on the unbridgeable gap between capitalism and socialism embodied in the two international power blocs.

On the other hand, there was the declaration that a British road to socialism could proceed through an alliance against monopoly capitalism with the struggling petty bourgeoisie and its political representatives like the Liberal Party. The party archives may well reveal some fascinating discussions about how the CPGB would proceed with the peaceful takeover and transformation of British capitalism.

The party's new reformist programme for transforming Britain peacefully was not popular amongst party union activists. The most important world for them continued to be the shopfloor. Their own strategies for British socialism revolved around encroaching on managerial prerogative and ensuring left-wing victories in elections for the shop stewards' committee and union branch. John Mahon's biography of Pollitt is eloquent in its coded way about the stony ground upon which Pollitt's enthusiasm for the new reformist road fell.[29]

Party union activists continued to emphasise the divide between capitalism and socialism, a polarity which had marked pre-war party propaganda. This Manichean perspective was embedded in unions' non-conformist past and shared with other left-wing union activists. Its strong persistence blocked the attempts of 'neo-reformists' like Jack Tanner to adapt trade union culture to reflect the changed realities of the post-war era – the unions' greatly expanded membership base and enhanced role in cooperating with capitalism via collective bargaining. The dense culture of British trade union activism remained fixed in the inter-war mould which had been forged by Communist/'reformist' cooperation.

Notes

1. Though some Trotskyist-leaning Marxists argue that Communists sold the 'rank and file' down the river at crucial points in the class struggle for the sake of the Comintern line, they agree that they were the (mis)leaders.
2. For a discussion of this common socialisation see Nina Fishman, *The British Communist Party and the Trade Unions 1933–45* (Scolar Press, 1994).
3. L.J. Macfarlane, *The British Communist Party: Its Origin and Development until 1929* (Macgibbon & Kee, 1966), pp. 218–19 and ch. X, pp. 221–42. Roderick Martin, *Communism and the British Trade Unions, 1924–1933: A Study of the National Minority Movement* (Oxford University Press, 1969), pp. 110–21 and 150–6.
4. N. Fishman, *The British Communist Party*, ch. 3.
5. Ibid., pp. 8 and 74.
6. TUC *Report*, 1935, p. 269.
7. Ibid., p. 275.
8. *DW*, 2 April 1937.

9. The sequence of events is summarised in N. Fishman, *The British Communist Party*, pp. 94–100. For a detailed discussion of the vicissitudes of the two rank-and-file movements and the Harworth strike, see chs 6 and 7.

10. Report of Campbell's speech in *DW*, 31 May 1937.

11. Ibid.

12. N. Fishman, *The British Communist Party*, ch. 10.

13. Eric Hobsbawm made this important observation at the Manchester conference during the session dealing with the CPGB and the Second World War. He was commenting on Monty Johnstone's paper which analysed material from the Comintern files not previously investigated.

14. *DW*, 20 December 1939.

15. *DW*, 29 January 1940.

16. AEU National Committee *Report*, 1940, pp. 212–13.

17. This episode is analysed by S.R. Broomfield in 'South Wales in the Second World War: the coal industry and its community', (University of Wales, 1979), pp. 547, 575–9 and 582–3.

18. N. Fishman, *The British Communist Party*, pp. 290–2.

19. Ibid., pp. 271–5. See also James Hinton, 'Killing the People's Convention: a letter from Palme Dutt to Harry Pollitt', *Bulletin of the Society for the Study of Labour History*, 39, 1979.

20. N. Fishman, *The British Communist Party*, pp. 287–90.

21. Ibid., ch. 11. For a different view of JPCs, see James Hinton's, 'The Communist Party, production and Britain's post-war settlement' in this book and his *Shop Floor Citizens: Engineering Democracy in 1940s Britain* (Edward Elgar, 1994). For productivity in war factories, see Alan S. Milward, *War, Economy and Society 1939–1945* (Pelican, 1987), pp. 184–91 and pp. 234–40.

22. N. Fishman, *The British Communist Party*, pp. 303–13.

23. A. Milward, *War, Economy and Society*, pp. 191 and 231–2. For coalmining, see Barry Supple, *The History of the British Coal Industry, Vol.4 1913–1946: The Political Economy of Decline* (Clarendon Press, 1987), ch. 11 and 12.

24. For party membership figures, see N. Fishman, *The British Communist Party*, Appendix One. At the 13th Party Congress in 1935 there were 294 delegates: 234 were in trade unions; 41 delegates were in the TGWU, 25 were in the AEU, 19 in the General and Municipal Workers (GMW); and 18 in coalmining unions. At the party's National Conference in 1942, of 1,196 delegates, 260 were in the AEU, 142 in the TGWU, 41 in the

GMW, and 72 in coalmining unions. At the 17th Party Congress in 1944 there were 754 delegates; 699 were in trade unions; 93 delegates were in the AEU; 81 were in the TGWU; 29 were in the GMW; and 52 in coalmining unions. The figures for the 18th Party Congress were almost identical to 1944. (Some of the delegates who were members of the TGWU would have worked in engineering, the proportion would have increased in 1942 and 1944.)

25. See Nina Fishman, 'Coal: owned and managed on behalf of the people' in Jim Fyrth (ed.), *Labour's High Noon: The Government and the Economy 1945–51* (Lawrence & Wishart, 1993).

26. The two statements were published together in December 1948 as a pamphlet, 'Defend democracy: Communist activities examined. Two statements of policy by the TUC General Council'. The pamphlets enjoyed a brisk take-up amongst trade unionists. The TUC files contain letters from branch officers of various unions, including the ETU, who were anxious to obtain cooperation in exposing Communists, to which cautious replies were sent. A short pamphlet rehearsing the two statements, 'The TUC and Communism', was published in March 1955.

    For the October statement see Hugh Armstrong Clegg, *A History of British Trade Unions Since 1889: Volume III 1934–1951* (Oxford University Press, 1994), pp. 308–9. For Clegg's assessment of the CPGB's post-war strength in the trade union movement and trade unions' responses, see pp. 307–15.

27. Joan Keating, 'Roman Catholics, Christian Democracy and the British Labour movement, 1910–60' (University of Manchester, PhD, 1992).

28. For the ballot rigging see C.H. Rolph, *All Those in Favour?* (Andre Deutsch, 1962). For Les Cannon, see Olga Cannon and J.R.L. Anderson, *The Road from Wigan Pier* (Gollancz, 1973). Cannon tried to interest the TUC in dealing with the ballot rigging. Turned down by Feather, he concluded an alliance with anti-Communist right-wing campaigners, including Woodrow Wyatt.

29. John Mahon, *Harry Pollitt* (Lawrence & Wishart, 1976), pp. 353–4.

Further Reading

The account of the early 1920s and the General Strike in Hugh Clegg is well worth reading: Hugh Armstrong Clegg, *A History of British*

Trade Unions Since 1889: Volume II 1911–1933 (Oxford University Press, 1985) His third volume contains more extensive consideration of Communist activities in unions: Hugh Armstrong Clegg, *A History of British Trade Unions Since 1889: Volume III 1934–1951* (Oxford University Press, 1994).

The official trade union histories do not usually consider the role of Communist activists. Unfortunately, this includes most of the volumes on the miners' unions and the engineers. A partial exception which is useful is Hywel Francis and David Smith, *The Fed: A History of the South Wales Miners in the Twentieth Century* (Lawrence & Wishart, 1980). Two South Walian autobiographies are helpful: Arthur Horner, *Incorrigible Rebel* (Macgibbon & Kee, 1960) and Will Paynter, *My Generation* (Allen & Unwin, 1972). See also Alan Campbell, Nina Fishman and David Howell (eds), *Miners, Unions and Politics, 1910–47*, (Scolar Press, forthcoming).

7 Sidestepping the Contradictions: the Communist Party, Jewish Communists and Zionism 1935–48

Henry Srebrnik

As J.J. Schwarzmantel has reminded us, 'there has ... been no lack of attention paid to the alleged deficiencies of socialist thought in developing a theoretical response to the phenomenon of nationalism.' Theorists of ethnicity such as Walker Connor and Ronaldo Munck have called the 'national question' the Achilles' heel of Marxism. 'The theory of nationalism,' wrote Tom Nairn two decades ago, 'represents Marxism's great historical failure.' Benedict Anderson maintains that nationalism has proved an uncomfortable anomaly for Marxists and for that reason 'has been largely elided, rather than confronted'.[1] After all, ethnicity was pre-modern, ephemeral, a troublesome factor that would surely disappear as capitalism, industrialism and urbanisation formed a relatively homogeneous working class. National consciousness was a superstructural phenomenon, national rivalry a function of capitalist competition and the economic laws of uneven development. In short, ethnicity was a diversion and a political bottleneck impeding class unity. Since Marxists considered themselves historical materialists, they insisted on applying only 'objective' or 'scientific' criteria in defining nationhood and expressed hostility to subjective or spiritual dimensions of ethnic identity. These were considered remnants of religious superstition, vestiges of a pre-bourgeois age.

Marxists were particularly obtuse in their analysis of the predicament Jews faced in the modern world. In medieval Europe considered an accursed people, theologically doomed to eternal punishment for the crime of deicide, they had occupied a special status within the political framework of feudalism, which organised the various Christian populations among whom they lived. As Joshua Trachtenberg has observed, 'In the Christian world the Jew was inevitably looked upon as a heretic – indeed, *the* heretic.' Judaism was 'a perverse deviation from the one true faith,' for Jews, unlike pagans, 'knew the truth and rejected it'.[2]

Christian dogma allowed Jews to exist demographically, socially, economically and politically only within very well-defined and circumscribed limits. It was no accident that they did not acquire their own territory; they were forbidden in most medieval jurisdictions even to own land or engage in agriculture, much less become one of the national branches of the European family. Their pariah status, which in some countries included their virtual confinement in segregated ghettos, would make it impossible for them, when the modern system of sovereign states replaced feudal Christendom, to attain the status of a nationality anywhere in Europe. Yet Marxist theoreticians, so solicitous of many other oppressed and disadvantaged groups in society, made no allowance for their plight.

One writer may indeed have got it right when he stated that 'the ideological origins of the Soviet stance on Zionism lie in the works of Karl Marx',[3] for whom Jews were not an ethnicity but rather a caste, in the parlance of modern sociology, a 'middleman minority' providing specialised economic services. For Marx, the '*chimerical* nationality of the Jew' was 'the nationality of the trader, and above all the financier'. The solution he proposed to their problems was radical assimilation into the structures of civil society.[4] Other adherents of Marxism did not so openly denigrate the Jews, but denied any claims to nationality that did not involve a territorial dimension; of course territorially based nationalities were not seen as being themselves ideological constructs, the legacy of Christendom. Lenin, therefore, argued that the Jews were simply a segregated caste, their ghettoisation the product of anti-Semitic persecution and isolation. His solution was a simple one: once democratic socialists assumed power, the Jews would be absorbed (as workers) by the societies in which they lived.[5] Stalin, presented as a Bolshevik specialist and spokesperson on matters of nationality, was, as Michael Lowy has pointed out, in his approach even more 'dogmatic, restrictive and rigid', his conception 'a real ideological Procrustean bed'. His 1913 tract 'Marxism and the national question' defined a nation as 'a historically evolved, stable community of language, territory, economic life and psychological make-up manifested in a community of life', and asserted that only when *all* of these characteristics were present was it possible to speak of a nation. Groups scattered as minorities within larger state units were not eligible for nationhood.[6] Stalin's pamphlet remained for decades the basic 'text' on nationalism for Communists; though amenable to exegesis, interpretation, gloss and commentary, it could never be denied outright. Even arch-rival Trotsky subscribed to Stalin's definition of a nation: 'This combined definition, compounding the psychological attributes of a nation with geographic and economic conditions of its development, is not only correct theoretically but practically fruitful,' he wrote.[7] The success of the 1917 revolution, the suppression of all rivals on the left and the imposition of dictatorial rule by Stalin meant that the Bolshevik definition of nationhood came to predominate in the USSR and, by extension, in all of the Comintern parties. Stalin's treatise became the 'scientific' basis of Soviet nationality policy towards the non-Russian peoples of the USSR, a centrepiece of the new Communist canon, and would remain politically inviolate until the collapse of world Communism as a movement.

Zionism, the most extreme expression of Jewish nationalism, was thus ideologically in error and politically an enemy. Since the Marxist–Leninist approach to the national question made it difficult for Jews to qualify for nationhood even in those areas, such as the old Russian Empire, where millions of them lived, they certainly could not lay claim to a territory to which they were linked only by religion and history. Zionism was also alleged to misdirect Jewish political energies. Even though fascist and Nazi governments had by the 1930s made anti-Semitism a fundamental cornerstone of their politics, Communists insisted that Zionism served to divide Jews from non-Jews and retarded the natural tendencies of Jews towards assimilation in advanced capitalist states. Zionists were even accused of being in league with fascism, since anti-Jewish legislation helped make the case for a Jewish state in Palestine. The Zionist project in Palestine was in any case a capitalist fraud and a ploy by British imperialism utilising Jews to subjugate the Arab population. Communists could brook no compromise with it.

The British Communist Party was in complete agreement with this analysis. It too accused German Jewish capitalists of having assisted Hitler and referred to Revisionist Zionism as a 'Jewish brand of fascism'.[8] The *Daily Worker* called the Palestine mandate a colony where British-supported 'rich financiers' exploited workers by cleverly cultivating 'race antagonisms'. It was simply 'capitalist robbery in its last stage', where 'Jews of every description slave for minimal wages in the illusion they are building the "Jewish National Home" under British protection'. The landmark Balfour Declaration of 1917, establishing the basis for Jewish settlement in Palestine under British auspices, had merely 'signed up the Jews on a long-term contract'.[9]

Zionism was always contrasted unfavourably to Communism. The former was narrow and parochial in its concerns and a false solution, wrote Aitken Ferguson in the *Daily Worker* in 1936, while 'Jews everywhere know that the Communist Party is the deadly enemy of all social injustice and race discrimination. It has fought and is still fighting for and with them wherever they are oppressed.' Even leftist movements such as the socialist–Zionist Poale Zion played into the hands of fascists and Mosleyites, by confirming that Jews were aliens to be sent packing to Palestine. Since they would merely become tools of the British government, Communists opposed Jewish immigration to Palestine to avoid 'further provocation'. This was 'not betrayal of the Jews. It is ordinary common sense.' Arab and Jewish workers needed to combat British imperialism collectively. Ferguson suggested that the proper answer to fascism was to fight for 'the unity of Jew and Gentile against Fascist terror and Fascist propaganda'. They had a common cause – peace, liberty and the struggle against exploitation, 'in a word, socialism'. The true task of the Jews in every country 'is to fight against oppression in their own country, shoulder to shoulder with their Communist fellow workers'.[10]

The CPGB central committee supported the Palestinian Arab revolt, organised by the Arab Higher Committee, which began in April 1936, and in June called on the Jews to join the Arabs in a joint struggle against fascism. Willie Gallacher, the CP's only MP at the time, defended the uprising during debate in the House of Commons. The party admitted that many found its support of the rebellion difficult to comprehend and the *Daily Worker* specifically pointed to 'considerable confusion' in the minds of many 'Jewish comrades'. It had to remind them that 'Zionism is not in the interests of the vast majority of the Jewish people. It is the expression of the interests of a group of Jewish capitalists which seeks to misuse the legitimate national feeling of the Jewish people for its own end' and indeed was willing 'to sacrifice the Jewish people in order to preserve and further their own interests'. The struggle of the Arabs in Palestine was 'not against their Jewish brothers' but British oppression. They were neither 'paid tools of Mussolini' nor anti-Semitic, but struggling against the 'ruthless oppression' of British imperialism. The paper called for the independence of Palestine and the withdrawal of British forces.[11]

An anonymous 'British resident' who was for a number of years the Palestine correspondent of *Labour Monthly*, the Communist theoretical journal edited by R. Palme Dutt, also justified the Arab uprising by noting that the native population there was struggling not against the Jews *per se* but against immigration sponsored by 'the interests of British and Zionist capital and British imperial strategy'. Zionism was not a Jewish movement but 'in reality a British colonising movement'. British imperialism wanted to impose a Jewish majority in order to further its own interests and also to prevent the Arab and Jewish inhabitants of Palestine from uniting 'on terms of equal citizenship' in a unified, independent state. Before the arrival of the British, 'Jews and Arabs lived peacefully together in Palestine', as they still did in Baghdad, Damascus and Alexandria. Not only would a Jewish entity in Palestine be little better than a British garrison state, he added, but it would exacerbate racial anti-Semitism in Europe by emphasising Jewish distinctiveness. He concluded that Jews would be better off supporting the democratic Arab movement for national independence under the leadership of Haj Amin al-Husseini, the Mufti of Jerusalem.[12]

The party, not surprisingly, opposed a solution that might involve the establishment of two ethnically based states and rejected the Peel Commission's partition plan unveiled in July 1937. The central committee called on party members to rally Jews in vigorous opposition to 'this alarming development'.[13] After all, noted the *Daily Worker*, the Arab–Jewish conflict was the product of British interference. Were 'Moslems, Jews and Christians' allowed 'to arrange their own lives in their own way', their 'good sense' would lead to communal harmony. Hence, all three religious communities needed to cooperate in order to defeat the partition plan. A leader added that 'a slicing up in this fashion solves nothing. It can only serve to fan and aggravate race enmity.' It was, the paper explained, the age-old policy of divide and conquer. A further editorial suggested as an alternative an independent and united Palestine where no groups would enjoy special privileges and where contentious issues such as Jewish immigration would be 'democratically settled by Arabs and Jews'. Gallacher challenged William Ormsby Gore, the Colonial Secretary, in the House of Commons in late July, pointing out that 'the basic right of the Palestinians to Palestine ... must be understood.' The Zionists did not represent the Jewish people but only 'a particular political trend', he added. Partition would not only be a 'menace' but would also 'encourage all the Jew-baiting and all the anti-Semitism that is being developed in Europe'. Gallacher again debated with Ormsby Gore in the House in early November 1937; defending the uprising led by the Mufti, Gallacher called the Tory government's policy a 'desperate expedient'.[14]

Many of the CP's more visible intellectuals weighed in with articles against partition. A future editor of the *Daily Worker*, J.R. Campbell, while declaring that the paper 'takes second place to no one in its struggle against the persecution of the Jews', called for an independent Arab Palestine, though allowing for minority rights for the Jewish population. The Zionist dream, he added, would only 'involve a war of the whole

Arab world against the Jews, and would lead to a greater loss of Jewish life than in all the European pogroms of the last generation'.[15]

One of the most forceful critics of Zionism in Britain was Reginald Bridgeman, who, while not officially a member of the CP, was 'unwavering' in his commitment to the anti-colonial programme of the Comintern. He served as the international secretary of the League Against Imperialism and for National Independence, a Communist-inspired organisation founded in Brussels in February 1927.[16] Bridgeman expounded his views on Palestine with great energy, in person and in print.[17] He insisted that Jews – even in Palestine – did not constitute a nation, but a religious faith; European Jews were 'totally different in outlook, manner and faith from Oriental Jews'. The conflict was one of class, not community: while the Arab masses were fighting heroically against 'Zionist enslavement' by the 'bourgeoisie', the workers had no such hatred for their Jewish counterparts.[18] In articles in *Discussion*, the CP's 'journal for political controversy', Bridgeman noted the relative lack of support for the Palestinian Arab uprising in the British Labour movement, 'much of which is subject to the Fascist influence of Zionism'. Communists, on the other hand, 'are opposed and have always been opposed to the whole system of colonisation'.[19] Ben Bradley, one of the party's specialists on India and other British colonial possessions, referred to the uprising as a struggle for liberation.[20] Bradley served as secretary of the party's Colonial Information Bureau, which in 1937 replaced the League Against Imperialism, and which included much material on Palestine in its publications, the *Colonial Information Bulletin* and *Inside the Empire*.

The novelist Sylvia Townsend Warner also contributed articles to the debate in *Discussion*. She understood that many Jews who had joined the CP due to its anti-Nazi stance might now feel betrayed by the party's position on Palestine. But they had to understand that the CP could not indiscriminately champion any 'vertical section of society', since some of its members were found among the wealthy rather than the oppressed. She equated Zionist ambitions in Palestine with Italian aggression in Ethiopia, the Japanese invasion of Manchuria, and British rule in India. In addition, she expressed her distaste for Orthodox Judaism, with its 'anti-social ... ritual food observances [and] system of mystical taboos', and stated that it was no business of Communists to encourage Jews in the 'delusion' that they were being persecuted because of their faith rather than for political or economic reasons.[21]

In their denunciations of Zionism, some of the Jewish party leaders took a back seat to no one. Jack Cohen, for many years prominent in both the Young Communist League and the CP in Manchester, stated that 'Our attitude towards Zionism is made clear by Stalin.' He called Zionism 'a *reactionary* nationalist movement seeking to imprison the Jewish masses within the four walls of a Jewish national state' and, like Lenin before him, attributed the progressive features of the Jewish people to their dispersion among other nations. Oddly enough, he simultaneously castigated some of his fellow Jewish Communists for denying or hiding their Jewishness and accused them of abandoning the struggle to defend Jewish rights against fascism.[22] The writer and film maker Ivor Montagu, scion of a prominent family in Anglo-Jewry, in July 1937 denounced the Peel partition plan as a 'naked imperial document' which only further 'deludes the Jewish masses' and would result in two mutually antagonistic states perpetually in conflict. Rather than analysing the issue in terms of two competing nationalisms, Montagu seemed more comfortable with analogies drawn from colonial settler states such as Rhodesia and referred to the 'anti-Arab "colour-bar"' among the Jewish leadership in Palestine.[23] Another polemic was directed against the World Zionist Organisation, which had approved the plan; their actions 'must make all Jews proud of their people blush with shame', he stated. 'The Zionists claiming Palestine speak with the accents of Mussolini claiming an Empire, or Hitler, or Japan in China.' Though himself thoroughly assimilated and far removed from his religious roots, Montagu took it upon himself to refute all Zionist claims based on religion as 'sanctimonious talk [which was] a perversion of Judaism'.[24] Even the socialist and Labour Zionists had to be condemned as simple nationalists, he argued; only in the USSR, through the 'great miracle' of socialist reconstruction, had the 'Jewish problem' been successfully solved.[25]

More closely linked to the Jewish community in London's East End, but equally a foe of Jewish nationalism, was Issie Panner, a Communist activist and intellectual who published in the Communist press under the pen-name 'I. Rennap'. During the Second World War Panner would become actively involved in the National Jewish Committee of the CPGB organised under the direction of the party's chief theoretician, R. Palme Dutt; he also wrote the party's seminal analysis of *Anti-Semitism and the Jewish Question*, published in 1942 by Lawrence & Wishart. His views gained wide currency, as he wrote not only for British Communist publications but for the world movement, in periodicals such as the Colonial Information Bureau's *Inside the Empire* and the Comintern's *World News and Views*. He also lectured on Palestine at Marx House and elsewhere in London.

Panner, too, opposed partition, instead submitting a proposal calling for a joint Arab-Jewish conference to create a democratic state where Jews would be granted 'inalienable democratic citizenship rights' alongside Arabs. In a free state, each community could exercise control over language, schools and local government, while immigration and land sales would come under joint jurisdiction. While Panner acknowledged the 'sincere aspirations of Zionist Jews for a life free from persecution', he deplored the fact that these desires served 'as a brake upon the Arab struggles for national independence' and he supported the Mufti's Higher Arab Committee as a 'full-blooded anti-Imperialist and full national independence' movement; it had 'the backing of the Arab people'.[26]

The CPGB published a pamphlet entitled *Palestine: Terror or Peace* in November 1938. In it the party described 'the reactionary character and role of Zionism' and emphasised that it had little following among Jewish workers. It was mainly 'Jewish big business' which saw in Zionism 'a chance of big profits from investments in the "Holy Land", which could be made under the cloak of National Idealism, and with Britain's benevolent protection'. In this way had Zionism managed to divert into escapist channels 'honest Jewish aspirations towards a better mode of life' among the rank and file and caused hatred between two peoples 'who have no natural cause for antagonism'. Jewish and Arab workers were enjoined to cooperate against the rising wave of fascist influence and intrigue 'among politically backward sections of the Arab people' in Palestine; the latter would have to recognise that those Jews already in Palestine had the same democratic rights to citizenship as they did. The CP called on the British Labour Party to demand a peace conference of Arabs and Jews which would work towards an independent state rather than a partition of the country.

By late 1938 the Peel partition plan was in any case dead, superseded in May 1939 by the Palestine White Paper which would throughout the Second World War severely limit Jewish immigration to Palestine and otherwise curtail Zionist activities. Though Jews throughout the world expressed outrage, the *Daily Worker* guardedly approved the proposals, which 'does make possible Arab–Jewish cooperation'; it called on Arab and Jewish 'progressives' to make certain it would be implemented. Gallacher was more critical, however, calling it a 'new effort of British imperialism to maintain its grip over Palestine while seeking to counteract the penetration of fascist influence among the Arabs' by providing for them limited concessions.[27] By late 1938, the CP was beginning to express concern over the political direction taken by the leadership of the Palestinian Arab community. Fascists, the *Daily Worker* claimed, were taking advantage of the 'uncompromising' policies of Zionism to whip up anti-Jewish feelings and were 'reaping a rich harvest'.[28] The *Colonial Information Bulletin*, too, began to provide a more balanced commentary, referring to some Arab leaders as 'puppets' (though still using terms like 'Brownshirts' to refer to right-wing Revisionist Zionists). More emphasis was now placed on the geopolitical machinations of British imperialism throughout the region.[29] The party leadership acknowledged that the situation had become more problematic and required careful study.[30]

Communist assertions and statements regarding the nature of Zionism and the role of Palestinian Jewry did not go unchallenged, of course, in other sectors of the left. Jews in the various socialist Zionist movements, and even some Jewish Communists, tried to counter Communist attacks. Bridgeman was said to have a 'deplorable ignorance of Zionist ideology' and a lack of sympathy for persecuted Jewry; he was told that it was impossible to divorce Zionism from Judaism, so that 'anti-Zionism must of necessity mean anti-Semitism'. Responding to Sylvia Townsend Warner, another critic observed that 'It is peculiar how Comrades who would never deny the role of the Party as champion of all oppressed peoples cannot stomach the Party as champion of the Jews.'[31] The party's Jewish bureau, while reiterating that Zionism 'as a whole is a pillar of imperialist domination', also found it necessary to 'correct some errors' in her analysis, reminding her that when the freedom to practise Judaism was attacked by 'the forces of reaction', Communists had to come to its defence.[32] Willie Gallacher was the subject of *An Open Letter* from a Palestinian Jew on a kibbutz, published by the Poale Zion socialist Zionists in London. His professions of sympathy for the oppressed Jews were 'superficial, sham', his reading of the history of Arab–Jewish relations 'nothing but a bad joke!' Most major Jewish capitalists were anti-Zionist, noted the pamphlet, and the movement was in reality a broad coalition of workers, the middle class and the intelligentsia.[33] Another Zionist tract by the journalist Joseph Cohen blamed Communists for stirring up Arab nationalist sentiment against the Jews in Palestine and ascribed to the CP a 'callousness towards Jewish needs'. Their conception of Zionism was 'fantastic' and 'doctrinaire', their bitter opposition to it 'ridiculous'. Jews who were Communists, he said, were 'utterly divorced from Jewish national life and not representative of the masses'.[34] Issie Panner, who belonged to the Workers' Circle or *Abeter Ring*, the influential east London Jewish friendly society, came under fire from comrades there. One member called him 'entirely ignorant of what is happening in Palestine' and accused him of spreading 'falsehoods'. Panner's analysis was 'logically unsound and factually inexact', because in Palestine the majority of Jews were not exploiters but workers, hence 'the Jewish masses are in a more advanced position in the struggle for socialism' and might one day create a 'Jewish Soviet Palestine'. Panner's response was that, on the contrary, Palestine would soon be 'writhing in crisis and chaos', while Jews in the Soviet Jewish Autonomous Region of Birobidzhan went 'from success to success, showing thereby that only under the dictatorship of the pro-letariat can the Jew find real freedom and emancipation'.[35] The *Daily Worker* in this period was told by one reader that it was 'utterly ridiculous' to refer to all Jewish supporters of Zionism as capitalists.[36] Some Workers' Circle members even tried to ban sales of the paper at Circle House in Stepney, and the organisation's central committee spent the better part of two meetings dealing with allegations that the *Daily Worker*'s utterances on Palestine were anti-Jewish.[37] In turn, Communists occasionally attempted to disrupt Zionist meetings.[38]

With the start of the Second World War Panner was at first hopeful that Arab uprisings would free Palestine from British rule. However, he was soon denouncing the Mufti, previously touted as a champion of Palestinian independence, as 'wily' and 'scheming' for his machiavel-lian attempts at playing the Axis and Allied powers off against each other. Panner now characterised the Arab leadership as 'rotten to the core', though he did not forget to direct some of his invective against 'reac-tionary' Zionist leaders such as David Ben-Gurion, who, he reminded his readers, continued to serve British imperialism. Panner warned the Zionist leaders that they would be thrust aside by Whitehall 'if they stood in the path of [British] war plans'. He soon afterwards published an account of how 'brutally' the colonial authorities in Palestine were sup-pressing Jewish opponents of the White Paper.[39]

Even as the Holocaust unfolded and prominent Communist theo-reticians such as R. Page Arnot wrote refutations of Nazi race theory, they continued to remind readers that Stalin 'throughout this century has devoted public attention to this very question' and that his 1913 work on the national question remained the 'standard text-book', a 'profoundly interesting and correct treatment'.[40] In a reading guide drafted in June 1943 Dutt recommended the standard Communist texts on the national question including works by Lenin, Stalin, Panner and Dutt himself.[41] The British CP minimised all separate Jewish political and military ini-tiatives, preferring to recognise Jews as citizens of the countries involved in the common fight against Nazi Germany. The party opposed the idea of raising a Jewish army from Palestine; when the British government finally acceded to the formation of a Jewish Brigade made up of volunteers from Palestine the *Daily Worker* was cool to the plan.[42] Some Jews in the Communist Party also continued to equate Zionism with Nazism. One anonymous 'Jewish correspondent', responding to critiques of the USSR made by the president of the World Zionist Organisation, Chaim Weizmann, suggested that Weizmann regretted 'the fact that there has grown up in Russia an enlightened generation of Jews over whom he has lost control and who refuse to regard themselves as members of a "chosen race", an idea, incidentally, which smacks horribly of Nazi ideology'.[43] Certainly the party worried about the growth of right-wing Revisionist-inspired movements such as the Irgun and 'Stern Gang'; when the latter group killed Lord Moyne, the British Minister Resident in Cairo, in November 1944, Issie Panner felt it would only encourage the growth of anti-Semitism in England.[44] Privately Dutt expressed the view that this action, taken by the 'extreme terrorist wing' of the Zionist movement, had 'injured the cause of the Jews'.[45]

As the war began to wind down, an editorial in the *Daily Worker* hoped that the existence of a Jewish community in Palestine would not be used as a pretext to delay the progress of statehood for the Arab nations of the Middle East.[46] When the CPGB 18th national congress met in November 1945 news of the murder of millions of Jews in Nazi-occupied Europe had become common knowledge; but in a resolution on 'the Jewish Question and Palestine' the delegates rejected 'the Zionist plea that the problems of world Jewry will be solved by the creation of a Jewish State'. Instead the congress endorsed a free and inde-pendent Palestine 'in which full Arab–Jewish unity will flourish', perhaps enabling some of the Jewish survivors in Europe to emigrate to Palestine.[47]

John Callaghan has recently demonstrated the close involvement of Palme Dutt, the CP's *éminence grise*, in the anti-colonial activities of the Comintern.[48] Since it was located in the very heart of the British Empire, the CPGB served as something of an international go-between, involving itself in the relations between the Soviet Communist Party and the various anti-imperialist movements in the British Empire and concentrating 'much of its energies and propaganda upon foreign and colonial affairs'.[49] Dutt had been editor of the *Daily Worker* during 1936–8, at a time when the Palestinian uprising dominated Middle Eastern news. In February 1947 he convened a conference of the

Communist parties of the British Empire in London, to press for recognition of the right to self-determination by the colonial peoples.

Chimen Abramsky was one of the chief theoreticians on the CP's National Jewish Committee (NJC), established in 1943 under Dutt's guidance, and later described himself as Dutt's 'blue-eyed boy' and chief collaborator on Jewish affairs. Abramsky maintained that Dutt effectively set the party's line on the Middle East during this period and even influenced Moscow's policy, 'as they themselves didn't know too much about it'. From 1944 on, Palestine became 'a burning issue' for the CP, and Dutt was 'the leading spirit' who conducted the campaign against Zionism in the party.[50] Another activist in the Jewish Communist movement, Alf Holland, referred to Dutt, in Yiddish, as *der rebbe, der kop* ['the rabbi, the brains'] of the CPGB, while Joshua Gershman, a prominent Canadian Communist, maintained that Dutt 'was very influential in setting world Communist policy on the Middle East. No question about it – Palme Dutt's line was accepted by the majority of [Communist] parties in the world.'[51]

The NJC was a subcommittee of Dutt's International Affairs Committee, which dealt with 'the Jewish question' along with other matters of colonial policy. Under the chairmanship of Lazar Zaidman, the NJC was to assist the party 'in framing its attitude to the problem of Palestine' as well as to attract more Jews to the party's colours.[52] After all, wrote Zaidman to a Jewish Communist in Melbourne, Australia, 'It should be realised that London is the place where all the various interests and views with regard to Palestine (and the Middle East) meet and are decided on.'[53] Abramsky remembered secret meetings which he and Jack Gaster, who in March 1946 was elected a London county councillor from Mile End, Stepney, held with various socialist Zionists from Palestine. One such visitor was Mordechai Bentov, later an Israeli cabinet minister. Phil Piratin, the Communist elected MP for Mile End in July 1945, has recounted having Chaim Weizmann approach him at a dinner in 1946. 'The next day, I asked Dutt what it was all about. Dutt said that Weizmann thought I had influence in Moscow!' Piratin noted that 'people were always coming and going from London to Palestine. We were meeting Arab comrades from Palestine and Jewish comrades from Palestine. This was an international discussion, with the tacit knowledge of our friends in Moscow also. I was in on discussions at high levels, with Russians.' Among the Middle Eastern visitors he recalled were Khaled Bakdash, afterwards a prominent Syrian Communist, and Shmuel Mikunis, a future leader of the Israeli CP.[54]

The CPGB's anti-Zionist stance for a time even enabled it to make common cause with such assimilationist and upper-class bodies in Anglo-Jewry as the Anglo-Jewish Association and the Jewish Fellowship, formed in 1944 to uphold the principle that Jews were a religious, not national, group, and to combat the Zionist 'take-over' of communal bodies such as the Board of Deputies of British Jews. Piratin and Gaster testified against the Zionists at the 1946 Anglo-American Committee of Enquiry in London. The CPGB executive committee remarked that the two men had helped 'clarify the Party's policy on the urgent problem of Jewry and the question of Palestine's future'.[55] So enamoured of the Communist position was Basil L.Q. Henriques, a prominent upper-class Jewish notable who was active in the Fellowship, that he penned a letter to Piratin stating that he was 'both amazed and delighted to see that [the CP presentation] was almost identical with that given by the Jewish Fellowship ... I am most anxious for you to become a member of the Fellowship ... our numbers would go up by leaps and bounds for the Jewish members of the Communist Party are only waiting for a lead from someone like yourself to join us.'[56] Anti-Zionist politics was indeed leading the party of the working class into some strange beds. At the 19th party congress, held in February 1947, the delegates demanded that Britain pursue a policy of 'peace and friendship with the Arab countries'.[57] While the CPGB did do a volte-face a few months later, when the USSR itself announced it now favoured the creation of a Jewish state in Palestine, like the Soviets it resumed its anti-Zionist politics in the 1950s. But by then most Jews in Britain had ceased to give any measure of support to the party or indeed even take much interest in its ideological positions.

While the national leadership of the CPGB, which included some acculturated Jews, adhered to the official Marxist–Leninist position on matters Jewish, the more ethnically conscious Jewish Communists working within immigrant and working-class Jewish neighbourhoods in east London and elsewhere often espoused a very different political outlook. As I describe elsewhere,[58] Communism thrived for a time as a specifically *ethnic* means of political expression, to the point where it might legitimately have been regarded as a variety of left-wing Jewish nationalism. However, although themselves often Jewishly educated and thoroughly steeped in Jewish culture, and concerned with Jewish issues, the Jewish Communists remained by ideological belief and organisational necessity wedded to the CPGB and to the policies of the Soviet state, including the assimilationist theories regarding Jewish nationalism. Even the NJC in its official documents adhered to the classical formula regarding Zionism: 'this reactionary doctrine is the counterpart of anti-Semitism; both deny the basis of national citizenship of the Jews in the countries where they live'.[59] Professor Hyman Levy, the noted scientist and a member of the NJC, informed a wider audience that a Jewish national home in Palestine would still be subject to pressure from the surrounding Arab world and would not in any way solve the Jewish problem. 'Jews in the past have survived when they fulfilled a progressive function in society' and worked 'to achieve equality and liberty for all peoples'. Only with the coming of socialism, he reminded his readers, would the Jewish problem 'vanish like a forgotten nightmare'.[60] Still, there was much disquiet over CP policy regarding Zionism among Jewish Communists, and the minutes of one NJC meeting in February 1945 make this clear: 'Very much confusion still exists amongst our comrades on many aspects of the Jewish Question.' Dutt felt it necessary to speak to the Jewish comrades, some of whom had 'a tendency to be swayed by backward ideas amongst Jewry'.[61]

Perhaps these debates were of less importance than they would become after the creation of the state of Israel in 1948, and so people were able to live with political contradictions; Bertha Sokoloff, onetime Stepney Communist Party secretary and borough councillor, has expressed this view.[62] But it was only a matter of time until Marxist–Leninist theory and Soviet foreign policy would come to haunt the Jewish Communists ideologically and would lose them the mass support they had gained in local political activities aimed at bettering the political and economic situation of their constituents. Mick Mindel, an active east London Communist and trade unionist and for many years an official in the National Union of Tailors and Garment Workers, felt that the party's Palestine policy was largely responsible for its later isolation. 'We are paying the price now,' he said in a 1978 interview.[63] Tom Rampling, another Stepney activist and Communist councillor after 1945, himself not Jewish, went even further: 'I found, and raised sharply with the party, that very many of the leading Jewish comrades were anti-Semitic,' he disclosed in an interview in 1979.

> Now I know this sounds ridiculous, and in fact they always insisted they were not anti-Semitic but anti-Zionist. But so anxious were they to prove that they were no longer tied to the old Jewish religious or national ties that they became in fact anti-Jewish.[64]

Recent studies of nationalism by Conor Cruise O'Brien and Donald Akenson have emphasised the religiously based nature of national identity among peoples such as the Afrikaaners, Jews and Ulster Protestants, whose complex foundation myths revolve around their relations with a deity, and whose sense of collective destiny therefore goes far beyond a common language, genetic kinship or territorial concentration. Their claims to land involve meta-historical concepts such as covenants with God, 'promised lands' for 'chosen peoples'. As Eugene Kamenka recently noted, while the Jews as a people have in a secular sense entered modern history through Zionist nationalism, that ideology has itself been able to rely on a very important precondition: 'This is the fact that the Jewish nation had been defined and given shape in that surprisingly early piece of national historiography that we call the Old Testament.' Communists never could come to terms with such forms of ethnic consciousness, thereby perhaps confirming Ephraim Nimni's suggestion that Marxists as well as others need to 'deconstruct the institution of the nation-state and ... look for novel ways of interpreting the right of nations to self-determination.'[65]

Notes

1. J.J. Schwarzmantel, 'Class and nation: problems of socialist nationalism', *Political Studies* 35, 1987, pp. 239–40; W. Connor, *The National Question in Marxist–Leninist Theory and Strategy* (Princeton University Press, New Jersey, 1984); R. Munck, *The Difficult Dialogue: Marxism and Nationalism* (Zed Books, 1986); T. Nairn, 'The modern Janus', *New Left Review* 94, 1975, p. 3; B. Anderson, *Imagined Communities: Reflections on the Origin and Spread of Nationalism* (Verso, 1983), p. 13.

2. J. Trachtenberg, *The Devil and the Jews* (Yale University Press, New Haven, Conn., 1944), p. 174.

3. W. Sharif, 'Soviet Marxism and Zionism', *Journal of Palestine Studies* 6, 1977, p. 78.

4. K. Marx, 'On the Jewish question' (1844), in T.B. Bottomore (ed.), *Karl Marx: Early Writings* (McGraw-Hill, New York, 1964), pp. 36–40.

5. See his 'Critical remarks on the national question' (1913), in H. Lumer (ed.), *Lenin on the Jewish Question* (International Publishers, New York, 1974).

6. M. Lowy, 'Marxists and the national question', *New Left Review* 96, 1976, p. 95; J. Stalin, *Marxism and the National and Colonial Question* (Lawrence & Wishart, 1947), p. 81.

7. L. Trotsky, *Stalin: An Appraisal of the Man and His Influence* (Harper, 1941), pp. 154–5.

8. *An Urgent Warning on a Most Important Matter: Jews and Fascism* (Coordinating Committee Against Fascism, nd but 1935), pp. 4–6.

9. *DW*, 14 March and 6 May 1935.

10. *DW*, 28 July 1936.

11. *DW*, 8, 20 and 26 June 1936, 28 May, 9 and 18 June 1936.

12. 'The events in Palestine', *LM*, July 1936, pp. 410–11, 417; 'Palestine: the imperialist view', *LM*, July 1937, pp. 450–1; 'The Palestine report', *LM*, August 1937, pp. 468–9; 'Open letter to a Zionist-Socialist', *LM*, April 1938, p. 251.

13. CPGB CC *Report* to 15th party congress, September 1938, p. 33.

14. *DW*, 9, 16 and 24 July and 4 November 1937.

15. *DW*, 18 January 1938.

16. See John Saville's entries on Bridgeman and the League Against Imperialism in J. Bellamy and J. Saville (eds), *Dictionary of Labour Biography*, vol. VII (Macmillan, 1984), pp. 26–50.

17. See for example the pamphlet *Palestine: An Authoritative Survey* (LAI, July 1936) and especially the section 'Zionism as a willing pawn', pp. 17–18.

18. *DW*, 8 May 1936.

19. 'Subject nations', *Discussion*, September 1936, p. 18; 'A reply to Zionist socialist', *Discussion*, December 1936, p. 19.

20. *DW*, 17 September 1936.

21. S. Townsend Warner, 'Communism and Palestine', *Discussion* February 1937, pp. 20–1.

22. J. Cohen, 'A reply to BP', *Discussion*, May 1936, pp. 9–11.

23. *DW*, 10 July 1937.

24. *DW*, 14 August 1937.

25. Review of W. Zukerman's *The Jew in Revolt*, *DW*, 28 July 1937.

26. *DW*, 15 July and 7 December 1938; 'The Arab Jewish conference', *LM*, January 1939, pp. 54 and 58.

27. *DW*, 19 May and 14 June 1939.

28. *DW*, 15 October 1938.

29. *Colonial Information Bulletin*, 15 April and 1 July 1939.

30. CPGB CC *Report* to 16th party congress, October 1939 (not held), p. 17.

31. Exchange between Bridgeman, Dr H. Edelston and A.R. Beiter, *Discussion*, March 1937, pp. 14–24.

32. *Discussion*, April 1937, pp. 22–3.

33. Sh. Lavi, *An Open Letter to Comrade Gallacher, on the Jewish Worker in Palestine* (Jewish Socialist Labour Party, Poale Zion in England, 1936), pp. 5, 9 and 10.

34. J.L. Cohen, *The Communist Challenge and a Zionist Reply* (Federation of Zionist Youth, 1936), pp. 1–2 and 15–16.

35. I. Goldenberg, 'Marxism and comrade Panner', *The Circle-Arbeter Ring*, December 1934, pp. 3–4 (English section). Panner's response in ibid., April 1935, pp. 4–5 (English section).

36. Letter from Q. King, *DW*, 24 June 1936.

37. *Circle-Arbeter Ring*, October 1936, p. 7 (English section).

38. See L. Richer's letter to *Jewish Chronicle*, 20 May 1938.

39. 'War effects in Palestine and the near East', *LM*, January 1940, p. 55; *World News and Views*, 9 March 1940, p. 142; *DW*, 2 July 1940.

40. R. Page Arnot, *There Are No Aryans: The Racial Theory Exposed*, *LM*, 1944, pp. 26–9.

41. Dutt papers, British Library, Cup. 1262 K4.

42. *DW*, 20 September 1944.

43. *DW*, 30 June 1944.

44. *DW*, 23 November 1944.

45. Dutt to Ben Bradley, 14 November, 1944, Dutt papers, British Library, Cup 1262 K4.

46. *DW*, 26 February 1945.

47. *Report* of CPGB 18th congress, November 1945, pp. 72–4.

48. J. Callaghan, *Rajani Palme Dutt: A Study in British Stalinism* (Lawrence & Wishart, 1993).

49. W. Thompson, *The Good Old Cause: British Communism 1920–1991* (Pluto Press, 1992), p. 97.

50. Chimen Abramsky interview, 26 May 1978; Abramsky to Shloime Perel, 7 December 1978.

51. Alf Holland, interview 16 June 1978; Joshua Gershman interview, 5 September 1978.

52. CPGB EC *Report* to 18th party congress, November 1945, pp. 10–11.

53. Zaidman to Isaac Gust, 31 May 1945, Zaidman collection, Sheffield University.

54. Phil Piratin interviews, 3 August 1976 and 30 November 1978.

55. CP EC *Report* to CPGB 19th congress, February 1947 (CPGB, 1946), p. 17.

56. Henriques to Piratin, 4 February 1946, Zaidman collection.

57. CPGB 19th congress *Resolutions and Proceedings*, p. 18.

58. H. Srebrnik, *London Jews and British Communism: 1935–1945* (Vallentine Mitchell, 1994).

59. *The Jewish Question* (CPGB, NJC, nd but 1944), p. 8.

60. H. Levy, 'The problem of assimilation', in J.J. Lynx, *The Future of the Jews* (Lindsay Drummond, 1945), p. 66.

61. CPGB NJC minutes, 11 February 1945, Zaidman collection.

62. Letter to author, 29 January 1979.

63. Mick Mindel interview, 5 November 1978.

64. Tom Rampling interview, 20 January 1979.

65. D. H. Akenson, *God's Peoples: Covenant and Land in South Africa, Israel, and Ulster* (McGill–Queen's University Press, Montreal, 1991); C. Cruise O'Brien, *God's Land: Reflections on Religion and Nationalism* (Harvard University Press, Cambridge, Mass., 1988); E. Kamenka, 'Nationalism: ambiguous legacies and contingent futures', *Political Studies* 41, 1993, pp. 80 and 84; E. Nimni, *Marxism and Nationalism: Theoretical Origins of a Political Crisis* (Pluto Press 1994), p. x.

Further Reading

Recent works on the Jewish community in Britain include R. Bolchover, *British Jewry and the Holocaust* (Cambridge University Press, 1993), D. Cesarani, *The Jewish Chronicle and Anglo-Jewry: 1841–1991* (Cambridge University Press, 1993) and T. Kushner, *The Persistence of Prejudice: Antisemitism in British Society during the Second World War* (Manchester University Press, 1989). For a general overview see V.D. Lipman, *A History of the Jews in Britain since 1858* (Leicester University Press, 1990). For the relationship between Jews and Communism see Sh. Kadish, *Bolsheviks and British Jews: The Anglo-Jewish Community, Britain and the Russian Revolution* (Frank Cass, 1992): There is also a body of memoir literature by Jewish Communists, including J. Jacobs, *My Youth in the East End: Communism and Fascism 1919–1939* (Janet Simon, 1978), I. Montagu, *The Youngest Son: Autobiographical Sketches* (Lawrence & Wishart, 1970) and P. Piratin, *Our Flag Stays Red* (Thames Publications, 1948).

8 The Communist Party and the *Daily Worker* 1930–56

Kevin Morgan

The *Daily Worker* was set up as the official organ of the British Communist Party in 1930. Now the *Morning Star*, it has, except for an 18-month wartime ban, maintained publication ever since. In 1946, ownership of the *Worker* was formally transferred to a non-party cooperative, the People's Press Printing Society (PPPS). The paper nevertheless remained the acknowledged voice of the CP until the factional disputes of more recent years.

A study of the paper's early decades raises a number of interesting questions. For CP historians the *Worker* remains, even after the opening of the archives, an incomparable source for the party's day-to-day outlook and political culture. Moreover, as the party's official mouthpiece, it provided a source of authority which, while formally accountable to leading party bodies, was imperfectly contained by the structures of democratic centralism. The defections of 1956 and battles of the 1980s mark the obvious crisis points, but there were muted tensions even in more disciplined times.

For social historians of Communism, the *Worker* reveals the face that the party presented to the world at large and thus tells us something of how the CP conceived of its 'public'. To whom was the paper addressed, in what language and with what shared assumptions? Did the *Worker* aim to challenge mores and taboos prevailing under capitalism, or did it work with the grain of mass culture to attain greater, or more immediate, ends? More specifically, was the paper intended as a popular daily on the Fleet Street model, harnessing mainstream journalistic techniques; or did it confront this dope with a purer vehicle of instruction, agitation and theoretical rectitude? Possibly, while leaning increasingly towards the former option, the paper never fully resolved this question, and hence perhaps the failure of its audacious attempt to break into Britain's press monopoly. But the basic cause of this monopoly, and transparent inequity of British liberties, was more fundamental. In a period of steeply rising newspaper readership, the *Worker* was the *only* new national daily even to see the light of day, as dependence on advertising revenues demanded circulations quite beyond the unconventional or undercapitalised.[1] It was only quite specific factors in the *Worker*'s case – notably a uniquely committed cadre of journalists, distributors and sellers – that made even the attempt to breach this monopoly possible.

It is to this second set of questions that this chapter is mainly addressed.[2] In terms of Raymond Williams's distinction between the 'pauper press' and 'respectable press',[3] the *Worker* was a pauper that, like the *Herald* before it, aspired to respectability, before each in its different way succumbed to the unequal contest. On its appearance in January 1930, however, the very last word to describe the *Worker* was respectable. Its launching owed everything to grandiose political imperatives and nothing to rational calculation. Its role was as a vehicle for the party's 'new line' of independent revolutionary leadership, and it was proponents of the new line who most clearly articulated its initial ambitions. They rejected the canons of Fleet Street, as they rejected every institution of capitalist society. This legacy of confrontation was one the *Worker* wrestled with ever after, producing tensions that were evident in its very first months.

By its founders the *Worker* was conceived as the directing organ of a class in struggle and particularly of its revolutionary vanguard. The point of its appearing daily was not so much to wean workers from other papers as to provide its own supporters with constant central direction in conditions of deepening revolutionary crisis. Its whole, mistaken, rationale was of events moving too swiftly for merely weekly contact, requiring instead a military speed of command.

> *Our Party is too slow to mobilise* ITSELF in this situation let alone masses of workers ... The 'DAILY' is therefore a matter of life or death for the new era of revolutionary struggle ... From lagging behind [it] will bring us abreast of events. It will become the MOBILISER, ORGANISER, MARSHAL, of the new battalions of struggle who enter the class front ... It can and will knit the Party into a quickly moving, highly politicalised organisation which can, overnight, get together and punch 100% on the central questions of each day.[4]

As befitted these objectives, the new *Daily Worker* rejected virtually every established newspaper practice. If a Fleet Street production was obviously beyond its resources, it was also contrary to its purposes. Editorially, the paper needed no distractions from the struggle, least of all the 'frills ... dazzle ... corruption and entertainment' of the popular press.

If it could not afford news agency subscriptions, its 'army' of worker correspondents would provide a steelier resource. Neither 'professional journalism' nor trade union agreements were to be respected. Disregarding hierarchies and job demarcations and imbued with a spirit of sacrifice, its staff would only thus keep costs to 'a revolutionary minimum'. Above all, the party's technical experts, particularly those infected by Fleet Street practice, were to be kept to a strictly subordinate role. 'The very conditions that have given them their professional training have also given them a technique which is alien to our purposes', wrote Palme Dutt, who had outlined a prospectus for the new paper.[5] It was Dutt in fact who exploded when a pre-publication mock-up by party journalists featured 'Jack the Ripper', 'Woman Exhumed' and 'Leicester Starters'.[6] To safeguard it from such horrors, the *Worker* had as its first editor William Rust, a Communist of scant journalistic experience but politically dependable and alert to deviations. Political control of the paper, Dutt warned, had to be 'ceaseless, vigilant and merciless to any weakness'.

Dutt's basic ideas, so often remote from reality, had in this case been practised with conspicuous success when seven years earlier he had launched the *Workers' Weekly*. 'Half a dozen helpers, students and workers, were got together at the centre to help put the material together', he wrote for *Pravda*. 'We took no notice of journalistic canons, but simply aimed to put together the materials as nearly as possible as written ...' Much of the *Weekly*'s material came from worker-correspondents and through its own distribution network it reportedly achieved a circulation of over 60,000. Such an achievement proved for many years to be beyond its successor.[7] The new daily operation strained to the utmost a much-weakened party and by any reckoning the venture was at first a failure. Projected circulation figures, even allowing for the inevitable wholesalers' boycott, had been in the order of 20–25,000, even 50,000. The actual circulation was barely 10,000 and the weekly deficit initially £500. If the Comintern bore the financial burden, it was its fragile British section that suffered the organisational consequences of so disproportionate an undertaking. The party's colonial and industrial departments briefly collapsed, its secretariat ceased to function properly and its membership losses continued, to an all-time low of around 2,500 in November 1930.[8]

The basic cause of failure lay in the CP's marginality to British politics and the consequent unreality of the whole project except in so far as the Comintern underwrote it. All that, however, was beyond discussion now that the paper actually existed. Instead, populists within the party sought editorial solutions to the *Worker*'s teething problems. The foremost critic was Harry Pollitt, the party's new secretary, who had earlier been opposed to the paper's premature launching. Pollitt, it should be remembered, had a lasting affection for Robert Blatchford's lively, colourful and irreverent paper, the *Clarion*. Now at the very outset he described the *Worker* as 'dull and dismal' and urged on it remedial studies of 'capitalist press campaigns'. Six months later, as he fretted over unbalanced books and unread newspapers, he raised the matter again more formally. 'We constantly talk about being close to the masses, of studying the needs and desires of the masses', he argued, 'but no one can say we carry this out in regard to the paper.' What workers wanted was more general news, sport, satire, light fiction, topical features. What they got was very different: 'Only strikes, deaths in the street, tear gas on a crowd, and so on.' In any case, too many party pronouncements made for 'a narrow Party political bulletin ... a daily edition of "Inprekorr"', which even its readers took only out of a sense of loyalty. One requirement was to relax the paper's merciless political constraints. Its staff, Pollitt argued, were 'a good group, but, afraid of making deviations, are unable to produce what is wanted'. What they needed was 'a free hand in the wide treatment of popular news', thus reaching out to 'those disillusioned masses who, fed up with the "Herald" etc., cannot afford to buy two papers daily, but get nothing save struggle and death in every page of our paper'.[9]

After some delay, during which Pollitt had discussions on the party's plight in Moscow, a resolution was adopted stating the new aim of a 'popular mass newspaper'.[10] The issue was far from resolved, however. As Dutt subsequently wrote to Pollitt: 'You have followed your line against ours from the beginning ... (the old opposition of news, racing etc and 'heavy political' matter, the Herald as the ideal of what the workers really want) although you are quite aware that it is completely contrary to our own.'[11] Dutt, it should be remembered, had a lasting affection for the Comintern's dense, turgid and unreadable paper, *Inprecorr*. His complaint of the *Worker* was not that it lacked popular appeal, but that it debased itself in striving for it. A perfectly digestible article of his, on 'Import boards, quota systems and tariffs', was even split into two parts, for which frivolity the editorial board inevitably earned Dutt's scathing reproach.[12] When in 1932 a 'workers' press commission' was established to review once more the paper's future, Dutt was therefore resistant to further concessions. In particular he took issue with the London Communist Print Group, which argued for the fullest use of professional skills 'to take the technique of the capitalist Press and turn it against the capitalists'. Among the group's members were Jack Flanagan and Willie Forrest, journalists with the *Mail* and *Express* respectively, who each afternoon sought to instil this lesson at the *Worker* before proceeding to their paying jobs. The appreciation of their efforts was not shared by Dutt. What, after all, were the techniques that these journalists presumed to teach the party?

> The expression of this highly developed technique of capitalist propaganda is not primarily the direct propaganda, the jingo teachings, etc; it is just the so-called 'general news' and 'sport' ... which it is our task to destroy (not take over) and replace by revolutionary working-class technique ... To the task of painting a false picture, of deadening thought, belongs the technique of the snippet, of the 'smart' paragraph, of personalities in place of politics, of high society and crime and bourgeois sport, of the 'scoop', the 'splash' and the 'sensation' ... The technique of arousing thought and consciousness and fight and responsibility is obviously different from that of paralysing and choking all thought and consciousness in triviality.[13]

Dismayed by so violent an enmity, Flanagan and Forrest quietly discontinued their efforts for the paper. Nevertheless, it was Dutt who was fighting a losing battle. Inevitably the issue got caught up with other controversies, notably that between Pollitt and Dutt over Communist work in the unions.[14] Jimmy Shields, who took Pollitt's side in this affair, also proposed a number of improvements to the *Worker*, including its more sensitive handling of trade union issues.[15] Dutt, meanwhile, remained one of Rust's keenest supporters and privately credited him alone with everything that was worthwhile about the paper.[16] Significantly, however, it was Shields who towards the end of 1932 replaced Rust as the paper's editor. That was a sign no doubt of the way the wind was beginning to blow.

Nevertheless, one should not necessarily read too much into the various changes of editor that followed. The post was one of a number constantly reshuffled among party leaders and, as one journalist recalled, 'although they considered the editorship most important, they were apt to make it secondary to some other changes'.[17] Of its pre-war editors, only Dutt had significant journalistic experience, and his was hardly the temperament of a daily newspaper editor. If that speaks for a certain continuing depreciation of journalistic skills and experience, the overall trend was in the opposite direction. Through successive editorships, including Dutt's in 1936–8, the paper now seemed to follow a consistent line of development. With every passing year it became brighter, more popular and more professional. General news and features now began to have their place, without of course displacing the paper's political message. 'Star' contributors had regular slots and Haldane's piece on science became a byword for quality popular journalism. Claud Cockburn of the *Week* provided the scoops and inside stories that the *Worker* had previously lacked. Weary eyes rested on diverting photographs, of Magnitogorsk or Gracie Fields. Readers were given not just a fighting political lead, but tips on what film to see, what horse to back and what jumper to knit their husbands.

Not everybody necessarily felt comfortable with the adjustments. Cockburn had previously worked on *The Times*, itself resistant for rather different reasons to the Northcliffe revolution. In the *Worker*'s grudging capitulation to lowly common denominators he detected exactly the sense of reluctant necessity he had previously encountered in Printing House Square.

> Campaigns were initiated for more hustle, modernity and snappy popular journalism all round. People sat gazing sadly at the *Daily Express*, with a view to imitating it. Over the problem of how to get snappier there raged discussions comparable to those at *The Times* office when some ruthless modernist ... [suggested] sticking in a crossword puzzle.[18]

Perhaps the cruellest development for the pure at heart was the reintroduction of racing tips. These had been featured in the *Worker*'s first few issues, but were swiftly expunged by higher bodies to an 'avalanche' of readers' protests.[19] Pollitt, showing that the spirit of compromise existed even in the Communist Party of 1930, vainly proposed printing results but no tips. It was in fact to be several years before the snares of gambling were openly condoned. Cockburn has described the editor's lugubrious mien as 'painfully, as though ... we had decided to go in for some kind of pornography', he explained the decision to cover greyhound racing.[20] Socialists of a more God-fearing variety had felt similarly woebegone when years earlier the *Herald* had gone the same way. Luckily, however, the party's tipsters had a happier knack with their forecasts than its theoreticians, and their many winners were worth more than a few readers to the paper.

As the paper sought a broader appeal, its earlier atmosphere of merciless vigilance and revolutionary quarantine was inevitably relaxed. Back in 1930, so able a comrade as Arthur Horner had, for his independent-mindedness, been ruled out as industrial editor and sent to Moscow instead.[21] Now a far more open spirit prevailed in which mere sympathisers and even unknown quantities were welcomed for their contributions. James Friell, the *Worker*'s popular cartoonist 'Gabriel', recalls that when he joined the paper in 1936 he was neither a party member nor even associated with it. 'Oh well, I suppose it doesn't matter', commented the then editor, Idris Cox, and Friell was straight away taken on.[22] The biggest capture of all was Cockburn, the *Worker*'s diplomatic correspondent, whom Pollitt charmed into joining the paper in 1934. Four years later Pollitt went so far as to offer the editorship itself to Willie Forrest, by this time covering the Spanish war for the *News Chronicle*. '[H]e never used words like "dialectical", "concrete", or "mechanistic"', Arthur Koestler recalled of this 'odd fish' of a British Communist, 'whereas he used words like "decency", "fairness", "that wouldn't be right" and the like'. Possibly that, as much as Forrest's journalistic talents, was what attracted Pollitt to him. Nevertheless Forrest declined to take up the offer, a matter presumably of some relief when only twelve months later he broke with the party over its wartime policy reversals.[23] Meanwhile the *Worker* continued to cultivate its Fleet Street contacts and made regular use of volunteers from other papers. Friendliest of these was Forrest's *News Chronicle*, whose editor and proprietors looked benignly on the several Communists or near-Communists on its staff. From such contacts the *Worker* looked for the inside leads that, in the absence of news agency subscriptions, were absolutely indispensable to it. It was in this way that Cockburn, who was well acquainted with Fleet Street pubs, filled so many of his column inches.

Inevitably this made for a rather free-and-easy atmosphere and even a certain amount of heterodoxy. Friell recalled a satirical house magazine that aimed some lively shafts at party bigwigs, particularly on the London district committee. It was called *Black Marx* and allowed no second issue. Friell himself had on his bookshelves Trotsky's *History of the Russian Revolution* and remembered well the shocked response of one colleague to his guileless 'Good book, eh?'[24] Apparently this sense of irreverence was to remain characteristic of the *Worker* office, and in the post-war period those drawn to cynicism and '"clever" derogatory remarks' about party, paper or workers were formally rebuked by the then editor, J.R. Campbell.[25]

In the late 1930s any such laxity accorded ill with Stalinist paranoia and heresy hunting, and the paper's political errors and 'criminal lack of vigilance' prompted demands from within the Comintern apparatus for a thorough purge. An internal report intended for Comintern secretary Dimitrov was particularly wide ranging and preposterous. Very often, its author complained, the *Daily Worker* made itself 'the bearer of enemy propaganda', instilling a daily dose of 'ideological poison' into its readers' minds. 'Can a system be recognised in these "mistakes"?' she went on.

> In my opinion, yes! The 'system' consists, I believe, in thwarting the correct line of the Party by so-called 'journalistic methods' in order to limit the penetration of Communist influence on the masses and inflitrate alien ideology into the Party and the movement.

What clearer example of sabotage, for example, than the demoralising front-page photograph it carried showing empty seats on a party congress platform?[26] Only one person seems to have paid for these idiocies, and that was Ralph Wright, the paper's literary editor. Publicly Moscow condemned his books page for welcoming texts by supposed Trotskyites (Karl Korsch) and Trotskyist sympathisers (Joseph Freeman). Wright also assisted with the 'Worker's Notebook' feature, criticised in *Inprecorr* for featuring 'literary cafe-crawlers' jokes' instead of 'proletarian, fighting humour'. Guilty only of political naivety and hardly even aware of having stuck his neck out, Wright was removed from the paper at the Russians' behest in 1939.[27]

Its new popular ambitions notwithstanding, the *Daily Worker* before the war could hardly yet be mistaken for the *Express* or *Herald*, nor even for their Communist equivalent. Subsequent editors remembered it fondly as a 'propaganda sheet', meaning that it still lacked a full range of news services and offered instead something nearer a commentary on other papers. At the same time, even as it removed the hammer and sickle from its masthead, it proclaimed its Communist identity with every Pollitt write-up and central committee manifesto. The particular emphasis on industrial and Labour movement news remained. Death and struggle retained their prominence, for with fascism threatening no Communist, least of all Pollitt, wanted a sunshine press. There were tensions there in every issue, as beauty tips jostled with faces of struggle, and epic cup ties earned headlines like the war in Spain. The paper was quite as fractured and contradictory as its readership.

Moreover, it had by no means become, in Dutt's earlier admonitory phrase, a mere 'professional production of a handful of technical workers ... for the benefit of the working class'.[28] On the contrary, only an enormous collective endeavour was sufficient to counteract the wholesalers' boycott and the paper's lack of resources. Organisationally, the *Worker* welded the party together in the performance of a common daily task: the collecting of news by worker-correspondents and party organisations; the waiting for the early train to pick up the latest edition, and then cycling off with it to newsagents and party contacts; the sales pitches at factory gates and street corners and the weekend canvasses of local estates. Most of all, perhaps, sellers were answerable for the paper's contents to their neighbours and workmates (and there must have been times, particularly in the autumn of 1939, when journalists and sellers alike must have wished the paper had remained a weekly). *Daily Worker* leagues were taking off towards the end of the 1930s, but the main responsibility remained with the party branches.

If the paper had achieved a measure of success by the war, that was therefore a reflection on the increasing vitality of the Communist Party itself. Daily sales were by this time around 50,000, with more on Saturdays making for a weekly sale in April 1939 of 377,000.[29] The real watershed in the paper's history, however, was the war itself. In that period the paper was suppressed by the government (from January 1941 to August 1942), bombed out by the Nazis (in April 1941) and robbed of key personnel by the call-up. It was certainly an achievement to end the war, as it did, healthier than ever and with serious ambitions of taking on the press barons.

For the wartime advance of the left, Communists included, there were obviously complex political reasons that are beyond the scope of this chapter. But for the share that the *Worker* had in this advance there are also more specific explanations. One was a new continuity of editorship. The upheaval within the party leadership at the outbreak of war saw the return to the *Worker* of its first editor, William Rust, who was as ambitious for the paper as he was for himself. Until his death in 1949 Rust threw himself into the task of extending the paper's influence, with only limited other responsibilities to distract him. Evidently he was an abler editor than his predecessors and, more importantly, he made full use of colleagues who were abler still. Chief among these was Allen Hutt, the party's most gifted and experienced journalist, whom Rust recruited to the paper immediately on its relaunch in September 1942. Political considerations ruled out Hutt himself as either editor or assistant editor and to his 'bitter disappointment and humiliation' he was passed over again on Rust's death and toyed with the idea of resigning.[30] No departure would have damaged the paper more. It was Hutt who, as chief sub-editor, saw the paper through the press and trained to a professional standard even the rawest of its recruits. It was his grasp of layout and typography that provided the paper with its award-winning design. It was Hutt moreover who introduced at the *Worker* the work disciplines, attention to schedules and clear separation of functions of a commercial newspaper office. That, according to Phil Bolsover, meant the end of a certain happy-go-lucky atmosphere of irregular hours, constant banter and everybody mucking in.[31] For whatever the paper's new professionalism achieved, Hutt deserves a large measure of the credit.

Before them Rust and Hutt seemed to glimpse a new era of opportunity for the paper. The Communist Party, its chief mainstay, had trebled in size. The campaign against the ban had brought the paper a huge fund of goodwill, both within the Labour movement and on Fleet Street. The wholesalers' ban was lifted and advertisers virtually queued up to cover the *Worker*'s precious newsprint. The fighting fund, having accumulated for 18 months with no paper to support, was now bringing in larger sums than ever. Press agencies and late editions were now within the *Worker*'s reach, as it began to compete on equal terms with its rivals. Only paper rationing, it was plausibly asserted, stood between the new paper and a genuinely mass circulation. Even as it was it reached 104,000.

It was in these circumstances that plans were drawn up for a more ambitious *Daily Worker*, owned by a cooperative, the PPPS, and 'equal in size, circulation and technique' to its capitalist rivals. 'Most forward looking people', ran the prospectus for the new society,

> have long been conscious that an urgent need of this country is a national daily newspaper which will be truly democratic in its ownership and editorial policy and also provide all the techniques and service that is associated with the mass circulation newspaper of today.

The prospectus failed even to mention the CP, for the paper aspired to voice no mere party interest but the very spirit of the new people's Britain in the making. To handle the expected circulation of 250,000, rising swiftly to half a million, a new rotary press was ordered and a building to accommodate it erected just a stone's throw from Fleet Street in Farringdon Road. The architect was Ernö Goldfinger and his clean modern lines expressed perfectly the period's confident rationality ('very different', noted Nikolaus Pevsner, 'from the style a Communist newspaper would care to display in Russia'[32]).

The paper's ideals were as close to Fleet Street as its new premises. Always the exhortation was to be brisk, modern, popular. 'The pace today leaves little time for contemplation', it was noted, 'and therefore the political content of the paper must be bright and palatable, serious but readily understood.'[33] Dutt's quota systems seemed as far away as the dingy Victorian warehouse in which the *Worker* had begun its existence. It was not so much a Bolshevik as a professional ethos that was now inculcated in the staff. As good journalists, they were urged, they

> should seek to acquire greater skill at the job they are doing, should feel a keen sense of responsibility regarding the quality of the work they turn out, should think and work as newspaper men and women, move in newspaper circles and accustom themselves to a quick popular response to all events.[34]

Although the paper did not actually join the Newspaper Proprietors' Association (NPA), it was indicative of its aspirations that it now claimed to adhere to NPA practices and recognised wage norms. Before the war its journalists had been paid only a fraction of the going rate, as and when resources permitted, and several spurned more lucrative positions to serve the cause. Even now, in fact, while technically paid the National Union of Journalists minimum, they were also required to sign covenants giving around half of it back to the *Worker*'s fighting fund.[35] That came about through union insistence that the paper be treated like the Fleet Street journal it claimed to be. Coveting the appurtenances of respectability, the *Worker* nevertheless remained reliant throughout on the loyalty and willingness to sacrifice that only the pauper press commanded.

In the end all its grandiose hopes were to be disappointed. Unavoidable delays meant that the first issue of the new paper appeared over two years later than originally intended, on 1 November 1948. In the intervening period the political situation had altered dramatically and with the onset of the Cold War the *Worker* was forced to retrench. Incautiously calculated advertising revenues never came anywhere near materialising and with rising production costs the paper had to make do with four pages, not the intended eight. Already it was locked into a vicious circle from which it would never escape. Inadequate revenues made for a poorer paper at an increased price, thereby choking its circulation. Sales immediately peaked at 120,000, then declined steadily to 63,000 by April 1956. It all turned out to be a colossal gamble that had not come off.

The basic explanation seems simple: that the paper's fortunes were so wrapped up with the CP's that it could not but share in the latter's post-war reacquaintance with adversity. That however is to understate the *Worker*'s failure. In the period from 1948 its circulation declined not only in absolute terms but even relative to the party's falling membership. As a cooperatively owned mass daily, distributed through the normal channels, fewer copies were sold proportionate to the party's size than during the whole period of sectarianism and wholesalers' boycotts.[36] The extent of the *Worker*'s decline therefore poses us again with more specific questions.

One obvious liability was that the broadening of the paper's basis in the mid-1940s had from the start been something of a fraud. The very last thing the PPPS was intended to do was dilute the CP's control of the paper or provide a democratic input into its editorial policy. Its sectional meetings were reportedly desultory affairs, ill attended and dominated by party caucuses. The paper's editorial board comprised only tame dignitaries of purely decorative function. 'It could have ceased to exist at any moment and not one ounce of difference would have been made to the running of the paper', claimed the *Worker*'s former news editor.[37] The paper's contents told the same story: viewpoints opposed to the CP's were never adequately presented, and to argue the case for Tito or Attlee, say, was virtually unthinkable. Eulogies of Stalin were perfectly acceptable, on the other hand, as were deadpan reports of monstrous show trials. In that sense the *Worker* remained a narrow party organ, attracting only readers prepared to swallow a very distinct political line. Its circulation, and its vaunted role as voice of the people, were thus inevitably circumscribed.

Paradoxically, the paper simultaneously suffered from the loosening of its ties with the Communist Party. Where once party work had revolved around the paper, sometimes as the branches' sole activity, now the wholesalers seemed to be doing the work for them. Soon it became more difficult to secure volunteers for street and factory sales and by 1955 the paper owed less than a tenth of its circulation to such methods. That was part of a general post-war decline in street politics, but much more sudden in its effects. The making of new readers in particular was not the function of newsagents. Furthermore, with the formation of the PPPS, King Street's direct interest in the *Worker* diminished, the palpable antagonism between Pollitt and Rust no doubt playing its part. In 1954 Phil Piratin was appointed the *Worker*'s circulation manager with a view to overcoming the continuing lack of liaison. 'My main failure', he reported two years later, 'has been to get the Party leadership to recognise its responsibility for continuous and sustained attention to the Daily Worker sales.' Having leapt at the chance of a conventional distribution, the paper let slip some of the loyalty and enthusiasm from which it had earlier profited. Only the fighting fund survived to foster that sense of commitment, which was why, according to Douglas Hyde, its appeals grew no less desperate even during the paper's wartime prosperity.[38]

An enduring dilemma was posed by questions of identity, function and readership. From readers and editorial professionals the complaint persisted that the paper was insufficiently popular. At sectional PPPS meetings, while political discussions seldom departed from prescribed rituals, sport, gambling and 'glamour' items aroused a lively response. Liverpool wanted more rugby league and less 'Southern bias', Manchester wanted golf left to the bourgeois press, and south Yorkshire, which received the Scottish edition, wanted less of Partick Thistle and more of decent local sides. ('Where's Sheffield? Fair's fair'). The West Midlands was concerned only with form and starting prices. 'Could there be more racing news on Saturday?' they asked in 1943. '90 per cent ... criticise the paper for lack of betting news', they followed up in 1944. 'Lamentations at Cayton's continued run of bad luck, a powerful influence in factory sales', they were at it still in 1954. The Glasgow readership was slightly more puritanical. 'For Saturday issues, proposed we feature film criticisms, news items from USSR, China and People's Democracies, and light features generally', the editor reported back the same year.[39]

Such views may or may not have been representative, the cross-section that attended such meetings being rather limited. They were augmented, however, by *Worker* journalists with their ears to Fleet Street who also called for a lightening of tone. Of course, the paper should 'at all times be controlled by the CP in all its aspects', one of them acknowledged.

> But surely a more dialectical approach is needed ... [to] the general public, who are not CP members and who desire their paper to be topical, pictorial or sporting ... the most powerful method of propaganda is the Press and yet you find the Daily Mirror and Daily Express powerful in their propaganda value ... but containing in their journalism a very small proportionate amount of political text compared with the Daily Worker.

A survey of party organisations produced similar findings. Noting the success of the popular press, most of the comrades favoured a lighter paper that, while retaining a 'sound core of Communist politics', would rather reduce its weight and prominence.[40]

That position was not uncontested, however. A minority of those surveyed favoured 'a more pronouncedly party paper' with 'more fundamental theoretical articles'. That was reinforced by a continuing strain of moral revulsion at the degradations of commercialism. 'Journalists ceased to regard people as responsible, thinking human beings, but as suckers, to be coddled or shocked by the latest stunt or "scoop"', ran a fervent denunciation of the modern press revolution. 'Suggestions and insinuations, headlines and short news "flashes" replaced argument and factual presentation of events … it is impossible to combine sensational commercial methods with really free and independent working class politics.' That wasn't Dutt, as it happened, but E.P. Thompson, writing for the PPPS in 1952.[41] It was an enduring strain in British radicalism that became entangled in this period with a note of wholesome anti-Americanism. Films, the diversion of millions, were as bad as comics. '[T]he levelling of all human feelings to a brutish level, the obscene decadence of them all', one reader reproached the paper's rather anodyne film critic, 'all this cannot be dismissed with a few words in passing; they are the manifestations of the deep tumours of a dying system, and as these they must be shown …' The same writer demanded a purge in the fashion department. 'Must the Daily Worker too follow the skirts of bourgeois French designers, sycophant American imitators and wealthy Bond Street parasites? … Pictures of "Miss Legs of California" and Royal Marine motor-cyclists belong strictly to the domain of the Daily Mirror.'[42]

Probably nobody now would disagree with that, and it is difficult to see what such concessions were ever going to achieve except to compromise the alternative values for which the paper claimed to stand. The party provided too narrow a basis for any serious competitor to Fleet Street and the *Worker* was never likely to have made a mass circulation daily. What it spoke to instead was a distinctive minority culture of trade union and political activism, loyal to the paper and finding within it news of its own unavailable elsewhere. In its clearer moments, the *Worker* acknowledged this. 'Because of our basic, inescapable political content, the paper is most likely to appeal to people who take a more or less continuous interest in politics from a Communist, Labour, Trade Unionist and Co-operative point of view.'[43]

In this culture the male wage worker had unquestioned pre-eminence, and it seems that this may have been one obstacle to the paper's wider acceptance. A characteristic iconography was of the factory worker, invariably male, striding towards the future in his overalls, wielding a spanner or punching through obstructions with his clenched fist. Not surprisingly, readers' surveys in inner London in the 1950s revealed that, its variety of features notwithstanding, the *Worker* was seen as the paper that father took.

It is referred to as 'Dad's paper' or 'Bill's Trade Union Paper' … almost without an exception an additional paper comes into the home to cater for the 'family' ... 60% of those visited ask for a 'brighter' paper – a 'family' newspaper. They ask for more pictures, personal items, 'comic' strips, sports features, features for women and youth, etc.[44]

It is significant perhaps that these insights resulted from a canvass of readers' homes: at the 'activist' meetings of the PPPS, by and large, the paper's need for brightness was discussed more in terms of racing tips and 'legs'. Mass-Observation in the 1940s had noted in exactly the same terms the distinct appeal to men not only of the *Worker* but of its Labour rival the *Daily Herald*. 'It's dad takes it' or 'My husband likes the Labour news' were typical responses of women *Herald* readers, and their menfolk agreed: 'It's the working man's paper after all.' Only *The Times* had a greater proportion of male readers, and if the women interviewed by Mass-Observation had a common dislike it was of the populist panacea of sports columns.[45] It is also fascinating that the unattractiveness to women of the Communist press had been noted even at the *Worker*'s outset. The warning came from the incomparably more experienced German Communist Party. 'It is ... necessary to watch that in our paper is sufficient social material (i.e. novels and stories from the life of women, etc)', Hugo Eberlein wrote to the British central committee, 'for we see everywhere that it is the woman in the family who puts up resistance to the regular taking of a communist paper.'[46]

That, of course, raises a whole research agenda in itself. It also prompts one last reflection on the *Worker*'s circulation peak in the late 1940s. That was a period of continuing unavailability of many goods on which to spend wages and accumulated wartime savings. It seems likely that, as in many cases a 'second' household newspaper, the *Worker* benefited from this frustrated spending power until, with goods back in the shops, readers gradually returned to buying just the one paper. 'Dad' had then to put up with the *Herald* or the *Mirror*. The obvious analogy is with working-class gambling, which reached its peak in the very same period and for precisely the same reasons.[47] It is not of course an analogy that would have appealed to the *Worker*'s founders.

Acknowledgement

I would particularly like to thank the former *Daily Worker* journalists who assisted me with interviews, information and comments on my original conference paper: Phil Bolsover, Willie Forrest, James Friell,

Douglas Hyde, Florence Keyworth, Bob Leeson, Alison Macleod, George Matthews, Sam Russell and Phil Stein.

Notes

1. The *Herald* was relaunched as a daily in 1919 and in 1929 sold to Odham's, which virtually threw gifts at readers to build up its circulation. But between 1920 and 1947, Williams's period of 'full expansion, to something like a full reading public', there were no other new dailies. See R. Williams, *The Long Revolution* (Penguin edn, 1965), pp. 195 ff.
2. It does not therefore purport to be a comprehensive account of the paper. In particular, the crisis on the *Worker* in 1956–7, when nearly half of the editorial staff left, requires a separate discussion in itself.
3. R. Williams, *The Long Revolution*, p. 210.
4. *Party Life*, 9 (new series) (CP Organising Department, 1929).
5. R. Palme Dutt, 'Towards the workers' daily', *Communist Review*, December 1929, pp. 628–43.
6. R. Palme Dutt to CP Political Bureau, 26 November 1929 (Dutt papers, British Library).
7. Dutt papers, British Library; *DW*, 1 March 1948.
8. CP Political Bureau, 2 and 15 January and 22 November 1930. Harry Pollitt to Political Bureau, 19 June 1930; William Rust, report to CI Anglo-American secretariat, 30 July 1930.
9. Pollitt to Political Bureau, 19 June 1930; Political Bureau stenographic report, 19 June 1930 (WCML).
10. CP Political Bureau resolution, *Communist Review*, October 1930, pp. 427–31.
11. Dutt to Pollitt, 6 July 1931.
12. Dutt to *DW* editorial board, 29 October 1930 (Dutt papers, British Library).
13. 'A popular workers' newspaper', *Communist Review*, May 1932, pp. 245–50; R. Palme Dutt, 'Bourgeois journalism and our press', *Communist Review*, July 1932, pp. 325–31; Willie Forrest interview, August 1994.
14. See K. Morgan, *Harry Pollitt* (Manchester University Press, 1993), pp. 78–80.
15. J. Shields, 'The "Daily Worker": a critical review', *Communist Review*, October–November 1932, pp. 5–11.
16. Dutt to Rust, 2 September 1931 (Dutt papers, British Library).

17. James Friell interview, August 1988.
18. C. Cockburn, *I, Claud* (Penguin edn, 1967), ch. 14.
19. CP Political Bureau, 16 and 23 January 1930 (CPA).
20. C. Cockburn, *I, Claud*, pp. 156–7.
21. CP Political Bureau, 15 and 16 January 1930. The proposal was Pollitt's.
22. Friell interview, August 1988.
23. William Forrest interview, August 1994; A. Koestler, *The Invisible Writing* (Collins/Hamish Hamilton, 1954), p. 335.
24. Friell interview, August 1988.
25. J.R. Campbell, speech to annual CP meeting of *Worker* staff, c. 1952 (Hutt papers, CPA).
26. Report on *DW* by 'Rosa Michel', 28 November 1938 and Comintern Cadres Commission report on CPGB, 14 January 1939, both in Comintern archives, Moscow (refs 495/74/39, 495/14/265; microfilms available in CPA). Translations from the German and Russian by kind permission of Monty Johnstone and Francis King.
27. James Friell, written statement to author, 12 March 1994; Philip Bolsover interview, May 1994; P. Dengel, 'Book reviewing is a serious matter', *Communist International*, August 1939, pp. 947–8; G. Friedrich, 'Cuckoo's eggs in the Communist press', *Inprecorr*, 11 June 1938, pp. 703–5.
28. *Communist Review*, December 1929, p. 632.
29. N. Branson, *History of the Communist Party of Great Britain 1927–1941* (Lawrence & Wishart, 1985), p. 57.
30. TS memorandum, 'Daily Worker editorial leadership: ideas about a managing editor', nd, c. 1944?; TS statement by Hutt (not submitted), 14 February 1949 (Hutt papers, CPA).
31. Philip Bolsover interview, May 1994.
32. N. Pevsner, *The Buildings of England: London except the cities of London and Westminster* (Penguin, 1952), p. 224.
33. *DW* souvenir festival programme, 1946.
34. William Rust, memoranda on 'The improvement of editorial work', June 1943, and 'Editorial work', December 1945 (Hutt papers).
35. See documentation in the Hutt papers.
36. See 'Review of Daily Worker circulation', 22 June 1956 (Hutt papers).
37. D. Hyde, *I Believed* (Heinemann, 1951), pp. 190–1.

38. Phil Piratin, TS report on his period as circulation manager, May 1956; 'Review of Daily Worker circulation', 22 June 1956 (Hutt papers). For the falling off of street sales see the reports of the Manchester and Neath sectional meetings of the PPPS, April 1954 (Hutt papers). D. Hyde, *I Believed*.

39. PPPS sectional meeting reports, April 1954; B. Niven, reports on visits to West Midlands, October 1943, July 1944 (Hutt papers).

40. E.A. Sullivan, TS memorandum to colleagues, c. 1957; 'The Daily Worker: its policy and content', TS memorandum, July 1956 (Hutt papers).

41. E.P. Thompson, *The Struggle for a Free Press* (PPPS, 1952), p. 17.

42. TS criticisms of D. Bourne of Nottingham, 12 September 1948 (Hutt papers) circulated to arts and features contributors.

43. 'The Daily Worker: its policy and content'.

44. Hutt papers.

45. Mass-Observation Archive, University of Sussex: file reports on women in wartime, July 1940; the banning of the *DW*, January 1941; and the *Daily Herald* readership, September 1942 and June 1948.

46. Hugo Eberlein to CP Central Committee, 8 October 1929 (CPA).

47. R. McKibbin, 'Working-class gambling in Britain 1880–1939' in *Ideologies of Class* (Oxford University Press, 1991 edn), p. 113.

Further Reading

The chapter's first two decades are described by William Rust in *The Story of the Daily Worker* (PPPS, 1949). This, while more informative than some official histories, is naturally reticent or misleading on any issue of sensitivity. A number of *Worker* journalists have published their memoirs including Claud Cockburn, *I, Claud* (Penguin edn, 1967), Douglas Hyde, *I Believed* (Heinemann, 1951) and Malcolm MacEwen, *The Greening of a Red* (Pluto Press, 1991). Two useful articles by Florence Keyworth on 'Women and the *Daily Worker/Morning Star*' appeared in *Link* (CP women's magazine) nos 29–30 (1980). Relevant materials in the Communist Party archives include papers of Ernie Pountney and Allen Hutt.

9 The Communist Party, Production and Britain's Post-war Settlement

James Hinton

Because Britain never had a mass Communist Party, historians of the Labour movement have been inclined to minimise the significance of the post-1917 division of world socialism for Britain's own Labour movement. Since the party was always a marginal player, its history could be left to the squabbling of hagiographers and sectarians, while serious Labour historians got on with the task of mapping the mainstream of Labour Party history, pausing only to regret (as in Pimlott's influential treatment of the 1930s) that the Communists, whose scheming served merely to muddy the waters for genuine radicalism, had ever been invented.[1] But Communists did more than muddy the waters. Out of all proportion to its formal membership, the Communist Party organised or influenced extra-parliamentary currents which did much to determine the force and direction of the overall Labourist tide in Britain. History with the Communists left out is likely to miss important aspects of the dynamics of the British Labour movement.

Nowhere is neglect of the Communists more debilitating than in writing about the peak of Labour's power in the 1940s. Both absolutely, and relative to the expansion of the Labour movement in general, Communist Party membership and influence was its height during this decade. Between June 1941 and the onset of the cold war in late 1947 the CP developed a reformist politics which, had Attlee's government responded favourably, might have contributed to the construction of a 'developmental state' in Britain – a practice of state intervention capable of tackling the deep-rooted inefficiencies in the industrial economy exposed by the 'audit of war'.[2] The Labour government, however, was not able to contemplate the kind of alliance with shopfloor militants which both the Communists and, more generally, the engineering unions were offering. The argument developed in this chapter stands in sharp contrast to the findings of a recent, sympathetic study of the Attlee government's attempts to stimulate industrial productivity, which presents a picture of trade union attitudes polarised

160

between a supportive TUC hierarchy and an indifferent rank and file.[3] This is simply to write out of history those thousands of trade union activists, many of them Communists, whose commitment to productionism between 1941 and 1947 must be an important factor in any reckoning of the potential for radical change during these years.

Unlike its post-war counterparts in a number of western European countries, the Attlee government did little to entrench worker participation in private industry. Much of what Communists and other reformers were demanding by way of planning and participation – tripartite planning committees at national and regional levels, statutory workers' councils – was not unlike measures that contributed positively to the institutionalisation of a productionist alliance in several of Britain's capitalist rivals.[4] In German industry, the statutory enforcement of codetermination helped to construct a collaborative 'productivity coalition' at the level of the enterprise which was widely seen as contributing to post-war economic success.[5] In France, as Herrick Chapman has argued, militants in aircraft factories, inspired by Communist productionism, were able to forge a positive alliance with technocratic state officials which contributed much to the capacity of the French aircraft industry to perform competitively despite fierce ongoing conflicts on the shop floor.[6] The contrasting experience of Britain's capitalist neighbours suggests that, had the proponents of planning and participation met with a more favourable response from the state, then a significant transformation of shopfloor attitudes to production might have occurred, even within a capitalist economic order. Certainly such participation would have enriched the quality of democratic life in Britain.

It may seem strange to suggest that the Communist Party was a potential agency of capitalist modernisation in Britain. But between 1941 and 1947 this was precisely the role that it sought: making capitalism work, first to win the war and then to consolidate the peace.

In line with their enthusiastic support for the war effort from June 1941, Communists ruled out the demands for nationalisation and workers' control which had figured so prominently in the politics of the factories during the First World War – and which were being pressed by the Labour left in 1941–2. While they had no doubt that a socialist society would be able to wage war more efficiently – was indeed doing so in the Soviet Union – the struggle to achieve socialism was bound to be both long and bitter; to unleash it now would destroy national unity and risk a fascist victory.[7] Nevertheless, much could be done to increase efficiency within capitalism, and most of what urgently needed to be done, though it did not involve changes in ownership, did involve a very real transfer of control over private industry both to the state and to the organised workers. The party's central 'reformist' insight rested on the fact that effective planning implied a transfer of authority from individual firms to state agencies. Any such transfer was likely to create opportunities for organised workers to seek the assistance of the state in their own attempts to encroach on employer autocracy in the factories. By allying themselves with state officials and enlightened management, militants could seek to break the stranglehold of employer autocracy and unleash worker creativity in industry.[8] Worker empowerment in no way contradicted the need for increased production. Indeed, a whole layer of production-minded militants in the engineering factories believed that it was only by allying itself directly with organised labour in the factories that the state would be able to acquire effective authority to persuade either employers or workers to put the needs of war production before private and sectional interests.[9]

This strategy held obvious pitfalls for a party whose industrial presence had been built around an aggressive economistic militancy.[10] One of the major weaknesses of Communist politics was the inability of the party leadership to explore these problems with its militants. So long as the main priority was the defeat of Hitler all talk about the implications of the wartime experience for any post-war strategy of transition to socialism was considered counterproductive.[11] Nevertheless, despite Communist anxiety that some of their militants were more interested in using the production issue to knock management than to inspire workers to greater efforts,[12] it seems probable that most Communist shop stewards buckled down to winning the war with a vague and unworked-out assumption that the increased status they won in the war factories would stand them in good stead when class struggle resumed after the war. The possibility that workers' organisation might be weakened by the processes of cooption unleashed by the productionist policy – possibilities which worried some more thoughtful stewards – were not seriously confronted.[13]

In 1944, emboldened by the writings of Earl Browder in the United States, the party leadership explicitly rejected the notion that the war period was 'a sort of interim after which we get down to the "real" class conflict with "our own" capitalists'.[14] Instead the party embraced the view that an objective basis existed for an alliance between 'progressive capital' and the Labour movement to carry through a 'state capitalist' reconstruction programme. While the construction of socialism was not yet on the immediate agenda, such a reconstruction would entrench organised labour in a way that would pave the way for a relatively painless assumption of power by the working class when conditions were ripe. Under 'state capitalism' the productionist initiatives of the workers would replace market forces as the main driving force of economic progress. To this end, the CP called on the Labour government to take workers into partnership, as the state's main agents in achieving the production targets set by the planners.[15] Party educationalists tried to wean members from the catastrophic view that only economic disaster could open the way to socialism, holding out the prospect that implementation of their planning demands would 'take key economic positions out of the hands of capitalists ... and put power in the hands of workers. Our aim should be – through confidence to power, rather than to power through disillusion.'[16] Or, as Harry Pollitt had put it in November 1945, pleading with the old-style class warriors skulking in the ranks: 'Are we never going to learn? I have been in too many campaigns which had as their main motive *against*, and not sufficient with the main motive *for* ...'[17]

How convinced the militants were by this commitment to gradualism it is difficult to say. No doubt many expected a frankly revolutionary policy to re-emerge in the fullness of time. But for the time being the class struggle had become a war of position within the emerging structures of 'state capitalism', designed to open up practices of democratic participation though which working people could gain the awareness, confidence and ambition to make the transition to socialism, by whatever means, when the time came.

During the war years Communist productionism helped to open the way for real changes in industrial relations. Hitler's assault on the Soviet Union encouraged engineering shop stewards to mount their own sustained and imaginative attack on 'managerial functions'. Ministry of Labour officials had long been worried by the capacity of shop stewards to draw them in as allies in domestic battles over trade union recognition, bargaining rights, facilities for meeting in the works, use of the canteen for meetings and similar issues.[18] Expanding the agenda of this burgeoning workshop organisation from wages and conditions of work to production issues was a natural progression for the shop stewards, and one that was, indeed, already under way before the change in the politics of the war encouraged Communists to place this issue at the forefront of workshop politics.

In October 1941 – in what was probably the largest mobilisation of shop stewards undertaken by the Communist Party at any time in its history – over 1,000 delegates assembled from factories in all parts of

Britain at the Stoll Theatre in London. Speaker after speaker denounced managerial incompetence and production hold-ups, demanded the establishment of production committees in the factories and (not least) pledged every ounce of worker effort to war production.[19] As the delegates reported back there was a major escalation of demands for the setting up of Joint Production Committees (JPCs). Where managements resisted, the Communists encouraged militants to produce detailed written accounts of production difficulties in the factory, and to use these to lobby support from union officials, workers in neighbouring factories, the press, Whitehall and Westminster. This activity helped to feed a major crisis of confidence over the capacity of Britain's employers to meet the needs of war production. By the spring of 1942 managements in over half of Britain's biggest engineering factories, together with about a fifth of the remainder, had succumbed to this pressure by establishing JPCs.[20] The Engineering Employers' Federation (EEF), traditionally the most adamant defender of 'managerial functions', did its best to stand against the tide. In the end it was forced to capitulate by Ernest Bevin's threat to legislate.[21] Ironically, the most substantial victory won by the new Communist strategy – the agreement of March 1942 which resulted in the establishment of JPCs in most of Britain's engineering factories – was achieved by an unlikely (and unspoken) alliance with the party's most powerful enemy.

In the aftermath of these events the employers were filled with foreboding: 'Nothing could be more harmful to production', wrote the Secretary of the EEF,

> than that managements should become imbued with an idea that their prerogatives are infringed, their status invaded, and their authority dissipated by a successful challenge from the workers, whether instigated by unofficial shop stewards or supported by a Governmental attitude

or, he might well have added, by both at once.[22] Employer fears for the integrity of 'managerial functions' were matched by triumphalism among the militants: witness the shop stewards at one London factory who explained to their members that the candidates for election to the JPC 'have behind them a powerful organisation with influence extending through every Government Department to the Cabinet itself, whereby they can force their decisions on the Management for better production'.[23]

As the last quotation suggests, for the reformers the establishment of the JPCs was only a first step towards a more radical participation of the unions in a chain of command linking worker power on the shopfloor into the administration of war production as a whole. The employers, however, were well aware of the dangers. Having been forced to concede JPCs, they were determined to limit the damage by restricting their authority to the affairs of the factory rather than allowing them to act as transmission belts for further state interference (and worker empowerment). As a Whitehall official explained after the war, allowing 'the system of JPCs [to] develop into a participation of trade unions in the organisation of production [above the level of the factory] ..., would have a reflex action on JPCs and would increase their specific gravity in factory affairs'.[24] To prevent this the EEF spent much of the war fighting to frustrate a variety of trade union attempts to open up links amongst JPCs in different factories and between the JPCs and the tripartite production machinery at regional and national levels. Denied the backing that the state had given to the original establishment of JPCs, the unions lost these fights.[25]

In this context, early hopes that the JPCs would unleash an avalanche of worker creativity in production were largely disappointed. It is probable that the committees did do something to increase production, mainly by their role in improving industrial relations. But the shopfloor was still the shopfloor, workers were still alienated, and the productionist enthusiasm of the militants found itself confronted by mountains of everyday cynicism and apathy. In the summer of 1943 – to cite just one example – a shopfloor versifier at Armstrong–Vicker's Openshaw plant characterised the productionists as a small minority surrounded by a 'careless and idle' multitude of 'low and slinking jackals':

> Of courageous honest purpose, we've just a little band
> Who defiance roar to slip shod work and against it make
>   a stand.

Conscientiously rebutting such pessimism about the qualities of the average worker, and blaming shopfloor cynicism on the uncooperative attitude of the management, the editor of the shop steward paper, Frank Allaun, nevertheless admitted that:

> there are rats and jackals in every factory. We should remember that we are living in the last years of a decaying society ... If we are brought up as wage slaves how can we all be expected to think like free men?[26]

And six months later he wrote, defensively:

I can think of several really first class engineers – charge hands,
Production Committee members, tradesmen, who attempted to
improve the running of our factory with both ability and enthusiasm.
Most of them have given it up as a bad job. They say it's banging their
heads against a stone wall … All credit to those few who, even if they
are called fools for their pains, carry on the fight for better production,
come what may.[27]

Creating free men out of wage slaves was, it seemed, a thankless task.
The JPCs were certainly more successful in many other factories. But
there is no doubt that by 1944–5 the shine had worn off the JPC
experiment, and many of its shopfloor promoters must have felt a
similar sense of misunderstood isolation.

Because the employers had successfully resisted any links between the
JPCs and the planning apparatus, the JPC experience did not create a
self-sustaining practice of worker participation in British industry
capable of opening the way to popular empowerment in a planned
economy. It may be that, however closely JPCs had been integrated into
the machinery of production administration, the mass of ordinary
workers would have remained uninterested in participation. We do not
know. What is clear is that, during the winter of 1941–2, the reformists
were able, often in the teeth of employer resistance, to build at least the
beginnings of a structure for shopfloor participation in economic
planning. What was not yet clear, in 1945, was whether the election
of a majority Labour government would open up the possibility of a
more decisive shift towards industrial democracy than had been possible
within the political context created by the Churchill coalition.

During 1946–8, the engineering unions – while fully accepting that
Labour had no mandate to nationalise the engineering industry –
repeatedly pressed the government to impose a system of participatory
planning on the private sector.[28] So long as the Amalgamated Engineering Union's (AEU's) charismatic president, Jack Tanner, maintained
his wartime alliance with the powerful Communist presence in the
union, there was no significant difference between CP and AEU
policies on these matters, and the AEU seems to have made the running
in the Confederation of Shipbuilding and Engineering Unions as a whole.
Complaining that employers were putting short-term profitability
before needs of national reconstruction – producing cars, radios and
household electrical goods rather than the capital goods needed to re-
equip British industry – the unions demanded the elaboration of detailed
controls which would effectively transfer the initiative in deciding

'types and quantities of engineering products' from individual firms to the planning apparatus.[29]

   This kind of detailed planning was not acceptable to Ministers,[30] nor were they prepared to provoke the employer hostility that would have been involved in meeting union demands for a structure of participation at regional, sectoral and national levels into which the JPCs in particular factories could be linked. Spelling out his rejection of the union's demands, John Wilmot, the Minister of Supply, explained: 'The engineering industries were privately owned; this was a fact which as they knew, was unlikely to be changed within the lifetime of the present Government. Ownership carried with it executive functions.'[31] In these words the Labour government ruled out any possibility that power in private sector industry could effectively be shared. There was no room within Wilmot's bald formulation for the project of a democratising alliance against employer autocracy which, however tentatively, had been struck between productionist trade unionism and some parts of the state machine in 1941–2 – and which the unions had hoped to revive and extend under a Labour government.

   The fuel crisis of January–February 1947 momentarily recreated the spirit of 1941–2 in British industry, as shop stewards and management struggled side by side to keep the factories open. In the south-west, for example, fuel efficiency committees were set up in nearly 500 factories. This initiative had the enthusiastic support of the shop stewards' movement – indeed the Bristol Communist Party had been working with the local Ministry of Fuel and Power controller to promote such committees ever since the war.[32] At the same time the tripartite regional boards for industry, whose limited wartime executive role had been downgraded at the end of the war, acquired renewed authority as the only means to hand to share out scarce coal and electricity supplies among competing firms.[33] The engineering unions pressed their demands for planning, with full support from the Communist Party and the Labour left. By linking factory production committees to the regional boards, argued Harry Pollitt, 'the JPCs and shop stewards can become the Government's main organised force for carrying through the plan … We need to break down the bureaucratic idea that planning means doing everything from Whitehall …'[34] To this end the left renewed its calls for legislation to enforce JPCs on reluctant employers, citing Czech, French and Scandinavian legislation on workers' rights to joint consultation.[35] In Coventry the local Labour Party and Trades Council backed local AEU demands for legislation to make JPCs compulsory, adding that they should 'be empowered to inspect the records and stocks, and to have access to all other information relevant to the successful carrying out of production processes in the establishment'. They also demanded the right to refer disputed issues directly to the regional board, and warned that 'without the mentioned authority the JPCs are useless and would be ineffective' in the fight to increase production.[36] At the AEU National Committee in June 1946 a resolution demanding statutory intervention had been withdrawn, but a year later the left pushed the issue to a vote and won by a majority of 46 to four.[37] Within two months even the TUC leadership, provoked by the refusal of employers to give anything more than lip service to joint consultation, was ready to back compulsion.

In the event sustained government pressure – including a new threat of compulsion from Stafford Cripps – forced employers to go through the motions, and by late 1948 there were as many JPCs in operation in the engineering industry as there had been at the peak of the wartime mobilisation.[38] But on the critical issue of linking the JPCs to the rest of planning apparatus the government was unresponsive, despite a brief moment in the autumn of 1947 when a convergence between union and left-wing demands, the views of a minority of progressive employers (these people did exist, they were not just a fantasy of the Browderist imagination) and Stafford Cripps appeared to create the possibility of a move towards a more forceful and participatory style of economic planning.[39] Although they understood that taking the workers into full partnership was one key to increasing productivity, Attlee's ministers were never prepared to push the issue of democracy to the point where it might undermine the employer cooperation which, in their view, was even more vital to Britain's economic recovery. Government policy was shaped by the priority given to establishing a *modus vivendi* with the employers – an orientation not compatible with the union agenda of releasing workers' creative energies through a radical democratisation of authority relations in industry.

Surveys suggest that the re-establishment of the JPCs in the late 1940s created little excitement on the shop floor.[40] As G.D.H. Cole pointed out in 1947, joint consultation in private industry made sense as a strategy of worker empowerment only 'to the extent to which [both parties] are acting under the auspices of the State ... and the power vested in the Government can be used to secure employers' conformity with the public interest'.[41] This is what the unions had argued for, and what had been denied. It should not therefore be surprising that the Labour government's campaign for joint consultation was subject to all the normal resistance of shopfloor workers to offers of responsibility without power.

In 1950 Harold Wilson, reflecting on his three years at the Board of Trade, circulated to cabinet colleagues his own diagnosis of what had gone wrong. In a lengthy paper Wilson argued that the key weakness of the government in its dealings with private industry was its inability to control the behaviour of individual firms: 'the real decisions which control our economic policy are taken at the board-room level ... Government has little knowledge of them and little influence on them ... we are virtually powerless as a Government to influence decisions at this level.' To tackle this problem, Wilson proposed a series of radical ideas for taking power to direct the key firms, including a plan to put government-appointed directors on their boards to represent the public interest. In discussing the role that joint consultation might play in advancing government policy Wilson showed a grasp – unique among Labour ministers – of the arguments that had been put forward by the engineering unions. JPCs, he noted, had been advocated not only as a way of harnessing the productive energies of the shopfloor, but also 'as a means of enabling the workers' representatives to put pressure on the management to bring the industrial policy of the firm in question more closely into harmony with national policy, e.g., on the export drive'.[42] This brought Wilson close to the Communist vision of JPCs acting 'not merely as an advisory chorus but as essential levers of the administrative machinery through which alone central decisions as to priority and allocation can be efficiently transmitted, right down to the individual factory and workshop'.[43] To act effectively in such a way, JPCs would have required a statutory basis and guaranteed access to the relevant information about production targets and achievements.

Wilson's paper provides evidence that a differently constituted Labour government, with different priorities, might have been able to respond positively to the ideas put forward by engineering trade unionists, Communists and others for an alliance between state intervention and shopfloor organisation to bring the power of the boardroom under democratic control. What is also significant, however, is that, having recognised this possibility, Wilson did not recommend that it be pursued. Instead he remarked: 'one reason why the Government has so far refused to contemplate statutory measures to enforce' the estab-lishment of JPCs was 'the danger that they might be used by extremist elements for furthering other policies'.[44] There was, that is to say, a critical *political* difficulty. The fault line between social democracy and Communism ran, broadly speaking, between the Labour government and its potential allies on the shopfloor. Any alliance between the shopfloor and the state would have to be, at the same time, an alliance between the Labour and Communist Parties.

This had been clearly spelled out by Jack Tanner, proposing Communist affiliation at the Labour Party Conference in 1946:

> It is said that the Communist Party would be an embarrassment to the Government ... As I think most of you are aware, during the war the shop stewards in the engineering industry played a very important part in increasing production through the Joint Production Committees, and it is ... generally known that a very large proportion of the leading shop stewards in the engineering industry are Communists. We urgently need a similar enthusiasm and a similar movement to that which we had during the war ... The efforts to increase production by the Communists ... would be very much more effective if they were also part of the mainstream of our movement.[45]

The relationship between Communism and social democracy was, however, ultimately determined by international relations. In 1941–2 the Communists had been able to provide the key to unlock shopfloor productionism only because Hitler had invaded the Soviet Union. Any attempt by the Labour government to mobilise similar efforts as a way out of the crisis of 1947 would have demanded similar support from Communist shop stewards – a support which, at the time, they were eagerly offering. The assumption of those who, overwhelmingly, voted down Communist affiliation in 1946 was that the Communists could not be trusted not to somersault again as dramatically as they had done in 1939 or 1941.[46] This assumption was well founded. By the time Wilson was writing, in 1950, the Communists were no longer interested in forging any kind of alliance with the Labour lieutenants of American imperialism. One could speculate as to whether things would have been different if the Labour government had listened with more sympathy to the ideas of planning and participation expounded by the engineering unions. Those non-Communists who backed affiliation argued that it was precisely by admission to the mainstream of Labour politics that the Communist Party could be won from its slavish dependence on Moscow.[47] But it is difficult, in retrospect, not to see this as a hopelessly optimistic judgement.

However inevitable its defeat Communist productionism was a significant presence in 1940s Britain, and one which, in happier circumstances, had the potential to make a major contribution to a more radical post-war settlement. There are, of course, other reasons – notably the power of finance and the depth of voluntaristic codes in the British political culture – which help to explain the failure of the Attlee government to establish the kind of 'developmental state' which, experience suggests, may be essential to industrial success in the late twentieth-century capitalist world. But the fact that the marginalisation of these 1940s proponents of participatory planning was probably inevitable is not a good reason for consigning them to oblivion. It is precisely by listening to voices drowned out by the clamour of history's winners that we may be able to understand where our society went wrong and how it might yet reform itself.

Acknowledgement

Apart from CP publications, the major sources are Board of Trade, Ministry of Labour, Ministry of Supply and cabinet papers in the Public Records Office; and the papers of the TUC, AEU, EEF and some individual CP militants in the Modern Records Centre at the University of Warwick. I have also used factory papers and the Manchester District AEU Minutes in the Working Class Movement Library, Manchester. I am grateful to the archivists in all three institutions for their help and advice, and for permission from the EEF to use their records. Other archival sources are listed in the Notes.

Notes

1. B. Pimlott, *Labour and the Left in the 1930s* (Allen & Unwin, 1986), *passim*.
2. C. Barnett, *The Audit of War* (Macmillan, 1986), ch. 8. On the 'developmental state' see D. Marquand, *The Unprincipled Society: New Demands and Old Politics* (Fontana, 1988).
3. N. Tiratsoo and J. Tomlinson, *Industrial Efficiency and State Intervention: Labour 1939–51* (Routledge, 1993), pp. 164–5.
4. Although Soviet examples were most frequently cited by the advocates of workers' participation in Britain, they were not unaware of the relevance of French or German models. David Kart, *Communist Review*, July 1947; Communist Party, *The Way to Win*, May 1942.
5. W. Streeck, 'Co-determination: the fourth decade', in B. Wilpert and A. Sorge (eds), *International Perspectives on Organisational*

Democracy (Wiley, 1984), p. 415 and *passim*; Report of the Committee of Inquiry on Industrial Democracy (Bullock Report), January 1977, Cmnd. 6706, p. 57.

6. H. Chapman, *State Capitalism and Working-class Radicalism in the French Aircraft Industry* (University of California Press, 1991). For a systematic comparison between the French and British experiences see J. Hinton, review of Chapman, *Social History*, 17, 3, 1992, pp. 523–7.

7. R.P. Dutt, *Britain in the World Front* (Lawrence & Wishart, 1942), pp. 132–34.

8. 'How to set up JPCs' (nd, February 1942?), Len Powell Papers, Modern Records Centre, University of Warwick; L. Powell, 'For a Real Ministry of Production', *Labour Monthly*, April 1942; E. Burns, *Labour's Way Forward*, (CPGB, July 1942); M. Dobb, *Economics of Capitalism: An Introductory Outline*, (nd, 1942?), p. 5. Contrast M. Edeleman, *Production for Victory Not Profit!* (Gollancz, 1941), pp. 124–5 and 177.

9. The most persuasive evidence that this 'layer' was more than a product of the excited imagination of a few Communist leaders are returns made by 1,200 shop stewards to the AEU's production enquiry of 1942, summarised in AEU, *Enquiry into Production Committees: Third Report on Production*, December 1942, in Michaelson Papers, Modern Records Centre, University of Warwick.

10. N. Fishman, 'The British Communist Party and the Trade Unions, 1933–1945' (University of London PhD, 1991).

11. 'Draft for Central Committee', 7 December 1942, Dutt Papers, British Library, K4; Political letter, 12 February 1942, Dutt Papers, British Library, K3; interviews with D. Hyde and Y. Kapp.

12. 'Some points on the production situation' (nd, early 1942?), Len Powell Papers.

13. Articles by E. Jennison and E. Frow in AEU *Journal*, December 1941, January, June 1942; AEU Manchester District Committee, *Minutes*, 23 December 1941; R. Croucher, *Engineers at War: 1939–1945* (Merlin, 1982), p. 170; N. Fishman, 'The British Communist Party', p. 290.

14. Nan Brewer, *World News and Views*, 26 August 1944.

15. 'Discussion guide on looking ahead', *World News and Views*, 23 August 1947.

16. 'Labour government and socialism', CP training manual, in Labour Party Archive, GS/1/4; H. Pollitt, Weekly Letter 46, 28 November 1946, CPA.

17. *Communist Policy for Britain* (CPGB, 1945), p. 32.

18. S. Tolliday, 'Government, employers and shop floor organisation in the British motor industry, 1939-69' in S. Tolliday and J. Zeitlin (eds), *Shop Floor Bargaining and the State: Historical and Comparative Perspectives* (Cambridge University Press, 1985), pp. 111–14; R. Price, *Labour in British Society* (Croom Helm, 1986), pp. 191–2; Deputy Chief Industrial Commissioner for Scotland, *Reports*, 10 August and September 1940, PRO LAB 10/361; North West Regional Industrial Relations Officer, *Reports*, 5 and 12 July and 6 and 13 December 1941, LAB 10/379; London Chief Conciliation Officer, *Reports*, 4 October 1941, LAB 10/357.

19. Engineering and Allied Trades Shop Stewards' National Council, *Arms and the Men* (EATSSNC), 1941.

20. *Trade Union Report*, Mass Observation Industry Topic Collection (nd, 1946?), p. 107; W. Hannington, *The Rights of Engineers* (Gollancz, 1944), p. 93.

21. J. Hinton, *Shop Floor Citizens: Engineering Democracy in 1940s Britain* (Edward Elgar, 1994), ch. 4.

22. 'Production advisory committees' (nd, March 1942?), EEF 237/3/1/313, Modern Records Centre, University of Warwick.

23. Handicar to Low, 3 July 1942, EEF 237/1/1/312 (London).

24. Bower, Briefs for Minister, 8 and 28 February 1946, PRO SUPP 14/137.

25. J. Hinton, *Shop Floor Citizens*, ch. 5.

26. *Factory News* (Armstrong–Vickers, Openshaw), August 1943, in Working Class Movement Library, Manchester.

27. *Ibid.*, January 1944.

28. J. Hinton, *Shop Floor Citizens*, ch. 8.

29. Meeting between Ministry of Supply (MOS) and National Engineering Joint Trades Movement (NEJTM), 13 February 1946, TUC 292/615.2/5, Modern Records Centre, University of Warwick; NEJTM, Memorandum on Post-war Reconstruction in the Engineering Industry, 1945, p. 9.

30. For example Bower, Brief for Minister, 8 and 28 February 1946; Downey, Notes on planning, 18 November 1946, PRO SUPP 14/137. Privately, however, Downey acknowledged that *ad hoc* tactical intervention designed to sort out particular bottlenecks would continue to be necessary during the transition period, and

might well prove permanent, given the rigidities likely to be created by full employment.

31. Meeting between MOS and NEJTM, 10 December 1946, SUPP 14/137.

32. *New Propeller*, March and April 1947; National Production Advisory Council for Industry, *Minutes*, 3 October 1946 and 6 July 1947, TUC 292/557.1/1.

33. J.W. Belcher to Lord President's Committee, 1 April 1946, PRO PREM 8 440.

34. H. Pollitt, *Looking Ahead*, August 1947, p. 75; *New Propeller*, July 1946 and September 1947.

35. *New Propeller*, June and October 1946, January 1947; *Metalworker*, August, October and November 1947. For pressure from trades councils for legislation on JPCs see TUC 292/225/3.

36. Coventry East Divisional Labour Party GMC, *Minutes*, 17 September 1947; Coventry Trades Council EC, *Minutes*, 2 October 1947; R. Williams, 'The meaning of industrial democracy', AEU *Monthly Journal*, September 1948. In a similar vein, the Association of Scientific Workers, many of whose members were well placed to understand policymaking at company level, declared that 'in the coming months and years it should increasingly be the function of [JPCs] to concern themselves not only with day to day problems but also to mould the policy of the particular establishment concerned to conform with the national interest.' *The Scientific Worker*, August 1946, p. 16.

37. AEU National Committee, *Report*, 1946, p. 238; *ibid.*, 1947, p. 274.

38. EEF Management Board, *Minutes*, 14 October 1948, EEF 237/1/1/45.

39. J. Hinton, *Shop Floor Citizens*, ch. 9.

40. National Institute of Industrial Psychology, *Joint Consultation in British Industry* (London, 1952), pp. 77, 80, 85 and 163; F. Zweig, *Productivity and Trade Unions* (Blackwell, 1951), pp. 238–40; Lloyd Roberts, 'Memorandum on joint consultation', 17 September 1948, LAB 10/722; Humphries, 'Joint Consultation in the Midlands', 28 October 1949, LAB 10/724.

41. G.D.H. Cole, 'Preface', in N. Barou, *British Trade Unions* (Gollancz, 1947), p. ix.

42. H. Wilson, 'The state and private industry', 4 May 1950, pp. 5, 10 and 13, PRO CAB 124/1200. For further discussion of Wilson's proposals see K. Middlemass, *Power Competition and the State: Vol 1 Britain in Search of Balance 1940–61* (Macmillan, 1988), pp.

181–4; J. Cronin, *The Politics of State Expansion: War, State and Society in Twentieth Century Britain* (Routledge, 1991), pp. 180–1.

43. *Labour Research*, September 1947.
44. H. Wilson, 'The state and private industry', p. 5.
45. Labour Party Conference, *Report*, 1946, p. 224.
46. 'The Labour Party and the Communist Party', 27 February 1946, Labour Party Archive, GS/1/4.
47. Labour Party Conference, *Report*, 1943, pp. 162 and 165.

Further Reading

This essay draws extensively on research undertaken for my book: *Shop Floor Citizens: Engineering Democracy in 1940s Britain*, (Edward Elgar, 1994). For a rather different evaluation of the role of the Communist Party from the one presented here see N. Fishman, *The British Communist Party and the Trade Unions, 1933–45*, (Scholar, 1994). The best account of the wartime shop stewards' movement remains Richard Croucher, *Engineers at War, 1939–1945*, (Merlin, 1982). Relevant assessments of relations between business, trade unions and the Attlee Government can be found in Nick Tiratsoo, (ed.), *The Attlee Years*, (Pinter, 1991).

10 West Africans and the Communist Party in the 1950s
Hakim Adi

This chapter is a preliminary investigation of the work of the Communist Party of Great Britain (CPGB) with West Africans in Britain and West Africa. The party was in contact with West Africans in Liverpool, Cardiff and Manchester and some other towns and cities, including London, where Nigerian and West African party branches were established. Here I concentrate on the party's work in London, but also give some idea of the extent of the party's influence in West Africa, especially in Nigeria.

The Party and West Africans before 1945

Before 1945 most West Africans in Britain were either students or seamen from Britain's four West African colonies: Nigeria, Gold Coast (Ghana), Sierra Leone and Gambia. Some were temporary residents, but more settled communities existed in Cardiff, Manchester, Liverpool and in parts of London. The CPGB had made some contacts with West African seamen in Cardiff and Liverpool before the war, but the most successful contacts were with the students, who established the West African Students' Union (WASU) in London in 1925.[1] WASU was a mainly London-based, anti-colonial organisation, which maintained links with West African students throughout Britain and Ireland, as well as with nationalists in West Africa.

By the late 1920s WASU had made contacts with Shapurji Saklatvala, and in 1927 became connected with Reginald Bridgeman and the League Against Imperialism (LAI).[2] Bridgeman remained a close ally of the students in the 1930s, and through them he and party members such as Hugo Rathbone made further contacts with nationalists throughout West Africa. At the time West Africans were also involved with the Profintern's International Trade Union Committee–Negro Workers and its journal *Negro Worker*. Some West Africans, including Bankole

Awooner-Renner and Isaac Wallace-Johnson, were educated in Moscow during the 1920s and 1930s at the University of the Toilers of the East (KUTV).[3]

During this period the CPGB relied on the LAI and other international bodies to carry out anti-colonial work in Britain's African colonies. However, in 1931 it was instrumental in the formation of the Negro Welfare Association (NWA) in London. The NWA, led by the Barbadian Arnold Ward, was affiliated to the LAI and both Bridgeman and Rathbone played an active role in its work, which included both welfare and politics. The NWA also established close contact with WASU and with nationalists in West Africa.[4]

In 1937 the party circulated a resolution to all branches instructing them to step up their anti-colonial work.[5] At the same time the party's Africa and colonial committees were involved in establishing the Colonial Information Bureau, which until 1939 produced the monthly *Colonial Information Bulletin*. In the early 1940s the Bureau published *Inside the Empire*, 'a quarterly journal on colonial and Indian affairs'. It was during this period that the party recruited its first West African member, J. Desmond Buckle, a medical student from the Gold Coast, who first became involved with the NWA during the late 1930s. Buckle remained a party member until his death in the mid–1960s. By 1943 he was a member of the party's colonial committee and subsequently worked in the international affairs and Africa committees. From 1950–54 he was the editor of the Africa committee's *Africa Newsletter*. Buckle also worked closely with the National Council for Civil Liberties and after 1945 in the international peace and trade union movements. Although a party stalwart, it seems that his obituary has yet to be written.

The Party and West Africa after 1945

The Second World War gave a new impetus to the struggle for self-government in the West African colonies. The support for the nationalist movements became much greater as expectations grew that the principle of self-determination would be applied to the colonies, especially by the new Labour government. Wartime conditions and the legalisation of trade unions had also led to a rapid rise in the strength and militancy of the Labour movement, which increasingly took part in the anti-colonial struggle. The war had weakened Britain and the old imperialist powers, but the prestige of the Soviet Union and the influence of Communism had never been stronger. Many more West Africans were drawn towards the international Communist movement.

After the war the CPGB took a more direct interest in the colonial question. Post-war Labour and Conservative governments recognised the need to transform the Empire into the Commonwealth, to reorganise the exploitation of the colonies both to solve Britain's economic problems and to cope with the struggles of the colonial peoples for independence. The party upheld the rights of colonial people for self-determination and independence, but at the same time argued that a new voluntary form of association was in the interests of colonial countries and Britain. In 1949, in *Britain's Crisis of Empire*, Palme Dutt argued that the Empire was bad for Britain, and that the country's economic recovery rested on first granting the colonies independence and then establishing new economic relations, which would enable the expansion and recovery of British industry through economic assistance to the former colonies. He argued that the British and colonial peoples were natural allies, fighting against a common enemy – Anglo-American imperialism. It was the duty of the party to strengthen this alliance and create the basis for 'a new close, fraternal association of the British people and the liberated peoples of the Empire'. This analysis was a central part of the party's post-war programme, *The British Road to Socialism*, launched in 1951.[6]

The convening of a number of international conferences at the end of the war served to link West Africans more closely with the world anti-imperialist movement. In 1945 meetings were held in London and Prague to organise new international youth and student organisations. When the International Union of Students (IUS) and World Federation of Democratic Youth (WFDY) were eventually formed their strong anti-imperialist politics attracted many young West Africans. In Britain, WASU was affiliated to the IUS and had its own representative, Bankole Akpata, on the executive of the WFDY.[7]

The meetings of the World Federation of Trade Unions (WFTU) held in London and Paris in 1945 gave the CPGB the opportunity to make closer contacts with West African trade union leaders. Meetings were held with T.A. Bankole, the president of the Nigerian TUC, who wrote an article, 'The Nigerian workers' movement', in *Inside The Empire*.[8] It is interesting to note that at the Paris congress of the WFTU Desmond Buckle spoke on behalf of the Transvaal Council of non-European Trade Unions. The party convened its own colonial conference in March 1945, attended by West African trade unionists and the students in Britain. In 1945, Desmond Buckle was involved in drafting the manifesto which announced the calling of the Manchester Pan-African Congress, which other party members subsequently attended. The party also participated in the strike relief committee established in London to give support to the Nigerian general strike. Close links were also established with the West African National Secretariat (WANS) formed by Nkrumah and others in December the same year, which had a membership including Wallace-Johnson, Akpata and Bankole Awooner-Renner.[9] Awooner-Renner's 1946 publication *West African Soviet Union* and his letter to Stalin, asking for land in the USSR for the poor and exploited of West Africa, give some indication of his sympathies.[10]

In February 1947 the party held a conference of the Communist Parties of the British Empire in London, at which Desmond Buckle presented a 'supplementary report' on East and West Africa and the West Indies. At the conference Palme Dutt stressed that 'The recognition of the democratic right of self-determination for all people is the cardinal principle of Communist policy.' But he only demanded immediate independence 'for those countries where the popular movements are well developed and have reached the stage of national consciousness', such as India, Egypt and Palestine. Apparently Palme Dutt considered that in Nigeria and the Gold Coast 'there is no developed national movement able to base itself on and speak for the people'; more importantly no Communist Parties existed there. He therefore argued that in these colonies the first step should be the fight for democratic and civil rights, which would facilitate the development of such a movement, and the curbing of the powers of monopolies, as part of the general struggle towards independence.[11]

The party now had its own contacts with West Africans in Britain and in West Africa. Through the WFTU, WFDY and IUS it also had significant international support. From 1947 the IUS published a monthly bulletin for colonial students and had established 'a Bureau of Students Fighting Against Colonialism', and the WFDY and IUS organised a two-yearly World Festival of Youth, which was first held in Prague. The festivals, visits, scholarships and hospital treatment offered to West African students by the WFDY and IUS in the people's democracies during this period were undoubtedly an important influence in recruitment. By 1952 eleven Nigerians were studying in East Germany and others, including Bankole Akpata, were at Charles University in Prague. Those Africans who visited eastern Europe were always favourably impressed and increasingly sympathetic to Communism.[12]

The West African student population in Britain remained the party's main point of contact with West African politics. By 1951 there were

about 4,500 West Africans, mostly Nigerians, living in London, where
the party concentrated its main efforts, but it also had links with smaller
groups of students and some workers in Manchester, Birmingham,
Cardiff and Liverpool. Disillusioned by the Labour government's stand
towards the colonies, many increasingly gravitated towards the CPGB.
In 1947 the party's Africa committee (a subcommittee of the International Department's international affairs committee) began the publication of the monthly *Africa Newsletter*, which by 1951 had sold nearly
700 copies, over half in Britain and nearly a third in Africa. It ceased
publication in 1954. From 1955–7 an *Africa Bulletin* was produced by
the Association for African Freedom, an organisation which was clearly
linked politically to the party, but about which there seems to be no
information.[13]

By 1948 Emile Burns was organising a class on Marxism for about
40 West African students in London, and in July of that year he was
enthusiastically received at WASU's annual conference.[14] Burns was able
to present to the conference some of the main points made in the July
resolution of the executive committee of the CPGB, which demanded
'full democratic self-government' for West African colonies, the abolition
of all discriminatory legislation, withdrawal of the British armed forces
and police, the replacement of European civil servants by Africans and
financial assistance for industrialisation and welfare in the colonies from
the British government. Indeed it was very much in line with WASU's
own political programme.[15]

By this time the party was in close touch with Amanke Okafor,
Edward Unwochei and other WASU members. Amanke Okafor had
written for *World News and Views* in March 1947, and in September 1948
the paper he presented to the WASU conference, 'Africa's historical contribution to civilisation' was reprinted in *Communist Review*. Both he
and Unwochei kept in close contact with Barbara Ruhemann and
Maud Rogerson of the Africa committee.[16] It is not clear how many
West Africans actually joined at this time. Clearly many were close
supporters and, in 1948, the party organised a special meeting for its
Nigerian contacts. The meeting was addressed by Palme Dutt who
presented 'a general statement of the party's position on the national
question in relation to the tasks of the national liberation movement and
the working class in Nigeria.'[17]

Okafor was one of a number of Nigerians who was sympathetic to
Marxism before he came to Britain. In 1945 he and members of other
Marxist groups in Nigeria had formed the Talakawa Party. This was 'a
political party of the working people of Nigeria', which aimed 'to achieve

a free independent and a socialist Nigeria'. Okafor had approached the CPGB when he arrived in Britain, and remained in close contact with the party until his return to Nigeria in the early 1950s. In 1949 he wrote a pamphlet, in collaboration with other Nigerian supporters of the party, entitled *Nigeria – Why We Fight for Freedom*.[18] H.O. Davies, a well-known nationalist and a founder member of the Nigerian youth movement, also contacted the party when he arrived in London in 1945. Davies soon rejected Marxism, but his initial education, by a CPGB member stationed in Nigeria during the war, shows the extent of party influence, which touched even the most bourgeois of nationalists. A number of other Nigerian Marxists, most of whom arrived in Britain as students, contacted the party during this period. They included Ayo Ogunsheye, Ade Ademola, M.A. Aderemi and others connected with a group in Nigeria which published *Nigerian Statesman*.[19]

Despite the presence of Desmond Buckle and Jonathan Tetteh,[20] another member of the Africa committee from the Gold Coast, the party seems to have had much less contact with students from the Gold Coast, Sierra Leone and the Gambia than it did with those from Nigeria. It did establish links with the London-based Gold Coast Union and Gambia League, but throughout the 1950s the party paid much more attention to Nigeria, Britain's largest colony. It hoped to train some of the students so that a Communist Party could be formed there. Unfortunately most of the Nigerians, both students and workers connected with the party, proved to be unsuitable for this task. At the same time the party found it difficult to stay on top of the many twists and turns of the movement for independence in Nigeria. It had to comprehend rapidly the role of the 'national question' and analyse political events in Nigeria almost on a daily basis. It was also unable effectively to organise and train Nigerians in Britain, so that they might find their bearings when they returned to West Africa. Almost as soon as Nigerians came into contact with the party, major ideological struggles broke out.

The Robeson Branches

However, West African and especially Nigerian support for Communism continued to grow. In 1950 there was a 'mass influx', and 150 Nigerians in London became party members. The basis on which so many Nigerians were admitted into the party remains something of a mystery, although party documents suggest that recruitment was through other Nigerian members. Because most had 'little political experience', they were not put into ordinary branches but into their own special 'Robeson branches' and this at a time when party leaders were urging closer ties between the peoples of Britain and the colonies. The recruitment seems to have been on a very casual basis, as it was later reported that the London district committee had no record of the names or addresses of Nigerian members. The Robeson branches attracted more recruits, but were soon objected to by the London district committee and the Central Organisation Department. They (rightly it seems) claimed that such basic units were contrary to party rules, even though other 'national groupings' existed within the party, and the London district committee ordered that the branches be disbanded.[21]

The most active Nigerians appealed in a signed letter to the International Department – which, it appears, had not been consulted by London district – that they were a special case. The International Department argued against the ruling. It pointed out that if it was accepted the party would probably lose most of the Nigerians, and that if they were split up this would lead to 'political confusion and disruptive tendencies from alien influences'. In particular the International Department was concerned that the divisions that already existed in the Nigerian independence movement, and which had already influenced some Nigerian members, would become more pronounced. But the Robeson branches were disbanded despite the problems such a measure was likely to bring.[22] However in 1951, the party's Africa committee (which had three African and six British members) formed a West African subcommittee of mainly Nigerian members. In London, the district committee now established an African and West Indian Advisory Committee, which in 1951 began to produce its own monthly paper, the *Colonial Liberator*.

Although the party had disbanded the Nigerian branches it continued to stress the importance of working with West Africans and other 'colonials', such as those from the Caribbean, who were living in Britain. In March 1951 the party held a conference to plan and further develop this work. In particular it aimed to take measures to 'tackle the problem of colonial women', make sure that colonial students and workers were organised and active in trade unions and student unions, secure maximum unity between colonial and British students and workers and involve 'colonials' in the peace movement. The party regarded WASU as the main organisation of West Africans in Britain and aimed to get all West Africans, workers as well as students, to join it. Party members within WASU were to be organised as 'fractions' on a national basis, and district committees were instructed to make sure that they appointed someone to take charge of 'colonial' work and liaise with the International Department. The party saw the opportunity of building 'close fraternal ties based on joint struggle' with those in the colonies through their 'representatives' in Britain. It saw the danger of the further development of racism in Britain, and the importance of building solidarity between colonial and British workers 'in their joint fight for peace and freedom from imperialism'.[23]

Party documents show that this work was considered both vital and urgent at the time. Apart from the work in London, progress had been made in Cardiff where the Colonial Defence Association was well supported. It organised and defended African and Caribbean seamen and produced its own paper *The Coloured Worker*. In Liverpool where the party was active in two organisations, the Colonial People's Defence Association and the New International Society (which produced its own paper *The Dawn*), there were also some advances. The party also had success with work amongst Africans and those from the Caribbean in Manchester, Birmingham and Leeds.[24]

In London the party's plans also seemed to be successful. In October 1951 Nigerian party members consolidated their leadership of WASU and were very active in a sit-in strike organised by colonial students at a government hostel. Over 70 West African students from Britain, organised by a special West African Youth Festival Preparatory Committee, attended the 1951 World Youth Festival in Berlin. Nigerian party members Uche Omo and Ade Thomas attended the IUS Council meeting in Warsaw as WASU observers. WASU was vigorous in its support of the IUS and strongly resisted attempts by the National Union of Students to disaffiliate from it. The party also had some influence in other African organisations based in London, especially in the Nigeria Union, which had members throughout Britain, and the Africa League which had a branch in Manchester.[25]

The Party and the Nigerian Independence Movement

However, in spite of these successes the party still experienced major problems when it tried to analyse the political situation in Nigeria. Amongst Nigerian members, and in the Africa committee and International Department, there was considerable confusion over the question of how the party should view the main nationalist organisations in

Nigeria, the leadership of the trade unions and the movement for independence. The main problems centred around the divisions which had developed in the independence movement between the politicians of two of the major nationalities in Nigeria, the Yoruba and the Igbo. These national divisions were also being used to split the independence and trade union movements, and became one of the most important issues in the political life of the country.[26]

A Yoruba cultural and political association known as the Egbe Omo Oduduwa (EOO) had been founded in London in 1945. Most of the Nigerians in London were Yorubas and some, including party members, joined the EOO, encouraged it seems by Emile Burns and Henry Collins.[27] In the summer of 1948 Edward Unwochei wrote an article in *Africa Newsletter* exposing the EOO as an 'imperialist sponsored' organisation which would sabotage the work of the National Council of Nigeria and the Camerouns (NCNC), at that time the main political organisation in Nigeria. Following the adverse response to this article in the Nigerian press, and criticism from some other Nigerian party members, Unwochei was asked by the International Department to write a second article repudiating his earlier views.[28]

For some years the Africa committee and International Department were unable to reach a common view on the political character of the NCNC and the Action Group (AG), the successor to the EOO. This led to significant divisions and uncertainty amongst Nigerian members. Indeed one member, O.A. Bamishe, actually formed and became secretary of the London branch of the Action Group. The problems were no doubt made worse by what appears to be the ease with which new members were admitted into the party. It was soon realised that many of the Nigerian members were politically unreliable, and when they returned home became inactive. In 1951 some of them, including Ade Ademola and Ayo Ogunsheye, were denounced as Titoists who were attempting to disrupt the Nigerian trade union and independence movements.[29]

Many of the Nigerians who had been recruited by the party objected to the way that it made statements on Nigerian affairs without fully consulting them. Their own class backgrounds (both Aderemi and Ademola for example came from the families of traditional rulers) led them to oppose the attitude of the party towards chiefs and other traditional rulers. Political events in Nigeria moved very rapidly, and it was necessary, but extremely difficult, for the party to fully analyse everything without making mistakes.

The June 1952 Political Committee Document

At the end of 1951 the International Department held a meeting with Nigerian members, chaired by Palme Dutt, to try and resolve some of these problems, but no resolution or clarification resulted. Barbara Ruhemann of the Africa committee was then asked to research the Nigerian political situation and to prepare a full report for the International Department and the political committee. The report was hastily written and even though five Nigerian members of the West Africa sub-committee were consulted, it seems they held diverse views. Two of these members were then invited to attend a meeting of the international affairs committee, which unanimously adopted the document. In June 1952 it was adopted by the political committee, and an article based on the document under Dutt's name was prepared for publication in *For a Lasting Peace and People's Democracy*. After adoption the document was presented to a meeting of Nigerian members by Idris Cox. Several made criticisms concerning its content and the fact that they had not previously been consulted. Eventually, in January 1953, four Nigerians prepared a written statement of their disagreements.[30]

Once again these disagreements centred on the party's characterisation of the AG as a 'political organisation of the compradore class', formed 'with imperialist backing'; and of Yoruba chiefs as 'a class of semi-feudal, semi-bourgeois compradores', who were 'completely reliable allies of imperialism and irreconcilable enemies of the mass of the people'. Unfortunately Dutt's article, 'People of Nigeria rise in struggle for freedom', was eventually published in January 1953, much to the annoyance of many of the Nigerian members. Dutt and Cox held two meetings with O.A. Bamishe and other critics, but could not convince them. Indeed not only would they not agree with the line taken by the political committee, they also raised the question of why the Robeson branches had been disbanded. To try to solve these and other disagreements Dutt proposed a general meeting with all Nigerian members 'with whom contact could be established'.[31]

The Nigerian Branch

The general meeting of Nigerian members finally took place in April 1953. By that time the London district committee and the Organisation Department had reversed their earlier decision and declared that a Nigerian branch might be formed. The April meeting therefore decided by ten votes to two to form such a branch which would 'carry through an unfettered discussion of all questions of political controversy in relation to Nigeria and the work of Nigerian comrades in London'. It is clear that many Nigerians felt that more political discussion was needed before a branch was established, and were concerned that they were being rushed into a decision. Apparently all present at the meeting agreed to participate, but four refused to be nominated to serve on the branch committee. However, within a month three of the members had resigned, and two, O.A. Bamishe and I. Dodiye, made a series of charges against the International Department and the party leadership. One of their main criticisms was that the party was 'not prepared to consider our views in preparing materials for the formulation of a policy concerning our country'. They argued not only that Nigerians were not consulted, but also that the party had 'rejected the elementary necessity of placing a reliable correspondent on the spot' in Nigeria. They also criticised the formation of the new branch, which they alleged was a 'manoeuvre' to 'fill the house with Nigerian comrades with different views from ours', in order to 'exorcise the bogey of criticism out of existence'. Bamishe and Dodiye were also extremely critical of party leaders. Dutt, they claimed 'arrogantly dismissed' their views, while discussion on the political committee document had been closed by 'the unilateral arrogant decision of comrades Dutt, Cox and co.', a practice which they felt 'smells of imperialist methods'.[32]

The Nigeria Commission

In May 1953, in response to the resignations and continuing political controversy, the party appointed a Nigeria Commission to look into all the allegations. Rather surprisingly perhaps, the Commission members were Dutt, Ruhemann, Cox, Burns and J.R. Campbell. Desmond Buckle, the Africa committee and some of the Nigerians, including Bamishe and Dodiye, were consulted or submitted evidence, but no West Africans were members of the Commission, which eventually met on over 30 occasions. The Nigeria branch also held a series of meetings, reportedly 'the first collective discussion of Nigerian Party members in the British party on the problem of the situation in Nigeria'.[33]

The evidence which the Commission heard from even loyal members, such as Ade Thomas, shows that there was general 'disquiet' over the International Department. Many Nigerian members were concerned that they were being segregated from British members. They claimed that their initiatives were 'not liked by the International Department', that they were not dealt with fairly. Many it seems were critical of what they felt were patronising and chauvinistic attitudes within the party. They claimed that the party's leaders were 'practising autocracy though professing democracy', and 'behaving like imperialist rulers'. As a result membership had declined. Thomas reported that only eight members attended one Nigerian branch meeting.[34] In 1954 the decline in membership was no doubt accelerated by an announcement by the federal and regional governments in Nigeria that no known Communist would be employed in 'essential public services' or the civil service. A similar ban had previously been announced in the Gold Coast.[35]

The Nigeria Commission Report presented in 1954 largely rejected the accusations made by Bamishe and Dodiye, but it did accept that the political committee document was 'too sweeping and over-simplified' especially in regard to the analysis of the EOO and the AG and the position of chiefs. Dutt and Burns were criticised for failing to take appropriate action to deal with the problems and controversies which had been developing since 1948. Further criticism was made of the decision to disband the Robeson branches. The new branch was to get 'the utmost political and practical support' from London district and from the International Department. Indeed in coming years Kay Beauchamp was appointed by London district to act as an unofficial secretary to the Nigerian branch. In 1956 she was joined by Molly Mandell, another representative of the district committee. The branch concluded its own discussions and issued a report in December 1953. Although this report has not yet come to light, it seems that the criticisms subsided.[36]

There is at present little information about the work of the new branch or its membership. It continued to work with WASU and other African organisations and Ade Thomas (who was also 'national organiser' of WASU) was initially its most prominent member. It was he who presented a report to the Second Conference of the Communist and Workers' Parties within the sphere of British imperialism, held in London in 1954.[37] Some time in the mid-1950s the branch was reorganised as a West African branch with Frank Oruwari, an ex-law student, as its secretary. Again there is little information about its work. It met monthly in order to study Marxism–Leninism and discuss West African politics. It also included more workers, such as S.O. Bello and George Okeleke. Oruwari, who was a member of the party's international affairs committee, remained branch secretary until his return to Nigeria in 1960. He was succeeded by George Okeleke, a factory worker in London. The branch now included Ghanaians and presumably some Sierra Leoneans, and had a membership of around 30.[38] In 1957 the West African branch was one of many which unsuccessfully submitted amendments to *The British Road to Socialism* at the party's special congress. It particularly objected to what many saw as attempts to propose a kind of 'socialist commonwealth'.[39] However, by 1960 the International Department reported that the branch was, 'a small closed circle' isolated from most West Africans in London, although it is clear that the party still continued its political work with West Africans outside the branch.[40]

The Party and the Nigeria Labour Movement

From the late 1940s the party maintained close links with some of the leading nationalists and trade unionists in Nigeria, and was also in contact with the many Marxist groups that emerged during this period. Perhaps the most important individual in communication with the party during this period was Nduka Eze, a Marxist union leader, who was one of the leaders of the NCNC, became president of the revolutionary Zikist movement and leader of the Nigerian National Federation of Labour (NNFL). Eze first contacted Harry Pollitt in 1950 after he led the formation of the Nigerian Labour Congress (NLC), which reunited Nigeria's trade unions after the break-up of the Nigerian TUC.[41]

In 1950 Eze was also instrumental in the publication of the *Labour Champion*, the Nigerian Labour movement's first daily paper, which sent Idise Dafe to Britain to be trained as a journalist by the *Daily Worker*. The NLC affiliated to the WFTU and sent delegates to the IUS Congress in Prague, the Congress of the International Union of Journalists in Finland and the Second World Peace Congress in Warsaw.[42]

Eze and other leading members of the NLC were in close contact with the party, which paid for at least one trade unionist to come to London for training. Officially the party's policy was not to interfere in Nigeria's politics, but this policy does not seem to have been upheld. Within the International Department there were two opposing views about Eze. Some maintained that his political stands showed that he was likely to be able to provide Marxist leadership to the Nigerian trade union and independence movement, but many Nigerian and some British party members were unhappy about the support given to Eze. When he was under political attack from the colonial government and other trade unionists in Nigeria some members of the International Department, such as Maud Rogerson, encouraged and even instigated further attacks. Eventually the Nigerian trade union movement was again split in two and Eze hounded from its leadership.[43]

The Party Press

From 1945 events in West Africa were regularly reported and commented on in *The Daily Worker, Labour Monthly, Communist Review* and *World News and Views*.

Desmond Buckle, who was also a TASS correspondent, was a regular contributor. But apart from Amanke Okafor's articles during the late 1940s it appears that no other Africans contributed. One of the most significant articles was the 'Statement of the executive committee of the party on the situation in Nigeria', published in July 1954 in *World News and Views*. Amongst other things the executive committee publicly acknowledged that the June 1952 political committee document on Nigeria had included political mistakes. The statement also called for the formation of 'a united anti-imperialist front' of all democratic and anti-feudal parties in Nigeria, and the formation of 'a united Marxist Party' to develop and lead this broad front. Despite the EC's optimistic view that 'all the conditions are ripe for this development', no such party was formed during this period.[44]

A Communist Party for Nigeria

There was some optimism within the party that a Communist Party could be formed in Nigeria. However the training of Nigerians in Britain for the task of founding such a party remained inadequate. Many returned just to pursue their careers or were totally unprepared for conditions in Nigeria. In 1953 Idise Dafe toured Nigeria on behalf of the CPGB, and arranged meetings with the main Marxist groups. His report was pessimistic and particularly lamented the fact that 'Our Nigerian comrades do return to our Fatherland and that is all we hear of them.'[45] A number of groups such as the United Working People's Party (UWPP), Convention People's Party and People's Committee for Independence emerged in the early 1950s, but they squabbled amongst themselves, each claiming that it could form the basis of a Nigerian Communist Party. Some of the leaders of these groups, such as Bankole Akpata, Ayo Ogunsheye and Uche Omo, had formerly been students in London, but the party found it just as difficult to reach agreement with them after their return home. Even a meeting in London in 1953, with the delegation from the UWPP, led to accusations that Dutt and others had received the delegation with 'unjustifiable contempt', mainly it seems because they had refused to recognise it as the sole Marxist party in Nigeria.[46]

Both publicly and privately the party urged the various groups to work together and end their squabbling, but without success. In 1956 Palme Dutt admitted in a confidential memo to the party's central committee: 'While the objective conditions are probably ripe for the development of a Communist Party, many initial groups attempting to fulfil this role show great weaknesses.' Dutt acknowledged that within the party there was 'considerable disagreement in estimating the political forces' in Nigeria, and that 'any differences of estimation in our press and other organs of the international Communist movement are quickly taken advantage of by the enemies of Communism in Nigeria'. He lamented the fact that 'no co-ordination or common outlook exists' and proposed closer consultation between the International Department and their counterparts in the French Communist Party and the Communist Party of the Soviet Union.[47] The British party, he admitted, needed international help. Whether such help was available is not yet clear, but not until 1963 was there a party in Nigeria organised on a country-wide basis which claimed to be guided by 'scientific socialist ideas'. This was the Socialist Workers' and Farmers' Party, formed in Enugu, eastern Nigeria, in October of that year.

Conclusion

During the 1950s the CPGB established close links with the Nigerian Labour and independence movements and with African Communists in Britain and Nigeria, but it encountered numerous difficulties in its political work with West Africans. In West Africa itself the Communist movement met with severe repression, which intensified with the onset of the cold war. Communist and Soviet publications were banned by the colonial authorities, Communists were hounded out of the trade union and independence movements and barred from government employment. The CPGB was unable to help fully to overcome the weaknesses in the emerging Communist movement in West Africa. Indeed the party was unable to overcome its own political differences and weaknesses, which were exacerbated, it seems, by the introduction of *The British Road to Socialism*.

Despite numerous 'colonial schools' the party was unable adequately to train its West African members so that they could orientate themselves in difficult conditions when they returned home. The policy of segregating them from other party members was detrimental to both West African and British members. British members took little interest in West African affairs, and West Africans little interest in British political life. And this at a time when the party was advocating building closer relations between the peoples of the colonies and Britain. The party's 'open door' recruitment policy allowed almost any Nigerian to join and then return to Nigeria, often damaging the movement there; some of those who were most disruptive even claimed to be CPGB representatives. The arrogant attitude of many former Nigerian members, when they returned home, may even have been encouraged by the widely held belief in the party that Nigeria was unable to produce its own political leaders without outside help.

The condemnation of Stalin and other revelations in Khrushchev's speech at the Congress of the Communist Party of the Soviet Union, in 1956, clearly led to divisions amongst West African student supporters of the party. So too did the allegations of corruption amongst some leaders of the WASU 'fraction', who it was claimed had stolen gifts presented to the union at the World Youth Festivals.[48] As Palme Dutt acknowledged, the weaknesses within the party and the emerging differences within the international Communist movement hampered the development of the Communist movement in West Africa. Both Ghana and Nigeria achieved political independence by 1960, but without the leadership of West African Communists.

Acknowledgements

I would like to thank Noreen Branson, Muriel Seltman, Jamal Narayan and the late Kay Beauchamp for their valuable time and information. I am also grateful for the assistance of the Marx Memorial Library and Communist Party Archives.

Notes

1. See H. Adi, *West African Students and West African Nationalism in Britain 1900–60* (University of London PhD thesis, 1994).
2. Ibid. pp. 82–90.

3. See W. McClennan, 'Africans and Black Americans in the Comintern schools, 1925–34', *International Journal of African Historical Studies* 26, 2, 1993, pp. 371–90; E.T. Wilson, *Russia and Black Africa before World War II* (Holmes & Meier, 1976); and M. Sherwood, *The Comintern and Colonies till c.1934* (Paper presented to SOAS African History Seminar, December 1993).

4. See H. Adi, *West African Students*. The CPGB also maintained some contacts in the Caribbean and with Caribbean workers and students in Britain. See M. Sherwood, *The Comintern, the CPGB, Colonies and Black Britons, 1920–1938* (Paper presented at the conference 'Opening the books – New insights into the history of British communism', Manchester, 1994).

5. *CPGB Circular to all District Committees*, 16 April 1937, Public Record Office, Kew (PRO) CO 323/1517/7046/1.

6. R. P. Dutt, *Britain's Crisis of Empire*, (Lawrence & Wishart, 1949).

7. See H. Adi, *West African Students*, pp. 217–24.

8. *Inside the Empire* 4, 1, April 1945, pp. 12–17.

9. M. Sherwood, 'Kwame Nkrumah: the London years, 1945–7', *Immigrants and Minorities*, 12, 3, November 1993, pp. 164–95.

10. B. Awooner-Renner, *West African Soviet Union* (WANS Publications, 1946). For his letter to Stalin see PRO CO 537/5263/47272/3/5.

11. *We Speak for Freedom* (CPGB, 1947), p. 28.

12. H. Adi, *West African Students*, pp. 226–7.

13. *Africa Newsletter* and *Africa Bulletin*, Communist Party Archives (CPA), Box 68, also International Department Report to Political Committee, 25 June 1953, CPA, Box 257A.

14. 'African Students in Conference', *World News and Views* (*WNV*) 28, 31, 7 August 1948, p. 330.

15. For the July resolution see *Communist Review*, December 1948, pp. 383–4.

16. A. Okafor, 'By the waters of Kuramo', *WNV* 27, 11, 29 March 1947, pp. 128–9; see also *Communist Review*, September 1948, pp. 278–85.

17. 'Nigeria Commission revised draft final report', 12 January 1954, p. 6. R. P. Dutt Papers, British Library, CUP. 1262 K4.

18. Nigeria Report, January 1956, p. 12. Ruhemann Papers Box 254, CPA. *Nigeria – Why We Fight for Freedom* (A. Okafor, 1950).

19. 'Draft discussion document on nature and personnel of the leadership of the Nigerian trade union and national movement', November 1951, Ruhemann Papers, CPA.

20. Tetteh was the victim of an openly racist attempt to exclude him from the work of the party's St Pancras borough committee by another party member. A full enquiry was held by the party's London district committee, which was chaired by Kay Beauchamp. Subsequently the party member responsible was expelled.

21. 'Nigeria Commission', p. 7. The branches were, of course, named after Paul Robeson, the well-known African-American singer and political activist. Robeson had been a patron of WASU since the early 1930s and had close links with the CPGB. In 1949 he wrote the foreword to Amanke Okafor's *Nigeria – Why We Fight for Freedom*.

22. 'Nigeria Commission', p. 8.

23. A report on this conference can be found in the Communist Party Archives.

24. Ibid. Some details of the activities of the New International Society in Liverpool and Manchester can be found in M. Herbert, *Never Counted Out – The Story of Len Johnson – Manchester's Black Boxing Hero and Communist* (Dropped Aitches Press, 1992). On the Colonial People's Defence Association see R. Ramdin, *The Making of the Black Working Class in Britain* (Gower, 1987), pp. 382–7.

25. H. Adi, *West African Students*, p. 219.

26. For example B. Ruhemann to R. P. Dutt, 17 June 1951, Ruhemann Papers, CPA.

27. 'Nigeria Commission', p. 9.

28. 'Draft discussion document', p. 2.

29. Ibid. For the party's view on the influence of Titoism amongst colonial students see J. Klugman, *From Trotsky to Tito* (Lawrence & Wishart, 1951), p. 196.

30. 'Nigeria Commission', pp. 11–12. Two of the Nigerians were Bamishe and I. Dodiye; it is likely that a third was J.O.B. Omotosho, a former member of the editorial board of *Africa Newsletter*.

31. Ibid. Also R. P. Dutt, 'People of Nigeria rise in struggle for freedom', *For a Lasting Peace and People's Democracy*, 9 January 1953, p. 4. See also O.A. Bamishe, 'Western Nigeria and chieftancy problems', 21 August 1952, Ruhemann Papers.

32. 'Nigeria Commission', p. 4.

33. Ibid., pp. 2–3 and 'Nigeria Commission', 3 June 1953, CPA.

34. Ibid.

35. See for example 'Witch hunt extends to Nigeria', *Daily Worker*, 14 October 1954 and 'Gold Coast expulsion', *Daily Worker*, 6 March 1954.

36. 'Nigeria Commission', pp. 28 and 37–8.
37. A. Thomas, 'Britain's largest colony', *Report of the Second Conference of the Communist and Workers' Parties within the sphere of British imperialism* (CPGB, 1954).
38. One West African worker, William Torston Ananaba, a Nigerian, had joined the party as early as 1948. See 'Comrade Ananaba – an African Communist', *Africa Newsletter* 3, 11, November 1950, p. 12.
39. Amendments to *The British Road to Socialism* submitted to the 25th Congress (CPGB, 1957), p. 10 (no. 318). Similar reservations were held by the party's West Indian members, see T. Carter, *Shattering Illusions – West Indians in British Politics* (Lawrence & Wishart, 1986), pp. 59–60.
40. Report of the work of the International Department, 2 March 1960, p. 6, CPA.
41. 'Draft discussion document', p. 7.
42. Ibid., p. 8.
43. Ibid., p. 11.
44. 'What next in Nigeria', *World News and Views*, July 1954, nos 32/33, pp. 630–3 and 649–52.
45. I. Dafe, 'Corrected report on visit to Nigeria', 27 May 1953, Ruhemann Papers.
46. 'Nigeria Commission', pp. 30–5.
47. 'Central Committee Confidential Memo', 1 March 1956, R.P. Dutt Papers, p. 8.
48. H. Adi, *West African Students*, p. 239.

Further Reading

There is almost nothing published on the politics and political organisations of Britain's African population during the post-war period. For more general information, especially on the period before 1945, see P. Fryer, *Staying Power – The History of Black People in Britain* (Pluto Press, 1984), and I. Geiss, *The Pan-African Movement* (Africana Pub. Co., 1968). See also R.J. Macdonald, 'The wisers who are far away: The role of London's Black press in the 1930s and 1940s' and C.J. Robinson, 'Black intellectuals at the British core: 1920s–1940s', in J.S. Gundara and I. Duffield (eds), *Essays on the History of Blacks in Britain* (Avebury, 1992). For a general survey of the anti-colonial movement in Britain during this period see S. Howe, *Anti-Colonialism in British Politics – The Left and the End of Empire 1918–1964*, (Clarendon Press, 1993).

11   Communism and the New Left
Michael Kenny

The reassessment of British Communism involves consideration of a wider range of organisations and traditions than the party itself. This is because, on occasions, Communists entered into a dialogue with other groupings, though more often their ideas emerged in opposition to the beliefs of rivals. The significance of non-Communist organisations in this story is also enhanced by assessment of the subsequent political careers and influence of former Communists, a relatively neglected group within British Communist historiography. An important question arises here, especially in the wake of the collapse of Communist Parties since 1989: are there any common features or patterns which characterise the political behaviour of former Communists? Obviously the answer depends largely on national context and individual biography. Yet we have little guidance from the study of past periods in Communist history to ascertain if any common trends occur in different countries: whether, for instance, leaving the party usually means a decline in political activity and involvement; and under what circumstances former members retain a socialist identity.

One way of approaching this question is to examine the few attempts made by ex-Communists to organise a political alternative outside the party. To this end, the history of the first New Left in Britain (1956–62), in which former Communists played a key role, is explored here. Whilst commentators on this movement have perceived the Communist heritage of some of its participants as important, the nature of ex-Communism in this context has been misunderstood. Two broad interpretations of the relationship between the New Left and former Communists can be discerned. First, commentators such as Nigel Young, in his influential study of the New Left in Britain and the US, present the persistence of Communist ideas and traditions as a malign influence upon the development of New Left politics.[1] New Left identity, in this view, depended upon the complete abandonment of old left positions, involving a wholly new political language and culture. Not surprisingly, the first wave of the British New Left fares badly in this account: 'a false start' is Young's abrupt and teleological characterisation of this movement.[2] This approach finds echoes in the work of other commentators and some contemporary observers who reflected anxiously on the undue influence ex-Communists might exert over their younger New Left comrades.[3]

Second, a number of former participants and later commentators suggest that the transition from party membership to New Left participation was essentially seamless for these intellectuals, and that their Communist heritage constituted one of the most important elements within the politics of the early New Left. Reacting against an older school of historiography which presented those who left in 1956 as proto-liberals,[4] this interpretation suggests that the ex-Communists who gathered around the *New Reasoner* (NR: the journal founded by Edward Thompson and John Saville in 1957) provided the fledgeling New Left with political experience and leadership. Drawing upon an unsullied, libertarian Communist heritage which had been displaced within the CPGB, this wing of the New Left developed an impressive and persuasive alternative, which was central to the new movement's success. Only the events of 1959–62, in which the NR journal merged with *Universities and Left Review* (ULR; a likeminded but different journal which was also founded in 1957) to form the *New Left Review* (NLR) in 1960, thwarted the development of a potent third current on the British left, founded upon the principles of socialist humanism. This position approximates to Thompson's various remarks on this period (especially in response to the turn taken by the NLR under Perry Anderson's editorship after 1962)[5] and appears in different forms in the work of David Holden, Bryan Palmer and Lin Chun.[6] Neither of these readings provides a satisfactory basis for understanding the relationship between the New Left and ex-Communists. Both tend to gloss over the question of how ex-Communists behave outside their party affiliations and culture, how they interact with the wider political culture and how they handle their 'transitional' identities, moving from orthodox Communism to new political positions.

One well-documented response to the abandonment of Communism arises from 'the god that failed' turn of former Communists at certain points of political rupture and ideological pressure. Yet, the switch to rampant anti-Communism in post-war Britain has been a minority preference. Most former Communists have remained sympathetic to liberal–left culture and political commitments, and many have held on to aspects of their political past. According to Mervyn Jones, ex-Communists in the 1950s displayed 'a habit of sharpness and intensity of argument, a seriousness about ideas, a tone that differed from the tone of the dominant liberal'.[7] One reason for the absence of a wholesale swing to anti-Communism lies in the richness and density of liberal–left culture and institutions in Britain in this period. In the late 1950s, the first New Left played a key role as an alternative to virulent anti-Communism, defining a space between the polarities of political debate in the cold war.[8] On the basis of this moment in the history of the left we can gain some insight into the larger question of the political identity of former Communists.

Above all, it is important to consider how those individuals who left the party in 1956–7, having absorbed in different ways the internal party culture illuminated by Raphael Samuel in his reconstruction of the 'The Lost World of British Communism', dealt with the legacy of Communist beliefs and culture.[9] Whilst certain elements of the Communist, and specifically Stalinist, heritage, were jettisoned, other aspects of this experience were retained in this new context. Yet historians have told us little about the nature of this transition, especially the process of rejection and reapplication of Communist orthodoxies. The major exception here consists of commentary on a number of historians whose work continued to show signs of their collaboration as members of the party's historians' group until the mid-1950s, including Christopher Hill, Eric Hobsbawm, John Saville and Edward Thompson.[10] The question of the transition from Communism to ex-Communism arises more obliquely from the insights of commentators who have stressed the complex and ambivalent nature of Communist identity and party life.[11] Thompson, reflecting on his previous party membership in 1963, neatly captured the paradoxical nature of his own (and many others') relationship to the party: he was part of a generation that gave intellectual allegiance to the party, yet 'which was nonetheless repelled by the alien and schematic manner and matter of its thinking'.[12] Leaving it did not induce for him (and others) the total, intellectual and psychic rupture it did for some.

This is not to suggest that those who founded the NR were in any way typical of the larger group of members who left in 1956–7. In many ways they were the exception, both in their intellectual orientation and small number. Yet their public creation of a dissident Communist position, within a larger New Left current, makes their experience exceptional and important. Unfortunately, we know little about the influence of this journal upon those who abandoned political activity altogether in 1956 or remained active in trade union politics.

Whilst most accounts of the New Left, like Young's, assume that this formation attempted a complete break from the past, a more dialectical conception of intellectual and political change may represent this movement more accurately. Aspects of the British Communist tradition significantly affected the political character of this milieu, not least through the ideas of Thompson, one of the dominant figures within this formation. In the brief sketch which follows I have drawn from the published reminiscences and contemporary correspondence of several individuals within the drama of 1956, especially Saville's own records, held at Hull University. Whilst I do not refer to these in any detail (though the political atmosphere they convey has influenced my interpretation), they are deployed in my larger account of the first New Left.[13] Here I highlight a number of recurrent themes within these different accounts and relate these to the New Left's later political development.

Three issues raised by these reminiscences are particularly important. First, they make clear that all of the high-profile group of intellectuals who left the party in 1956 did so with great reluctance. This suggests that the transition from a Communist to ex-Communist (New Left in this case) identity was more complicated than is conventionally suggested and did not necessarily involve a dramatic break from previous orthodoxies. A large part of contemporary Communism consisted of a shared sense of purpose and mutual respect at the self-sacrifices demanded by party membership and activism, as well as the experience of social and political isolation engendered by the pervasiveness of cold war culture. As Saville recalls:

> [w]e were highly committed Party members who had come through the tough and difficult years of the Cold War – more difficult than is often appreciated – and we had personal experiences of those who had left the Party to cultivate their own gardens, or of those who had left to become, in our eyes, renegades.[14]

Coming to terms with these values outside the party was a difficult process which, in many cases, took years rather than months. The disgruntlement that appeared in many quarters in 1956 rarely undermined these core commitments but was the result of a mixture of political, constitutional and ideological anxieties: about the leadership's support for Soviet policy; about the validity of Khrushchev's argument that the removal of the 'cult of personality' had eradicated the main features of Stalinism (the central argument of the 'secret speech' at the Twentieth Congress of the CPSU in February); about aspects of Soviet history – for instance Hyman Levy's revelations about anti-Semitism on his return from the USSR; and about the CPGB's reluctance to allow a genuine debate to occur on these questions in the party press (a process vividly described by Malcolm MacEwen).[15] The ambivalence many felt within the CPGB is neatly captured in Doris Lessing's exploration of party life through her fictional character Anna Wulf in *The Golden Notebook*:

> Yet when I leave the Party, this is what I am going to miss – the company of people who have spent their lives in a certain kind of atmosphere, where it is taken for granted that their lives must be related to a central philosophy. This is why so many people who would like to leave, or think they should leave, the Party, do not.[16]

The diffuse opposition which arose in 1956, especially once the first issue of Saville's and Thompson's internal discussion journal the *Reasoner* appeared, pitched their arguments in the terms of Communist loyalty and tradition. Indeed, as Samuel suggests, their continued belief that the party in some sense belonged and would respond to the feelings of its members fired their indignation.[17] Their initial objective was reform. Saville remembers how he and Thompson viewed the *Reasoner* as compatible with party traditions and culture.[18] In this they were fairly typical: MacEwen recalls that of the external submissions to the Commission on Inner-Party Democracy which the leadership set up to head off criticism, 'virtually all ... were intended to strengthen the Party, not to weaken it, and came from people who even at that date would rather have reformed the Party than abandon it'.[19] One of the key questions faced by those pressing for reform was whether, when avenues were closed within the party, they should voice dissent from outside. Saville's account of 1956 stresses the reluctance with which he and Thompson considered publishing outside the party press, testimony to their refusal to break with Communist convention, unlike those members who published a letter of protest in *Tribune* and the *New Statesman*.[20]

Second, these accounts highlight the extent to which the Soviet invasion of Hungary was a catalyst which persuaded many to leave. The project of reforming and democratising the party receded against the backdrop of events in Hungary in early November. These fundamentally shifted the terms of the argument: the blatant immorality of Soviet actions and the CPGB's 'unequivocal'[21] support for these opened a wide rift within the party. Calls for reform seemed unrealistic and insignificant against the backdrop of the invasion, whilst for those who fell behind the leadership's line, the core elements of Communist identity ensured that reform could not be countenanced when the party was under such external pressure. This explains the increasing hostility, noted by contemporaries, which was directed towards the *Reasoner* in the latter months of 1956. An interesting counterfactual question arises, however, if we consider what would have followed had the invasion not occurred. According to the reminiscences of those involved in these events, it is clear that the willingness to work within the party's traditions and structures still exerted a strong pull. Given the dominance of the Conservatives nationally, and their unwillingness to abandon imperial pretensions, as Suez made clear, as well as the unfavourable political situation within the Labour Party where the left were marginal, the party would have continued to appeal to many as the repository of alternative values. Saville recalls a contemporary letter in which he argued that, '[h]ad not Hungary occurred I was prepared to stay in and continue the fight so long as the ban on discussion was not complete'.[22] On the other hand, the reform project would probably have been contained within the party, leaving a strong tide of disgruntlement. Whatever the answer, posing this question clarifies the extent to which party loyalties were still firmly in place in November 1956.

In fact, the elements of Communist identity given above were too deeply embedded to be simply jettisoned: indeed, they helped the formation of an organised opposition grouping. Accounts of the conditions in which the *Reasoner* was produced by Thompson and Saville describe the self-sacrifice, sense of isolation and common purpose which were also central to party culture.[23] The desire to retain moral clarity and a Communist sense of purpose, however difficult circumstances may have been, played a central role in sustaining this enterprise. In political terms, the argument shifted from party reform towards the search for the 'lost tradition' of British Communism, leading to re-examination of the theoretical Marxist tradition and calls for a new history of the party.[24] Most importantly, the *Reasoner* and, subsequently, the NR attracted a number of ex-Communists to the project of defining a libertarian Communist alternative.

Third, it is clear that the break from Communism and the formation of the New Left were neither caused by nor encouraged the development of a coherent alternative model of political organisation. Opposition spread from the particular form of democratic centralism practised by the party to the merits of this organisational principle in 1956. MacEwen's account of the party's Commission on Democracy emphasises that among those who produced the minority report (MacEwen, Christopher Hill and Peter Cadogan), the main concern was the balance between democracy, meaning unconstrained internal discussion, and the need for centralism.[25] Yet no substantial, alternative model was available. This was evident in the critique mounted in the *Reasoner* and also in Thompson's keynote article in the first edition of the NR, 'Socialist Humanism: An Epistle to the Philistines': the Stalinist interpretation of democratic centralism was rejected, yet no concrete alternative was offered. This had a number of consequences for these ex-Communists when they participated in the New Left, not least because they brought with them untransformed expectations about political organisation.

These points illuminate aspects of the first New Left. They undermine the conventional view that 1956 represented a neat and complete break of perspective for former Communists, leading directly to the emergence of a New Left. In fact, a more complex process occurred within the NR group, whereby older orthodoxies coexisted with the development of newer ideas outside the constraints of party membership. Undoubtedly the absence of the restraints of party life encouraged rethinking and more pronounced opposition to Stalinism. Yet several features of party culture – the most influential context which the key figures in the NR had known – were reproduced in this new setting. Above all, the sense of the party as a particular kind of moral community, described by Samuel, was redeployed to energise the NR. It maintained a sense of 'membership', loyalty and purpose which were wholly absent from its New Left counterpart, the ULR.

The intellectuals who broke from the party and were involved in the NR project (including Kenneth Alexander, Alfred Dressler, Derek Kartun, Doris Lessing, Ronald Meek, Randall Swingler and Peter Worsley) did not shift simply and unproblematically from one coherent world view (orthodox Stalinism) to another (New Left ideology). In fact, the ideas of this group were always diverse: a range of political and intel-lectual experiences were brought into the NR. Whilst much emphasis has rightly been placed on the influence of the historians' group on some of these figures, equally fruitful areas of study might include their different wartime experiences, their diverse political histories and the various intellectual routes though which they passed into the party in the previous generation.[26] Consideration of this range of experiences makes redundant the notion of a single Stalinist politics which these figures simultaneously renounced. Equally, it is inaccurate to posit a new position to which they all adhered after 1957. Certainly, the NR provided a distinctive and highly creative milieu in which a number of political and theoretical anxieties were 'worked through' by ex-Communists and others. Yet, contrary to the impression left by commentators who assume that this milieu was coherent,[27] no single programme or perspective emerged out of these deliberations. Indeed, the reminiscences of those involved, as well as their contemporary correspondence, provide a different picture altogether: of a group which remained bound by many of the codes and conventions of Communism, yet began to develop a diverse and stimulating agenda in the unfettered atmosphere outside party life, developing a particularly sharp analysis of Stalinism.

The ideological dimension of this transition was particularly important. Differences emerged within this milieu despite the shared sense of direction it maintained. Two examples illustrate the tendency for disagreement to undermine the project of the NR's founders in the new, uncertain context which they inhabited. In terms of international relations, rethinking Communist orthodoxy meant abandonment of 'two camp' thinking and a pronounced hostility to the Soviet Union's role in the cold war. In particular, the NR placed tremendous emphasis upon events in eastern Europe, highlighting the different sources of opposition to official Communism. This encouraged a strong commitment to 'positive neutralism', involving support for a non-aligned bloc led by Britain. Yet the emphasis on non-alignment led some to develop an affinity for different countries (Yugoslavia and Cuba especially) as potential models for revolution now that the Soviet model was discredited. This process, common to both wings of the New Left, ultimately led to the celebration of the 'third world' as an arena of vital significance in contemporary politics, yet which was absent from the majority of Marxist writings. This tendency culminated in the theoretical internationalism of the NLR under Anderson's influence after 1962, yet was already evident in the first New Left and, indeed, within the NR: Peter Worsley, author of the influential text *The Third World*, was prominent within this milieu. The drift towards such commitments and consequent disillusion about the prospects for political advance within Britain disturbed Thompson greatly, inspiring his critique of the historical revisionism of Anderson and Nairn.[28]

More generally, the heterodoxy of New Left political culture encouraged a reassessment of Marxist beliefs. This process was difficult to contain and unfolded in numerous, and sometimes conflicting, directions. Whilst the NR was dominated by Thompson's and Saville's already developed positions on the Marxist tradition, others began to voice doubts about a number of socialist beliefs, and engaged non-Marxist radicals in close debate in a context when they were less sure of their intellectual bearings.[29] This was a complex, and often liberating process, which undoubtedly prefigured the rethinking of Marxism of later decades. For influential ex-Communists like Saville and Thompson the retention of a creative and flexible Marxism was relatively unproblematic – the continuation of a previous perspective. This rested upon a confidence about the continued applicability of Marxist beliefs which had emerged from a particular and difficult dialogue within the party, and which at times smacked of an 'orthodoxy', encouraging hostility towards those in the NR who moved rapidly away from a Marxist perspective in this period.[30]

Significantly, Thompson developed an ethical alternative to actually existing socialism in his contemporary writings, which he called socialist humanism. In several articles in 1957–8 he re-emphasised the centrality of morality to socialist thinking, bypassing both the anti-humanism of orthodox Communism and Trotskyism as well as the individualism and voluntarism of contemporary liberalism.[31] This project constituted Thompson's earliest excursion on the terrain of epistemology. His celebration of humanist language and commitments heavily influenced New Left politics and, arguably, underlay some of the theoretical assumptions behind his major text, *The Making of the English Working Class.* Yet, even here, Thompson showed signs of a continuing commitment to certain traditions within Communism, alongside the influence of factors particular to his complex and singular intellectual formation. Traits of the Marxism which he had absorbed within the party resurfaced, for instance, in the teleological commitment at the heart of socialist humanism. Thompson, like vulgar historical materialists, presumed that socialism was the guaranteed outcome of the historical process. This assumption generated tensions with some of his more heterodox New Left comrades, for whom such an idea was increasingly problematic in the conservative political climate of the late 1950s and early 1960s.[32]

The continuing purchase of Communist traditions was evident elsewhere within the NR milieu: Communist internationalism was deployed to highlight colonial injustices and express solidarity with nationalist liberation struggles; despite a pervasive rhetoric about alliance with radical sections of the Labour movement (often articulated in the style of the popular front), the political trajectory of the Labour Party was closely followed and frequently criticised in a vein familiar to Communists; and a number of important debates took place, shaped by the historical perspective of former members of the historians' group, for instance about the impact of the welfare state, 1957–8.[33]

This context helps explain some of the tensions which distinguished the first New Left milieu. Whilst some commentators have interpreted the fusion of the original two journals into the NLR in 1960 as evidence of the formation of a distinctive New Left movement, the persistence of divisions between and, indeed, within these journals was equally significant. As I have suggested elsewhere (*The First New Left*), the key to the controversial history of the early years of NLR lies as much in the process of fusion in 1959 as in the more obvious date of 1962 when Anderson was entrusted with editorial responsibility. As Stuart Hall, the journal's editor for its first twelve issues, suggested at the time, this 'marriage' was not accompanied by a serious political dialogue about the nature of the New Left as a movement and the role of the journal.[34] On the contrary, a number of resentments were stored up as the focus of New Left activity shifted to London, leaving Thompson, the dominant figure within the first New Left, feeling increasingly impotent. Interestingly, his views were not always shared by his NR colleagues, some of whom played a key role in the early editions of NLR, not least in attempting to smooth relations between Thompson and the editorial office in Soho.[35]

The tension between the different wings of the movement was exacerbated by a deeper difference which can also be partially explained in terms of the NR's Communist heritage. Whilst sections of the New Left, especially in London after 1957, revelled in the notion of spontaneous, non-bureaucratic organisation, many ex-Communists were appalled at the lax and 'naive' culture which such attitudes engendered, reproducing the distrust of the extempore and improvised noticed by Samuel within the CPGB.[36] Whilst they were also keen to avoid the implications of full-scale bureaucratisation, they found spontaneist ideas difficult to swallow after their experiences of disciplined political organisation. Here the conventional values of Communism were re-invoked: the correspondence between Saville, Thompson and intimates, (1960–1), is dominated by the belief that the New Left required more discipline, better organisation and a more mature sense of purpose. From 1959 Thompson increasingly felt that many in London were prone to political self-indulgence and organisational anarchism, an accusation he pursued vigorously in his struggle with the NLR office.[37] The tension between ex-Communists and others cannot be adduced as the sole explanation of these differences: other factors such as age, political experience, geographical context and tensions between regional locales and the metropolitan centre in London were also important. Yet many of these differences arose, at least initially, from the different contexts in which the journals appeared: unlike the NR's emergence from an embattled relationship with the CPGB, ULR began in the very different atmosphere of Oxford University and put down roots in the 'golden triangle' between Oxbridge and London. Many in its milieu were from non-English backgrounds, bequeathing a particularly cosmopolitan emphasis within the journal.[38]

Communism played a minor part in the story of ULR too. Samuel, one-time participant in the historians' group, was one of its founder members and initiator of New Left activities in London. Its pages were frequently home to the ideas of ex-Communists, especially Thompson who engaged closely with its ideas. Yet ULR developed an altogether different style and distinctive political interests, charting shifts in the nature of post-war capitalism. Its writers tended to cast a far more critical eye on a number of socialist orthodoxies. Whilst some aspects of this project overlapped with the politics of NR, the trajectory of these concerns took ULR away from the NR's orbit. This difference was astutely sensed by Thompson. His important critique of Williams in 1961 was also an attempt to challenge some of the dominant ideas of the ULR milieu.[39] He highlighted the latter's emphasis on alienation, rather than exploitation, and its writers' tendency to use systemic explanation and cultural language rather than the discourses of class and socialist mobilisation. Whilst cultural politics and social description were not alien to the NR, its emphases were altogether different. Thompson's political analysis, for instance, drew upon the experience and language of the popular front, especially his notion of a broadly based, social coalition against private-sector monopolies.[40] As the two journals entertained the prospects of merger, their differences became more important. Here the ex-Communist culture of the NR was once again salient. As their correspondence attests, both Saville and Thompson remained sceptical of the political motives and abilities of individuals from the ULR group who appeared inexperienced, unreliable and unschooled in the traditions of the British left.

The New Left was therefore characterised, from its inception, by internal divisions which were impossible to resolve. Some of these can be usefully explained with reference to the different political backgrounds from which its participants came. Once the New Left was unified as a formation – a problematic process which occurred between 1959 and 1961 – these diverse strands were brought together in a creative yet combustible mix. The beliefs of ex-Communists existed uneasily alongside the predilections of others in this formation, for instance Trotskyists, supporters of direct action politics in the peace movement and newly politicised youth, attracted to the London New Left club and coffee bar in Soho. Attempts to unify the New Left failed without exception. Yet the creation of a new political space, outside the two main parties of the left, was an important project, influencing many who participated in this formation. The combination of New Left and ex-Communist sympathies was an unpredictable mix, the impact of which varied on an individual basis. Ex-Communism was an important part of the story of the New Left, which has been obscured by those who assume that this movement achieved, or should have attempted, a clean break from older political traditions.

The New Left was an eclectic formation which drew upon a range of political and intellectual experiences. Much of its identity arose from its dialogue with and critique of old left positions. Ultimately, the movement's rapid demise and failure to sustain its fragile institutions suggests that the diversity of these experiences was never transcended. One reason for this was the survival of Communist ideas and identity, of a libertarian kind, in the group which formed around the NR. Whilst Communism was not the sole political influence within this grouping, figures such as Thompson and Saville drew heavily upon the experiences and expectations of their party backgrounds in the course of the New Left's life. This generated mistrust towards younger activists who operated in different contexts, yet also enriched the political culture and ideas of the movement. The New Left offered a serious alternative where 'intellectuals' could participate in a culture which was not entirely cut adrift from mainstream politics, yet remained insulated from both orthodox Communism and social democracy. In this sense, New Left identity remained loosely connected to, though also removed from, the politics of Communism. Indeed, the notions of a distant dialogue and mutual influence, rather than dichotomous opposition, might be extended beyond this period. Some evidence exists that party members were affected by the NR's critique of eastern European Communism, for instance Willie Thompson's interesting remarks about the influence New Left ideas exerted upon him before he joined the CPGB.[41] Additionally, the 'brokerage' role played by New Left intellectuals for Gramscian ideas, culminating in the Communist University of London schools in the 1970s (which involved figures from the first New Left) and the political turn taken by *Marxism Today* from the late 1970s, has been highlighted by David Forgacs, but remains a largely unexplored source of influence.[42]

This brief assessment of the first New Left highlights the limitations of positing a simple dichotomy between Communist and New Left politics. More generally, this episode reveals the importance of non-Communist organisations and traditions in determining the political development of former Communists and raises the more general question of what factors shape their subsequent political allegiances. In particular, it suggests that even for the most coherent and virulent opponents of Stalinism, aspects of the Communist heritage continued to shape political choices and preferences, however profound their break from Communism appeared. Unfortunately, this unusual example of collective political action by former Communists has been misrepresented by commentators on the British New Left. In fact, the relationship between Communism and this movement was more important and complex than has conventionally been suggested.

Notes

1. N. Young, *An Infantile Disorder? The Crisis and Decline of the New Left* (Routledge & Kegan Paul, 1977).
2. Ibid., p. 148.
3. See, for instance, J. Cameron, 'The New Left in Britain', *Listener*, 8, 15 and 22 September, 1960; J.G. Watson, 'Politics and culture', *Socialist Commentary*, September 1960, pp. 19–21.
4. See especially H. Pelling, *The British Communist Party: A Historical Profile* (A. and C. Black, 1975), pp. 114–81.
5. See especially 'An open letter to Leszek Kolakowski', in *The Poverty of Theory and Other Essays* (Merlin, 1978), pp. 303–403.
6. D. Holden, 'The first New Left in Britain: 1954–1962' (University of Wisconsin–Madison, PhD, 1976); B. Palmer, *The Making of E.P. Thompson* (New Hogtown Press, 1981); and L. Chun, *The British New Left* (Edinburgh University Press, 1993), pp. 10–13. Interestingly, few others who participated in the NR milieu appear to share this view.
7. M. Jones, *Chances: An Autobiography* (Verso, 1987), p. 119.
8. See M. Kenny, *The First New Left 1956–62: British Intellectuals after Stalin* (Lawrence & Wishart, 1995).
9. R. Samuel, 'The lost world of British Communism', parts 1–3, *NLR*, 154, 156 and 165, 1985–7, especially part 2, *NLR*, 156, pp. 63–113.
10. E. Hobsbawm, 'The historians' group of the Communist Party', in M. Cornforth (ed.), *Rebels and their Causes: Essays in Honour of A.L. Morton* (Lawrence & Wishart, 1978), pp. 21–47.

11. See K. Morgan, *Against Fascism and War: Ruptures and Continuities in British Communist Politics* (Manchester University Press, 1989).

12. E. Thompson, *Where Are We Now?*, internal discussion document, submitted to the NLR board April 1963, Lawrence Daly papers, Warwick University, Mss 302/3/19.

13. See M. Kenny, *The First New Left*, ch. 2.

14. J. Saville, 'The twentieth congress and the British Communist Party', *Socialist Register*, 1976, pp. 1–23, especially p. 7.

15. M. MacEwen, 'The day the party had to stop', *Socialist Register*, 1976, pp. 24–42.

16. Doris Lessing, *The Golden Notebook* (Grafton, 1987), p. 338.

17. R. Samuel, 'The lost world', part 2, p. 79.

18. J. Saville, 'The twentieth congress', pp. 9–11.

19. M. MacEwen, 'The day the party', p. 33.

20. J. Saville, 'The twentieth congress', p. 7. See also E. Hobsbawm, interviewed by Gareth Stedman Jones, '1956', *Marxism Today*, November 1986, pp. 16–23, especially p. 19.

21. J. Saville, 'The twentieth congress', especially p. 15.

22. Ibid.

23. For instance ibid., p.21.

24. See the first issue of the *Reasoner*, 1956.

25. M. MacEwen, 'The day the party'.

26. For an account which incorporates some of these elements, see M. Bess, 'E.P. Thompson: the historian as activist', *American Historical Review*, 98, 1, 1993, pp. 18–38.

27. See, for instance, D. Holden, 'The first New Left' and C. Bamford, 'The early New Left in Britain 1956–62: the politics of commitment', (Edinburgh University, PhD, 1983).

28. See Thompson's critique of this tendency and the later New Left's reliance on Sartre and Fanon, in *Where Are We Now?*.

29. The NR published contributions from outside its immediate circle and encouraged debate on theoretical questions. See, for instance, the responses to Thompson's celebration of socialist humanism from Charles Taylor and Harry Hanson in *NR* 2, 1957.

30. See M. Kenny, *The First New Left*, ch. 4.

31. E. Thompson 'Socialist humanism: an epistle to the Philistines', *NR*, 1, 1957, pp. 105–43; 'Socialism and the intellectuals', *ULR*, 1, 1957, pp. 31–6; and 'Agency and choice', *NR*, 5, 1958, pp. 89–106.

32. See M. Kenny, *The First New Left*, ch. 3.

33. This debate was prompted by J. Saville, 'The welfare state: an historical approach', *NR*, 3, 1957–8, pp. 5–25. See also P. Smith,

'The welfare state', *NR*, 5, 1958, pp. 110–14; and D. Thompson, 'Discussion', *NR*, 4, pp. 125–30.

34. Letter to Edward Thompson, 20 June 1960, John Saville papers, University of Hull (*New Left Review* 1959–63 file).
35. See M. Kenny, *The First New Left*, ch. 2.
36. R. Samuel, 'The lost world', part 2.
37. See M. Kenny, *The First New Left*, ch. 2.
38. S. Hall, 'The "First" New Left: life and times', in R. Archer et al. (eds), *Out of Apathy: Voices of the New Left Thirty Years On* (Verso, 1989), pp. 11–38, especially pp. 19–20.
39. E. Thompson, 'The long revolution: I and II', *NLR*, 9 and 10, 1961, pp. 24–33 and pp. 34–39.
40. W. Thompson, 'Revolution', *NLR*, 3, 1960, pp. 3–9.
41. W. Thompson, *The Good Old Cause: British Communism 1920–1991* (Pluto Press, 1992), p. 14.
42. D. Forgacs, 'Gramsci and Marxism in Britain', *NLR*, 176, 1989, pp. 70–88.

Further reading

For the first New Left, see R. Archer et al. (eds), *Out of Apathy: Voices of the New Left Thirty Years On* (Verso, 1989) and N. Young, *An Infantile Disorder? The Crisis and Decline of the New Left* (Routledge & Kegan Paul, 1977). On the Communist Party in 1956, see M. MacEwen, *The Greening of a Red* (Pluto Press, 1991).

12 Sex 'n' Drugs 'n' Rock 'n' Roll (and Communism) in the 1960s

Mike Waite

Most studies of the British Communist movement refer to the Young Communist League (YCL) only in passing, perhaps to illustrate a point about the party itself. This is a belittling of young people's political activity which is general amongst those who study history, only partly excusable by the fact that people who have provided accounts of their lives as young activists tend to remember these periods as brief, if intense, preludes to longer and more 'effective' stretches of work as adult politicians. It is also an expression of an assumption that, although nominally independent, the YCL was always merely the youth section of the Communist Party of Great Britain (CPGB), mainly significant as an element of its recruiting machinery. This assumption is fed by the facts that its work was closely monitored by the party, and league leaders were always approved by the 'adult' organisation – at least until the 1980s. The party subsidised many YCL activities and publications and, more generally, YCL activists took their lead from the party as they adopted their 'lines' and developed their approach to politics. Its political subordination to the party meant that there was rarely a need for organisational or administrative measures to keep the league in check.

This conventional wisdom does not tell the whole story. It buries facts such as that the YCL of the late 1920s made much of the running in bringing about the change of line to the ultra-leftist 'Class Against Class' thesis. It forgets that during the late 1930s the YCL in many places was much bigger and more active than the party, the focus for microcosmic versions of what popular front politics might have looked like had they taken off in this country. Most of all, it obscures untold stories of fascinating battles which took place within the British Communist movement. These battles expressed the varying priorities and agendas of different generational cohorts within the movement, and reflected the difficulties the movement had in regenerating and renewing itself as the heroic moments of 1917 and the anti-fascist struggles of the 1930s and 1940s receded into history. This chapter focuses on the ways in which tensions and differences developed between the YCL and the party during the 1960s, a decade which saw the formation of the second of the two 'political generations' which shaped the history of British Communism, the first having been the generation which formed in the mid- to late 1930s, in opposition to fascism and war.[1]

For many years, from the early 1930s on, it is true to say that there were few examples of *political* conflict between the YCL and the party in general. Certainly, the fault lines within British Communism over the infamous changes in policy at the beginning of the Second World War and over the events of 1956 ran *through* the league and the party in similar ways, rather than *between* the party and the league.

This gave credence to the ritual claims made by John Gollan in the late 1950s and early 1960s that he had never had to discipline the YCL – a point he was making to contrast favourably the league with the successive Labour youth organisations which had often been trouble-some to Labour Party leaderships. This was partly because of the tensions spontaneously created by relatively radical youth for a parlia-mentary party seeking respectability and electoral success, and partly because these tensions had been exploited and young people's radicalism had often been used for their own ends by first Communist and later Trotskyist entryists who had operated within Labour youth organisa-tions.[2]

In fact, there were already elements of wishful thinking in Gollan's claim by the late 1950s, of more or less wilful blindness to the complex and conflicting currents forming within the movement he so desper-ately wished to keep 'united'. There were unmistakable signs of the 1930s generation of Communists becoming exhausted, and losing the ability to determine all the political priorities and outlooks of the movement. One example is that the period saw the first significant separation in approach between the YCL and the party to a policy issue for 30 years – over the Campaign for Nuclear Disarmament (CND). Many Communists were initially suspicious of and hostile to CND, an inde-pendent campaign, after a decade and more during which 'peace' politics had been dominated by Communist initiatives such as the British Peace Committee. They also had mixed feelings about CND's central demand of unilateral disarmament, preferring the approach of working for multilateral disarmament. But the fact that many young people – including YCL members – were joining CND and enthusi-astically supporting events such as the Aldermaston marches led to some leading members of the YCL arguing openly for a change in line. When Communists did switch to backing CND in 1960 it was Monty

Johnstone, who until recently had edited *Challenge*, who was first to offer a public admission that Communists had been wrong to withhold support from the campaign.[3] Over the next years, YCL members came to play a key role in CND, and in Young CND, and many recruits to the organisation came from contacts initially made in the peace movement. This was of great help in rebuilding the membership base and moral standing of the league which had been very badly damaged by the events of 1956.

The relationship between the YCL and the broader peace movement also had an impact on the political culture of the league. The presence in CND of activists influenced by 'New Left' politics and other currents opposed to Stalinism led to many young league activists sharing in the new political moods which emerged after 1956, which involved at the least a contingent and more often a quite critical relationship to the Soviet Union. This created some tension between YCLers in CND and the party leadership. Terry Monaghan remembers:

> being called into a meeting along with similar activists, and the 'progressive' work we were doing was acknowledged, but no apparent reason for calling the meeting emerged, and I suspect that they were just trying to work out what they were dealing with.[4]

When conflicts developed between the loyalty to Soviet policy expected by the party, and the concern of working for peace which had brought many young activists into politics in the first place, they often privatised the latter. Young people were often not inclined to locate and shape their commitment to 'peace' within a complex strategic outlook which required Communists to support every changing nuance of Soviet foreign policy, on the grounds that the 'defence' of the Soviet Union was a key part of effective peace campaigning. Thus there were significant numbers of voluntary and forced resignations from the YCL when Khrushchev resumed nuclear testing after a moratorium.

Political differences between league activists and the party around CND were linked to the broader social development of youth culture, and it is possible to identify the clear emergence of generationally based cultural conflict within the Communist movement in this period. There had been precursors of such cultural conflict before, certainly as far back as the early 1930s, when there were disagreements between the CPGB hierarchy and league members in London and some other cities over 'outlandish dress' and the singing of 'unsuitable songs'. But such cultural conflicts were far more important in their own right by the beginning of the 1960s, meaning that for the first time they became the predominant and defining aspect of some disputes, rather than being a secondary expression of some other generationally rooted tensions over political or organisational questions.

Sharply expressed differences of approach and conflicts between the YCL and the party during the 1960s were expressions of the wider emergence in society of youth cultures through which young people developed and displayed senses of their own identities *as* young people. Followers of movements such as the teddy boys, beatniks, mods and rockers and hippies were using the increased leisure time and disposable income which young people gained in the early post-war decades to create styles and identities which emphasised the differences between themselves and members of the older generation. Older Communists participated in the 'adult' disapproval which greeted successive youth cultures, even if the ways they expressed their concerns over the growing and much-discussed 'generation gap' avoided the crudities of the general moral panics. Nevertheless, the traditional Marxist approach could not allow Communists of either the YCL or party to see that:

> to teens in the mid-1950s, Rock'n'Roll carried, encoded within its arcane language, the promise of a new world: a world where they did not have to do National Service, where they didn't have to keep on hearing stories about the war, where they could reject sacrifice, where they could have sex and consume freely, where they could drift, cruise, run wild.[5]

Even where they began to understand what the new forms of youth culture meant to young people, Communists did not necessarily approve or consider relating to the new interests of youth in a positive or imaginative way. The goals and outlooks formed by participants in youth subcultures seemed anarchistic, individualistic and just too new when set against the traditional concerns of the left. These comments by a Clydeside shop steward in the 1960s reflect the unease which resulted from the inability and unwillingness of the Communist movement to key into the emerging interests of young people, and

> echoed the complaints of many socialists during the so-called youth revolution: 'Most of the lads in the yard have grown their hair long; they are more interested in drugs and discos than in going to college. They've lost interest in any ideas of self-improvement that even some of their parents have.'

The left-wing 'tradition of self-improvement and rational recreation could simply not compete against the glittering array of youth cultures'.[6]

This traditionalist suspicion of 'the youth revolution' was not shared by newer or recently strengthened currents on the left. The New Left was desperately keen to link itself to the many positive associations which the concept of 'youth' carried in the late 1950s and 1960s. This was a period when 'youth' was widely and convincingly used as a metaphor for a better life: for hope, excitement, creativity and spontaneity, in contrast to the stigmatisation and victimisation of groups of young people which has shaped mainstream discourse more recently.

New Left coverage of youth issues largely took the form of commentary, rather than actually being shaped by the voices of young people themselves. However, many of those who had broken from Stalinism, and who had developed a more generous and layered conception of the nature of politics, were able to recognise that the upsurge in youth radicalism of the 1960s was primarily expressed in cultural forms – dress, music, lifestyle, 'permissiveness' over sexual matters. Some Communists identified the problem presented by the wide gap between the way in which the movement related to such forms of culture and the way in which young people more generally did. Recognising that this expressed the severe difficulties the movement was now having in regenerating itself, some YCL leaders attempted to develop a politicised relationship to youth culture, and braved the disapproval of older traditionalists in a variety of ways.

Many of these simply showed that young Communists followed and helped shape the fashions favoured by much wider numbers of their generation. In his history of British Communism, Willie Thompson has noted that the 1960s saw a weakening of constraints and censures in relation to the way in which party members were expected

> to be respectable in a general sort of way, to take their lead in social mores and behaviour, in dress and appearence, from the cultural ethos of the skilled working class which numerically dominated the party ... activists were expected to present exemplary models of working-class virtue.

At the beginning of the decade 'a District Secretary could still compel a prominent YCLer to shave the beard which the Secretary regarded as incompatible with the image he wanted young Communists to project: by 1970 such a notion would have appeared laughable.'[7] This process was by no means straightforward, and the 1960s saw many arguments and scenes between younger and older Communist activists over this kind of issue.

As well as stopping shaving and letting their hair grow long, some YCLers sought to relate to the emerging musical tastes of young people. The league leadership increasingly saw youth cultural activity as expressing positive, vital qualities which corresponded to their own left-wing values. A 'cultural explosion' around 1963 and 1964, which led to the emergence of new forms of rock and roll, expressed by young bands from working-class backgrounds such as The Beatles, The Rolling Stones and The Who, was positively welcomed by the YCL, which moved away from its earlier purist insistence on traditional folk as the musical form most compatible with its politics. But when *Challenge* went so far as to put a big picture of The Beatles on its front cover, followed by a page two exclusive interview, there was some disquiet.[8] Should stories about 'trade unions and young people' and 'festival time in Hungary' really have been relegated to pages three and seven? The mid-1960s saw genera- tional and political battles widely played out over the question of what music should be promoted as ideologically sound. For example, the Mandela Club, set up in Glasgow (with resident band The Jay Hawks), died a death partly because of party disapproval; a consequence of which was the setting up of a rival folk club (with Ewan MacColl as its honorary president). This proved to be even more short lived.

More sustained initiatives helped convince leading Communists that giving the young ones some scope could pay dividends in terms of contact with potential recruits. Jackie Heywood remembers that Wembley YCLers formed a band called The Bow Street Runners, who played at a YCL rhythm and blues club every Sunday night at the Railway Hotel, attracting 300 young people.[9]

What some young people got up to in the dark corners of the Mandela Club and the Railway caused concern to the older party members who paid superintendent visits to 'the gigs' from time to time. Sexual morality became an important focus of tension between those seen as puritan traditionalists on the one hand and 'permissive', 'decadent' YCLers on the other. But debates over sexual matters were not only shaped by differences of opinion between the generations. There were fierce debates *within* the YCL, shaped by changing attitudes towards sexual questions and women's oppression throughout the 1960s, which were indicative of how the decade saw the opening up of major debates within the Communist movement, and particularly in the YCL. During this time the men who wanted to define left agendas and centre them around their conceptions of 'class politics', with little regard for other questions, began to lose the control they wanted and had assumed was automatically theirs.

Back in the 1950s, *Challenge* had often run so-called 'health and beauty' competitions, in which young women members of the YCL were asked to send 'photographs (with negatives if possible)' of themselves 'hiking, swimming, cycling, working round a camp, playing tennis, climbing. And 100 words about yourself'.[10] Increasingly confident that this kind of thing was what most *Challenge* readers wanted, the editors began putting 'cover girls' on the paper in 1956 – partly perhaps to take readers' minds off the controversy on Hungary that was splitting the movement. Such an exploitative and cynical attitude to the portrayal of women was also, of course, expressed by some of the powerful men within the league.

There was definitely something of a change in tone during the early 1960s, reflecting changes in the YCL leadership. The *double entendres* and pin-up style portrayal of young women recruits to the YCL was replaced by a more positive type of presentation, and a sensible, sober tone in the discussion of sex. 'Beauty queen "cattle shows"' were attacked as money-making rackets even by male contributors to *Challenge*, and by the mid-1960s, the paper was for the first time beginning to deal with sexism and society's waste of women's abilities as serious issues in their own right. But there was a reversion to what was soon to be seen as sexist language and inappropriate portrayal of women later on, particularly when *Challenge* was relaunched as a monthly magazine. This was a period which saw the contraceptive pill becoming widely available, and a cultural movement around ideas of liberation – defined in terms of women being free to make themselves available to men – led to an increasingly open approach to sexual relationships. The still mainly male editorial team of *Challenge* celebrated these aspects of the period in a variety of unfortunate ways. Invitations to subscribe to the magazine and requests for donations took the form of pictures of young women in unmistakably seductive poses alongside such slogans as 'Care to make me happy? Then send a contribution to *Challenge*'s development fund.'[11] Discussions of sexual issues moved away from the straightforward tone that had been established in the mid-1960s, and began to include details that seemed intended to excite.

It is of course important to understand such a style and approach in a historical context, to think about how it would have been 'read' in its day, rather than simply to judge it by the 'politically correct' standards that have been established since. Most people on the left at the time saw the 'sexual liberation' of the 'swinging sixties' as more than a mixed blessing; it was widely welcomed. Any qualms people had about the way that it was actually serving as a cover for exploitative behaviour by men were often suppressed as a form of puritanism. And *Challenge* was trying quite consciously to compete with 'underground' magazines such as OZ and *International Times*, by combining aspects of their style with the promotion of Communist politics. Thus the questionable ways in which women were sometimes talked of and portrayed in the magazine expressed the many positive ways in which *Challenge* was shaped by the outlook of the times generally, and the culture of the 'hippie' and 'underground' movements in particular. It should however be noted that opposition to puritanism, and a belief that there was nothing 'dirty' about sex or shameful about contraception, was promoted by the YCL in a way which was *even then* criticised as exploitative of women. From such starting points, the way that sex and sexuality were talked of and presented in *Challenge* became increasingly informed by the language of the emerging women's movement – many of whose members had been active on the student left in the years around 1968 – and had quickly become disappointed at their male colleagues' failure to apply the principles of fighting oppression and discrimination to the problems faced by women.

Though it was less fully debated than questions of sex and women's rights, the issue of drugs provided another focus for fierce debates on 'the youth of today', both within the YCL and between the YCL and older activists in the party. One illustrative anecdote from the early 1960s concerns the three leaders of the YCL who decided to hold a meeting on the question, 'Should drugs be legalised?' Gollan heard of this, and summoned the YCLers. They had made an agreement to enter his room in an exaggerated parody of a military march, and then to salute in mock subordination. Gollan went into spluttering apoplexy, telling his deputy to 'deal with them'. The YCLers were told that if they went ahead and held the meeting they would be expelled. In spite of being ominously reminded that 'the Party could close down the League', they left the King Street offices in the same ridiculous march, and decided to call the party leadership's bluff. No action was taken,[12] perhaps because the controversial question of drugs never became a major campaigning concern for the league. It never developed a clear line on such questions as legalisation, and tended to settle for describing drug use as an inappropriate response to the negative aspects of life in capitalist society. Socialism, then, would resolve the difficult question of what attitude to take to drugs. It was sometimes suggested that forming socialist commitments this side of the revolution would be sufficient to tidy up this messy matter

– several articles in *Challenge* seriously argued that selling the paper on street corners would provide a better buzz than any drug on the market.

The fact that even raising the issue of drugs could create paranoia in the higher echelons of the party illustrates the concern with which the YCL's attempts to engage with young people's current interests and lifestyles was watched. From the late 1960s into the 1970s, increasing attempts by the YCL to repose its politics in relation to where young people were 'actually at' fuelled significant debates within British Communism about how to view and relate to youth culture.[13] A major debate on this issue in *Marxism Today* from 1973–5 discussed many of the deep splits between traditionalists and modernising, Eurocommunist, currents which were to shape the remaining years of the party.[14] What lay behind this was a set of agendas and confusions about how to relate to spontaneous developments in civil society, linked to changes in the composition and consciousness of Communists' intended and actual working-class constituencies. For traditionalists, particularly older comrades schooled in patterns of discipline and in a hierarchical culture where political questions were decided at the top and communicated down the line, the uncertainties and conflicting tendencies within youth culture made it frightening and foreign. It was not clear how it could be disciplined, or how an order could be imposed so that there could be a return to the days of simply hitching the interests of the 'youth' constituency to familiar, pre-determined programmes of class politics.

Even the most radical of leading YCLers in the 1960s centred their approach to youth issues on the need to separate out the 'nonsense' from the potentially progressive tendencies within youth culture, so that these could then be shaped and harnessed for the cause. The key notion of the league in the mid-1960s was to translate the self-evident mass rebelliousness of the generation into Marxist–Leninist revolutionism.[15] That this seemed possible was not simply the result of theoretical conviction, but reflected the experience YCLers had of encouraging, amplifying, shaping and organising trends in youth culture. Whilst this was ever only really effective in particular localities, the YCL had made a sustained (and in many ways successful) attempt to project a left-wing agenda on to youth culture nationally with the 'Trend is Communism' campaign from 1967 onwards. Largely financed by a legacy to the party, the key element of the campaign was the mass distribution in youth clubs and schools of a large, garish leaflet, which introduced itself to readers as possibly the first piece of Communist literature they had seen. A high point of the campaign was the organisation of an International Youth Festival at the Derbyshire Miners' Holiday Centre at

Skegness, held alongside the 26th YCL Congress at the end of May 1967. In addition to political debates and meetings, there were performances by top pop groups such as The Kinks, poets such as Adrian Mitchell and folk singers from Britain and abroad. According to Tom Bell, rising through YCL ranks at the time, the 'Trend' campaign 'captured the imagination of a lot of young people. The leaflet gained so many applications to join that the league was flooded out with them all.'[16] Apart from directly winning recruits to the YCL, the approach exemplified in the 'Trend' campaign helped lend a radical hue to the wider youth scene. Young Communists were not simply dedicated followers of fashion, but in much of their activity helped to make left-wing politics fashionable.

Although in retrospect this approach seems almost classically Leninist, many in the party saw it as an abandonment of concern with the real questions of politics – the need to defend the socialist countries, the requirements of the Labour movement etc. Looking back in anger to 'Trend' in 1987 a traditionalist supporter of a factional grouping which was to split from the CPGB decided that it had been 'the first major campaign masterminded by revisionists … in many ways the forerunner of the "Politics With Style" type of campaign pushed [in the 1980s] by *Marxism Today*'.[17] Thus we can see that, in the 1960s, the wider differences between the YCL and the party over cultural questions provided the context for the focussing of political differences over more traditional questions. Significant arguments about the structure of the league, and tensions in its organisational relationship with the party took off at this time. Assertions of the need for top-down discipline, and the political subordination of the league to the party, were resisted by those who argued the need for more horizontal models of organisation and approaches to political work, based on what young Communists had in common with their 'ordinary' peers rather than on the political commitments which differentiated them. Concern about the logic of the YCL's strategy informed the beginnings of internal opposition. Tom Bell has remembered that political differences underlying what had seemed to be little more than differences in style increasingly came out into the open. 'The real split between the Stalinist tendency within the YCL and the majority began to emerge … At the Congress of '67 in Skegness we had quite a big split on issues like *Challenge*, style of work etc.'[18] During the 1970s, this split surfaced in a debate over two models for the YCL. One argument was for a smaller but potentially more effective vanguard type organisation, which would train up cadre to run political education classes and intervene in trade union disputes; the other was for a league geared to 'mass work', which would provide many points of contact between YCLers and ordinary young people, by requiring activists to sustain and make inputs into social, sporting and cultural life.

Such emerging splits expressed the way in which the Communist movement, in common with the wider left, was shaped and affected by the cohering of a new political generation. This was the first large new cohort of left activists whose approaches and world view were shaped by a particular series of events since the anti-fascist generation of the 1930s, and the last political generation to throw up figures who played a role in the evolution (and dissolution) of British Communism.

By the late 1960s, there were many significant adherents of Marxism who had ceased to aspire to monolithic unity, thus creating the space for a variety of complementary and competing foci of left activity. Thus many thousands of young people becoming active over the Vietnam war, students' campaigns and many other issues did not feel that they must necessarily follow – or define themselves primarily in opposition to – the Communist line. Many other organisations existed, as did looser, 'non-aligned' tendencies inspired by new left themes, readings of European Marxist writers and anarchism. Although this can now be seen as positive, allowing debate on and modernisation of the left, the 'loss' of young people to other left groupings and the break-up of Communist-dominated 'unity' was seen as tragic by the orthodox in the movement. They reacted by seeking to impose their outlooks ever more strongly on those young recruits who did join the YCL and CPGB around 1967 and 1968. But they found that many of the new recruits – even where they were amongst the daughters and sons of party members who filled YCL ranks – were increasingly immune to Stalinist orthodoxy, having been influenced by the new and more critical political moods, and by such developments in youth culture as the mocking of authority and the rejection of deference.

The most clearcut example of the political differences which developed between the YCL and the party in this period is that the two organisations took diverging positions over Czechoslovakia. The party had moved far enough away from slavish subservience to the Moscow line since 1956 to express reservations over the 'intervention'; but the league leadership went further, condemning the August 1968 'invasion'. This was not merely the difference between two words. The league promoted its line in clear and outright forms, some of which seemed calculated to mock and upset the Stalinist old guard within the party. It also provoked the (fairly large) traditionalist minority within the league to begin factional activity, establishing patterns of conspiracy and open subversion of leadership decisions and political policy at branch and district level which were to become more and more familiar in the league and the party itself during the 1970s and 1980s. The front cover of *Challenge* after the invasion offended not only the political line of pro-Moscow 'tankies', but also targeted their puritan sensibilities about sex and appropriate language. The obligatory seductive blonde 'hippie' girl swayed provocatively by the side of the words 'If you think socialism means tanks rolling in at any time, you're bloody wrong.'[19] Protests outside the Czechoslovakian embassy, and the heckling of Soviet fraternal delegates to the 1968 YCL Congress at Scarborough, confirmed the extent to which the league had diverged from the party in being able and prepared to recognise and openly oppose Stalinism.

Although the question of what attitude to take on Czechoslovakia became something of a touchstone for many YCLers' political identity, this was not the only issue on which differences in policy and approach between the YCL and the party developed in the 1960s. Criticism of 'Stalinism' had already been well developed by the league at a time when the concept could not be easily mentioned within the party. In parallel with this the league was developing a serious political debate about Trotskyist politics, breaking with the reliance on slander, misrepresentation and weak polemic which had been established in the 1930s. The enthusiasm of some league members to tackle such issues corresponded to the organisation's need to compete for the affiliation of several thousand radicalised students and young workers. Some of the new organisations centred on Trotskyist or Maoist activists who had hitherto pursued relatively insignificant projects since their decisions to reject the 'official' Communist movement. The battle over how to regard and present Trotsky was one of the proxy ways in which differences between traditionalists and younger modernisers in the movement were fought out. Simply including a line drawing of Trotsky on an early 1970s front cover of the YCL journal *Cogito*, which featured twentieth-century revolutionary leaders, proved too much for some of the leaders of the party. Recalling an incident which suggests that top CPGB officials still had enough power to reverse details of YCL decisions, Jackie Heywood remembers that she was telephoned by the then leader of the league who regretted to have to tell her that she should shred all the *Cogito* covers she had produced and turn out a new one that did not include old Leon.[20]

The fragmentation of the left which started in the late 1960s, and continued into and beyond the 1970s, mirrored the increasing significance of identity, culture and lifestyles as sites for political activity and commitment. The emergence of the women's movement, and the raising of other agendas from outwith (and sometimes in opposition to) traditional left priorities presented challenges to Communists and others on the left. The fact that the Communist Party was – to a limited degree – able to take account of and relate imaginatively to these developments was largely the result of the 'class of 68' moving into the party, fighting out and eventually winning (in the pyrrhic victories of the party's final congresses) arguments which had been initially signalled and rehearsed in the league in the late 1960s. Different models of political intervention combined with diverging attitudes towards youth culture. On the one hand there was suspicion and a wish to control youth culture, while on the other enthusiasm, interest and a wish to learn from and participate in it. This divergence can be seen as prefigurative of the contending models of left politics and understandings of changing patterns of social life which claimed the loyalties of the warring members of the shrinking and disintegrating CPGB in the late 1980s.

In relation to the narrower life of the movement, the greatest significance of the differences which emerged in the Communist movement in the 1960s lay in the fact that many of the YCL leaders who then showed themselves to have largely broken with Stalinism were representative of the tendency that was to develop more and more in the Communist movement over the next decades. As some of the YCLers of 1968 moved into the party through the 1970s, support in the CPGB for reform, and for the Communist project to be redefined in terms which broke from the official ideology of 'Marxism–Leninism', became stronger and stronger. This corresponded with the formation of a cohort of intellectuals and activists who increasingly promoted policies based on their identification with Eurocommunism and their reading of Gramsci, and cohered a project around *Marxism Today* which necessarily brought them into conflict with generally older and more traditionalist party members. The outlooks of this strata were shaped by the times in which they had become active, as well as by their locations in such fields as the middle ranks of trade union officialdom. These developments not only resulted from generational factors, but corresponded to more general disagreements and problems that were exercising the Communist movement internationally, and it is clear that the 'generation gap' as it affected British Communism in the 1960s was one of the beginnings of what was to become the end.

Notes

1. For a careful discussion of the 1930s see Kevin Morgan, *Against Fascism and War: Ruptures and Continuities in British Communist Politics 1935–1941* (Manchester University Press, 1989). The concept 'political generation' seeks to identify a cohort grouping of a significant number of people of similar age who become involved in political activity during a particular period, and who are similarly influenced by the particular historical circumstances of the period. They usually develop to some degree a shared age group consciousness as a unique age group and display a set of attitudes and behaviour at odds with those of other age groups in society.

2. See Willie Thompson, *The Good Old Cause: British Communism 1920–1991* (Pluto Press, 1992), p. 124.

3. Monty Johnstone, *World News* (CPGB, 4 March 1961), p. 116.

4. Terry Monaghan, response to author's research questionnaire, 1990.

5. Jon Savage, *England's Dreaming: Sex Pistols and Punk Rock* (Faber & Faber, 1991), p. 47.

6. Philip Cohen, 'Losing the generation game', in James Curran, (ed.), *The Future of the Left* (Polity Press/*New Socialist*, 1984), p. 109.

7. Willie Thompson, *The Good Old Cause*, p. 152.

8. *Challenge* (YCL, December 1963). Thompson recalls that the front cover 'resulted in gratifying sales figures, even if many casual purchasers at street sales were less gratified, not realising at first what they had bought', *The Good Old Cause*, p. 153.

9. Notes on a meeting between Jackie Heywood and the author, February 1991,

10. *Challenge*, (YCL, 28 April 1957), p. 2.

11. *Challenge*, (YCL, February 1968), p. 11.

12. Verbal contribution to discussion at Manchester conference, 30 January 1994, by Jude Bloomfield.

13. See my article 'The YCL and youth culture' in *Socialist History* 6 (Socialist History Society/Pluto Press, 1994).

14. Martin Jacques provided the opening and closing contributions to the debate. 'Trends in youth culture: some aspects', *Marxism Today*, (CPGB, September 1973), pp. 268–80, and 'Trends in youth culture: reply to the discussion', *Marxism Today*, (CPGB, April 1975), p. 111 ff.

15. Graham Stevenson, 'The Young Communist League of Great Britain: anatomy of decline' (unpublished manuscript, nd, but 1984).
16. 'The Bell Tapes: part two', *Challenge*, (YCL, October/November 1979).
17. Kenny Coyne, 'An unmistakable warning: the liquidation of the YCL', *Communist Campaign Review* (Communist Campaign Group, Winter 1987).
18. 'The Bell tapes'.
19. *Challenge* (YCL, nd, but August or September 1968).
20. Notes on a meeting between Jackie Heywood and the author, February 1991.

Further Reading

The main source for this chapter, as for the related paper which I presented to the Manchester conference, is my unpublished 1992 MPhil thesis, 'Young people and formal political activity: a case study: young people and Communist politics in Britain 1920–1991'. Copies are available for consultation through the library and Department of Sociology of Lancaster University, and through the Democratic Left/Communist Party of Great Britain archives in England and Scotland.

In addition to Thompson's *The Good Old Cause*, cited in the Notes, further sources providing information on the YCL and the CPGB during the 1960s were Frank Parkin, *Middle Class Radicalism: The Social Basis of the British CND* (Manchester University Press, 1968) and David Widgery, *The Left in Britain 1956–1968* (Penguin, 1976).

13 Young Turks and Old Guard: Intellectuals and the Communist Party Leadership in the 1970s

Geoff Andrews

Much attention has been given to 1956 as a watershed in the relationship between the CPGB and its intellectuals. The decisiveness of this moment is not hard to see. Prior to this, and in the 1930s in particular, the CPGB exercised a strong hegemony over left-wing intellectuals who were attracted to its Marxist analysis and humanitarian causes, but whose intellectual work remained largely divorced from that of the party. It also put emphasis on developing its own intellectuals, encouraging serious reading and a growing range of specialist groups. The year 1956 seemed to change all this. The exodus of leading intellectuals was seen as evidence of the incompatibility between creative intellectual energy and Communist Party membership. The general conclusion seemed to be that the future of Communist intellectuals rested on one of two possibilities. Either they would lead a 'life of compromise' and 'surrender to party values', as Neal Wood put it, or they would leave the party altogether.[1]

Yet the CPGB in the 1970s offered an alternative possibility. By the mid-1970s the intellectual and cultural renewal of another decisive moment – 1968 – had come to fruition in the CPGB when its intellectuals were again seeking hegemony over the rest of the left as well as inroads into the party's strategy – in the Communist universities, the party's economic committee, student politics and the Eurocommunist movement. Therefore while the recurrent tension between intellectuals and the Communist Party leadership remains the main theme of my argument, the political context of this relationship is substantially different from what had gone before. In their intellectual energy, the degrees of political autonomy sought and resistance to 'ideological conformity' the intellectuals looked for a fundamentally different relationship with the party from that of their predecessors. Their aim was essentially a much bigger political role for intellectuals in the party's overall strategy.

In interpreting the specificities of this relationship it will be necessary to adopt a broader Gramscian concept of ('organic') intellectuals, as those involved in the production of ideas, as innovators and strategists, and which allows focus on their ideological and organisational functions rather than on the more restricted ('traditional'), concept of intellectuals as isolated 'men of letters'. Such a distinction becomes particularly useful in a period when the role of the intellectual itself was being transformed through technological change and educational expansion.

The following discussion will be broadly divided into two parts: the first will consider the development of the critical and 'Gramscian' outlook; the second will assess the effect the 'Gramscian' and 'Euro-communist' intellectuals have on the strategy of the party. While recognising the dangers of implying homogeneity among intellectuals, my argument will be that there was a distinctive critical political and intellectual trend – to be described at different times as 'Gramscian' and from the mid-1970s as 'Eurocommunist' – which grew and developed in this decade and which provides a framework for the political and strategic differences with the leadership.

The 1970s' intellectuals were a substantially different group from their predecessors – in social background, intellectual influences and political socialisation. The expansion of higher education in the 1960s meant that not only was there a rise in the number of intellectuals but a greater diversity in their social origins. Many of the new generation came from working-class backgrounds and were first-generation university students. This is an important distinction as research into the earlier periods has identified the upper-middle-class background of intellectuals as an important feature in the way they were perceived by others in the party (sometimes given as a reason for lack of discipline) as well as a reason for their own deference to party traditions.[2] By contrast, in the social milieu of the 1970s many intellectuals showed an increasing reluctance to conform to the prevailing cultures of the party, perhaps mirroring a similar contempt for other forms of authority.

The changing political climate of the period 1967–9 was formative in shaping their political outlook. Many had been involved in the growth of radical student politics, including the formation of movements such as the Radical Student Alliance (which Communist students helped to set up[3]) and the rise in support for Trotskyist groups, such as the International Socialists and the International Marxist Group. The events in Paris in May 1968 and in other parts of Europe, notably the 'hot autumn' in Italy in 1969, were the culmination of militant student action which had less extensive, though none the less significant consequences in Britain with student occupations at places such as the London School of Economics and the universities of Manchester and Essex. These events, together with developments such as the anti-Vietnam War movement, provided new forms of politicisation, while the crushing of the Prague Spring by the Soviet invasion of Czechoslovakia heralded a new crisis in the international Communist movement.

These events had a mixed impact on the fortunes of the party in its links with the new generation of intellectuals. On the one hand many Communist students, for example, found their views directly under threat and challenged from a growing and, at its peak (1967–8), vibrant ultra-left. 'Being a communist', as a student at Essex university in 1968 recalls, 'was just about on the edge of left-wing respectability.'[4] On the other hand, the party's decision to condemn the Soviet 'intervention' in Czechoslovakia (as it officially described it) contributed to a new – albeit limited – degree of strategic independence and innovation in the party and was a key factor in the decisions of intellectuals to join or remain in the party. Many young intellectuals in the CPGB found inspiration from the radical politics and cultural transformations of the time. Although the Communist Party was often seen as a conservative force in student politics at this point – not helped by a traditionalist National Student Committee (NSC) – it began to have other attractions for those seeking commitment to an organisation that was serious about theory and strategy. For some it was the 'saneness' of the party in the prevailing left political climate which appealed; for others it was the party's links with the Labour movement and its working-class membership. For many the international links were important. And though the emphasis shifted here from subservience to the Soviet Union to the inspirational model of the Italian Communist Party, belonging to an international movement maintained its attractions. The anti-Vietnam War movement, the relationship with Cuba and Chile and the anti-apartheid movement were all sources of inspiration to a new generation seeking a political home. Therefore despite the unprecedented degrees of political and intellectual autonomy which they sought, and the increasing distrust of the leadership, the party became and remained throughout the 1970s a central focus for their energy.

From the late 1960s the party leadership, concerned about the intellectual vacuum that had existed since the exodus in 1956, gradually sought ways of involving a new generation. The executive committee's (EC) *Questions of Ideology and Culture* statement of 1967 which rejected dogmatism in favour of 'the widest variety of artistic approaches, subjects and styles' opened up new possibilities for intellectual innovation. The leadership also sought a *rapprochement* with intellectuals who had taken a critical line in 1956 but had chosen to remain in the party. Notable amongst these was Monty Johnstone, a consistent critic of the party's attitude to Stalinism, who up until this point had remained isolated and ostracised by the party, having been refused publication of his views on many occasions. However, even after he was 'rehabilitated' in 1967 (having appeared on an edition of 'Late Night Line Up' endorsing the party's protests over the trial of Daniel and Sinyavsky), Johnstone was still underused by the party leadership and became instead a recognised spokesman for the new generation throughout the 1970s, particularly on questions to do with 'socialist democracy'.[5] Another response from the leadership was to assimilate younger thinkers into the party hierarchy. This was the main reason for the election on to the EC of Martin Jacques in 1967, secured through the traditional system of patronage and recommendation, months after he graduated from Manchester University.[6] The leadership, encouraged by an older generation of intellectuals such as James Klugmann and Brian Simon, also put on initiatives aimed at involving the new generation. In addition to supporting the first Communist University of London (CUL) held in 1969, these included a meeting held under the auspices of the party's cultural committee (also in 1969) on 'The role of intel-lectuals today', at which concern was expressed by the new generation over the theoretical weaknesses of the party and the need for open discussion. It was apparent to the senior members of the cultural committee that 'the party is lagging behind in the field of ideological work' and that there was 'the need to develop a clearer approach to the role of intellectuals in the party'.[7]

For their part, intellectuals sought a consistently more critical view of the party leadership, in particular of its strategic weaknesses, its the-oretical ambiguities and its relationship with the international Communist movement. The more critical perspective reached the extent of organising along factional lines, though this was often an informal 'networking' of people of like-minded views, both poorly organised and – necessitated by party rules – clandestine.[8]

An early example of such clandestine factional activity was the setting up of the Party Group which, as well as providing a forum for discussion, had a more specific objective of organising for changes in party policy, particularly at the 1971 party congress. The Party Group had arisen out of the Smith Group, a discussion group consisting of party and non-party members, set up by Bill Warren, a party member and lecturer, in 1970 and based mainly in London.[9] The Party Group was concerned at the party's lack of theoretical rigour, particularly the 1968 version of *The British Road to Socialism* (BRS), the party's strategic programme. The party's theoretical and strategic weaknesses meant that it had a flawed analysis of the nature of class alliances and antagonisms, exemplified by the 'mechanical collation' of different interests under the concept of the anti-monopoly alliance. Further weaknesses included the failure to clarify what it meant by democracy, including an inability to develop 'industrial' or 'workplace' ideas of democracy. A particular criticism was made of the party's 'economism' and its failure to go beyond the 'trade union defensive level' in working-class struggles.[10] It exaggerated the revolutionary potential of the unions and ignored the restrictions and limitations of trade union bargaining. The Party Group also condemned the party's inability to confront patriarchy within its own ranks and its lack of commitment to feminism.

These criticisms – posed at the time interestingly as criticisms of 'revisionism' and 'reformism' – have a revealing resonance for the later disputes over the party's strategy, where the party's deference to trade union orthodoxy stifled theoretical debate, where it never clarified its understanding of class and maintained an obscure if gradually more sympathetic approach to democracy. What was also demonstrated was the disquiet felt by intellectuals in the Party Group that full-time party workers had responsibility for theoretical work.[11]

The work of the group centred around the circulation of papers and ideas for discussion. It had organised a small network of support in some London branches and proposed an amendment to the 1971 congress on the need to challenge 'the hold that social democratic reformism has on the working class'. Its members also called for a better understanding of the reasons why young people and students were attracted to the ultra-left, and proposed an alternative resolution to the EC one on 'Women and society', which challenged male chauvinist attitudes within the party.[12] More ambitiously it circulated a 'Manifesto for the renewal of the party' which offered a way out of the 'sterile revisionism which now dominates the party'.[13]

Despite some limited successes in winning support for rethinking in the party the Party Group began to dissolve in 1972. This was a consequence of lack of organisation and clarity on some of its objectives, but also because members of the group were moving in quite different directions, which indicated that the Party Group, while a forerunner of what was to come, was more heterogeneous than the later groupings of intellectuals.[14] One of its strongest political commitments had been to feminism, and in this respect leading feminists from the group (notably Beatrix Campbell) became involved in a more fundamental struggle with the party. Campbell and other feminists in the party were critical of the lukewarm support given by the National Women's Advisory to the women's liberation movement (WLM) as well as the more general class reductionist attitudes and the limited representation of women members. One response was to form, together with other Marxist–feminists outside the party, *Red Rag*, a journal of Marxist–feminism closely linked to the WLM. It was 'first and foremost a feminist journal, because feminism is the political movement which emerges as women's response to their own oppression'.[15] The response from the party leadership confirmed its suspicion of independent thinking and organisation over which it could not exercise any control. *Red Rag* had been published without consultation with the party leadership (worse still the first issue had been printed on the press of the International Socialists). Members of the editorial collective were called in after the publication of the first issue and told of an EC decision not to publish further issues, which they took no notice of, presumably seeing the ideological significance of the feminist movement far beyond the confines of the Communist Party.[16]

The party leadership's eventual 'tolerance' of *Red Rag* was an indication of the way in which its suspicion and at times hostility to new thinking was tempered by a paternalistic view of the new generation of intellectuals. It was supportive of events which enhanced the party's standing with broader movements. In particular it welcomed the growth of the party's student membership, which in the early to mid-1970s was the fastest-growing section of the party. It made positive attempts to widen its influence among students, and to counter the influence of the ultra-left. However, its enthusiasm was modified by a traditional view of intellectuals as those who should stick to their specialist areas of interest and not involve themselves in the strategic aspects of the party's work. By all accounts they rated low in comparison to other elements, notably the party's industrial cadres, while the strategic and theoretical work of the party remained largely the preserve of the full-time workers. Therefore their enthusiasm for new ideas was only to the extent to which it modernised the party's appeal. Once these started challenging traditions, strategy and structures they reverted to defensive postures.

Confirmation of the party leadership's commitment to winning the new generation of intellectuals was the removal of Fergus Nicholson, the party's long-serving national student organiser, and his replacement by Dave Cook in 1972. Nicholson and his supporters on the NSC, who had been in the majority during the 1967–9 period, had kept their distance from the new thinking generated by student radicalism, preferring to concentrate on the day-to-day business of the National Union of Students (NUS). As well as leading to hostility on the NSC itself this had caused a rift between Nicholson (who became a long-standing opponent of Eurocommunist reform) and the leadership. It was clear to the party leadership that the NSC had become marginalised from the new movements, a position which contrasted sharply both with some local Communist student branches (who were seeking broader alliances) and the existing strategy of the national leadership of the Young Communist League.[17]

Dave Cook's appointment, although not initially a popular decision with student activists at the time,[18] was a major factor in the revitalisation of the NSC and the increase in the party's student membership, which reached a peak of just under 1,000 in February 1973.[19] His organisational flair and ability to engage with the 'new social movements' (as they came to be known) contributed a new intellectual openness and pluralism, exemplified in his influential pamphlet *Students* (1973). This, although orthodox in its strategic commitment to the anti-monopoly alliance, in which the leadership of the working class was crucial, identified a new progressive role for students within the context of the expansion of higher education. From this moment the contribution of Communist students in the 1970s took on two important dimensions. First, Communist students played a prominent strategic role in the Broad Left, set up officially at a conference in Leeds in 1972, and which consisted of Communists, Labour students and the non-aligned left. It had as its purpose a 'mass popular' student movement which would seek a 'mandate for progressive change, combined with higher levels of democratic participation and involvement'. It rejected both the 'revolutionary vanguardism' of the ultra-left and the narrow electoralism of mainstream Labour politics. It sought alliances with the women's and anti-racist movements and respected the autonomy of each, prominent feminists being among its leading members. Great emphasis was put on democracy as a common thread uniting all progressive movements.[20] The key role of the CP within the Broad Left was to be 'an innovator of strategy and theory, unifier of democratic forces and the transforming agent of political forces'. In its Gramscian mode much weight was given to the role of students as 'trainee organic intellectuals', a recognition of the relative autonomy of their conditions and work as intellectuals.[21] The Broad Left won consistent majorities on the NUS executive committee with Communists often the leading figures, among them Sue Slipman, who was NUS president 1977–8.

Significantly, the students – following a succession of Eurocommunist national student organisers[22] – had moved towards a perspective of broad democratic alliances some time before the party as a whole accepted the basis for such a strategy. Here it is important to distinguish between the Gramscian concept identified and practised by the Broad Left and the existing Communist tradition of unity and popular fronts. The students put emphasis on the extension of democracy within the student movement which would be based on important 'structural reforms', such as the 'democratization of higher education' in the traditions of 'progressive democracy'.[23] Though exercised at a more theoretical level, this followed the innovations of the YCL of the 1960s, in particular the focus on popular culture as a key terrain of political struggle. Following Gramsci the Broad Left both identified tensions between non-economic groups and sought alliances between them. It was the NUS and not the party that provided, as one intellectual put it, 'the real lessons of pluralism'.[24]

Closely related to the strategic role of the Communist students in the Broad Left was the second major contribution: the role of student and university branches as centres of intellectual rigour and vitality. The sharp increase of critical forums, reading groups and local CP student journals suggests that this was a major source of recruitment as well as ideological innovation. The strongest student branches such as Essex, Cambridge and Manchester combined effective politics with successful series of 'alternative' or 'critical' seminars, with in-depth study of the recently translated works of Gramsci, and the new texts of Balibar, with the vogue for the heavy theoretical Althusser texts being particularly apparent in places such as Keele and Cambridge.

The main arena for this intellectual renaissance was the CUL, which became a prominent and popular forum for the development of Marxist theoretical alternatives across a range of disciplines. It was here also, particularly in the later CULs that the intellectual momentum for Eurocommunism took off with the meeting of different strands of intellectuals from the party: feminists, students and academics as well as those involved with party journals, advisory committees and full-time party work.

The first CUL in the summer of 1969, initiated by Fergus Nicholson, had been held in 'splendid isolation' from the revolutionary changes and upheavals that had occurred the year before. There were none of the prominent non-party New Left intellectuals who were to play an important role in the peak years of CUL. Instead the lecturers were either full-time party workers or the older generation of party intellectuals (giving the impression to some of a party 'finishing school'), and the main attention was on providing theoretical weight to immediate political issues rather than a broad examination of wider aspects of Marxist theory.[25]

The major breakthrough in CUL numbers as well as a qualitative change in the content of the courses from the early 1970s reflected enthusiasm for new theoretical trends within Marxism, the influx of students into the party and the new dialogues that started to take place between party and non-party intellectuals. Its range of specialist courses grew, in part a reflection of the plethora of party journals and specialist groups that were forming.[26] The CUL offered specialist courses on a range of subjects from Social Anthropology to 'Science and Hegemony', as well as an increasing range of popular cultural evening activities. It began to gain a reputation as a generator of Marxist heresy and a focus for the key debates between prominent Marxist thinkers. Its balance of theoretical rigour and a lively, open atmosphere gained it a reputation and significance beyond the confines of the party, a situation made clear in the growing number of influential non-party participants, and annual coverage in the national press. As a leading CUL participant remarked:

> When you can stuff a university with 1500 people and more professors per square inch than anywhere else ... When you can put on courses with a Marxist interpretation of virtually every living thing, then what you've got is a theoretical perspective which has shown a lot of confidence; it's saying 'actually we have an alternative way of under-standing the world'.[27]

The impact of CUL did not go unnoticed by those hostile to the left who perceived its growing reputation – together with the broader revival of Marxism – as a threat to academic freedom. *Attack on Higher Education: Marxist and Radical Penetration* (known as the 'Gould Report' and published in 1975), identified CUL participants and Communist Party influence in higher education and prompted a major debate between right and left educationalists, in which Communist intellectuals took part over the content of courses and the influence of Marxism.[28]

The CUL was never an entirely autonomous organisation. The leadership (through the PC), while being generally supportive – no doubt seeing the CUL as a major public face of the party which brought it intellectual esteem in some influential areas – retained the right to vet speakers, and the extent to which the leadership could be pushed on questions of controversy was always a consideration amongst the organising group.[29] The most notable occasion of intervention by the party leadership was over an invitation to the Soviet dissident and scientist Zhores Medvedev to speak in 1977. The PC's intervention (after Medvedev had already agreed to participate) was officially on the grounds that Medvedev was not 'currently engaged on scientific work', though this did not impress those who had invited him, who organised a petition for CUL participants to sign. A group of New Left intellectuals and Labour MPs around the Bertrand Russell Peace Foundation sent a letter of protest to the *Morning Star* complaining of a 'serious infringement of the standards of open-minded discussion ...' by 'higher communist organisers'.[30]

Despite its diverse range of participants, the concept of the CUL – linked to the Gramscian notion of the 'collective intellectual' – remained important to the objective of transforming the party, through the meeting of intellectuals and the party's wider membership. In this respect, as the CUL organisers' records indicate, the limited involvement of Labour movement activists and other sections of the party was seen to be a serious concern. Despite concessions and courses geared to part-time students, this was not ultimately realised and there is some indication of a schism between the intellectual work of the CUL and the party's industrial activity, an element which was reflected in many areas of the party's ideological work.[31]

In turning to the implications of the intellectual rejuvenation for the Communist Party's overall strategy, it is important to reiterate the caution that the leadership exercised in dealing with the increasingly critical intellectuals. Its support for the CUL did not easily extend to an incorporation of the ideas into the party's strategic goals. An indication of the lack of influence can be derived from a survey of the party's educational material during the 1970s. Here there was a major distinction between the content of the courses at party education schools and those offered by the CUL, with the former dominated by classical Marxist texts. Typical in this respect was an 'About Marxism' publication in 1974 which was used, at the height of the Gramsci and Althusser boom, as the central text for party education, giving an impression to the membership that there had been little development in Marxist theory since Lenin.[32] The party was also reluctant to employ 'critical' intellectuals at party education schools, with sessions led by industrial organisers and national and district officials.

A main reason for the lack of penetration of new ideas was that the official channels of ideological influence, such as the advisory committees, remained dominated by representatives from the PC who had the role of chairing, reporting back and generally interpreting the respective discussions. This was in part, of course, due to the democratic centralist structures of the party. This bureaucracy was accompanied by an atmosphere of suspicion and a fear of the untried, perpetuated by the higher moral authority afforded to the industrial cadres over intellectuals. Throughout the 1970s the party preferred to employ national officials and industrial organisers rather than 'critical' intellectuals in educational instruction.

Although it was not until the 1977–9 period that the clash between the intellectuals and the party leadership came to a head over political strategy, there were earlier indications of what was to come. Important examples of this were the struggles on the economic committee, a key advisory committee of the EC. The debates were significant because some of the most advanced criticisms of the party's industrial strategy which went to the heart of the party's overall political position were argued and formulated here. Younger and distinctively 'Gramscian' members of the economic committee included Dave Purdy, Pat Devine, Bob Rowthorn, David Currie, John Grahl and Bill Warren: leading professional economists in their own right. On the same committee were the party's industrial organiser Bert Ramelson and prominent trade union leaders such as Ken Gill and Mick McGahey.

The disputes became intense from the 1974 period of industrial struggle over the Labour government's social contract. The major issues which dominated discussion at this time were the causes of inflation (identified as the main economic problem facing post-war capitalism) and the political and industrial strategy needed to deal with it. The party's position (reflected in Bert Ramelson's two pamphlets, 'Heath's War on Your Wage Packet' (February 1973) and 'The Social Contract – Cure-all or Con-trick?' (December 1974)) was that inflation was the consequence of a multiplicity of factors to do with the world capitalist system, such as the rise in world commodity prices, the growth of multinationals, the crisis of the international monetary system and the collapse of fixed exchange rates, and very little to do with wage demands. Therefore the party's alternative economic strategy strongly opposed all forms of incomes policy, proposing instead price freezes and import controls. The principle of free collective bargaining would provide the basis for mass mobilisation and the deepening of the political consciousness of workers.

The alternative Gramscian position was based on an analysis of post-war capitalism that had been developing since the late 1960s. Some of the arguments had first been put forward by Bill Warren in the *New Left Review* and were made within the Smith Group and the Party Group. According to Warren, the party leadership had made a serious error in the late 1960s by committing itself to supporting all wage struggles and being opposed to all incomes policies.[33] In the mid-1970s *Marxism Today* had initiated a debate on inflation and incomes policy where the alternative argument was set out by contributions from Pat Devine and Dave Purdy. In short their argument was that inflation was the outcome of competing claims on resources, arising from conflicts between capital and labour under conditions of full employment, and the extended role of the state in maintaining social welfare.[34]

The rival strategy advocated incomes policy as the means to resolve the problem of allocation of resources. However the proposal for incomes policy had a much wider strategic significance, in which a Gramscian perspective can be identified, and probably for the first time linked to a distinctive strategy for the party. Incomes policy needed to be a central part of a long-term perspective based on the construction of unity amongst different class and social groups. In this respect the alternative approach was critical of the party's policies and strategy for its 'economism' and 'sectionalism'. It was not enough to base a strategy on the immediate interests of workers. Moreover 'militant economism' would lead to the isolation of the trade union movement and strengthen already existing sectional divisions between groups of workers and other sections of society. The working class needed to make sectional compromises for the greater good. 'Free collective bargaining' could not address the problems of powerlessness and unrepresented groups of workers (women, in particular), nor did it provide an answer to long-term ideological objectives or the problems of socialist transition. Therefore the view was that the leadership was missing important opportunities to make a strategic intervention. At its height the optimism of the alternative approach was that the working class could become a 'hegemonic' class, and assume a 'national–popular leadership'.[35] This view related to debates elsewhere on the socialist left, where divisions were growing on issues such as workers' control, the nature of the relationship between the Labour Party and the unions and the role of economic planning. Innovations such as the Upper Clyde Shipbuilders work-in (1971–2) were followed in the late 1970s by the publication of the

Bullock Report on industrial democracy and the Lucas Aerospace initiatives, which gave wider credence to the prospect of an alternative strategy for the Labour movement.[36]

The importance of these issues for the party's strategy led to heated discussions on the economic committee where the intellectuals and the industrial and political leaders 'were constantly at loggerheads'.[37] Despite substantial, arguably majority, support on the committee for the alternative position, the party line prevailed. It seems likely that the leadership was not prepared to risk a breach with its industrial links. Bert Ramelson's role as both industrial organiser and the PC representative on the economic committee was crucial in chairing the meeting and feeding back to the EC and PC. Ramelson also sat on several other party committees and regularly consulted James Klugmann (editor of *Marxism Today*) on 'controversial' articles submitted on the economy and industrial strategy. The last-minute refusal to publish a party textbook on economic strategy after all the articles had been commissioned and submitted by different members of the economic committee indicates the further unease felt by the leadership at the implications of the alternative position.[38]

The intellectuals' high point of influence came during the peak period of Eurocommunism, between 1976 and 1979. The Eurocommunists in the CPGB were never a homogeneous group and some, while broadly identifying with its objectives, chose not to use the term.[39] Indeed it was often used as a pejorative term to label any who dissented from the leadership. Eurocommunism was also an inadequate description of the feminist critique of the party's strategy and there were different degrees of criticism and discontent with the leadership. Some – particularly younger rank-and-file – Eurocommunists wanted a more open confrontation with the leadership, and above all over its commitments to the Soviet Union and industrial strategy, while others with more senior positions within the party, notably Martin Jacques and Dave Cook, saw themselves involved in a 'war of position', seeking necessary compromises for long-term advance.[40]

However it was the coming together of these different positions and the continuity of an earlier Gramscian perspective whose roots had been present in the 1967–9 period and the Broad Left, and consolidated at the CUL and the journals and specialist committees, that a Eurocommunist intellectual identity can be distinguished. The leadership's explicit rejection of the term as one (in the words of Gordon McLennan, general secretary from 1975) 'intended to create differences in the

Communist movement' illustrated the growing divergence between the alternative positions.[41]

Aided by the election of leading Eurocommunist intellectuals to more senior positions in the party,[42] their ideas took on a greater significance in the renewal of the party's strategy and attempts to transform its structures. The Eurocommunist influence was not restricted to intellectuals and was having a growing influence within different spheres of the party, including its industrial work, with emerging criticisms of national industrial policy from younger organisers, such as Pete Carter in the Midlands, who was a member of the EC from the late 1970s. Following political victories in the districts and regions came broader political and cultural initiatives such as the People's Jubilee at Alexandra Palace in 1977 which attracted 11,000 people and gained wide press coverage. The group was united on the need for a strategy of broad democratic alliances relevant to the conditions of western Europe, in which social divisions other than class were adequately expressed and the autonomy of the movements which represented them was respected. It was a position which was increasingly critical of the Soviet Union and the party's ideological ties with that system, being particularly upset by John Gollan's astoundingly banal 20th anniversary 'reassessment' of the Khrushchev revelations in 1956 (the 'Gollan speeches'[43]). Despite this, the wider European developments such as the joint declaration of Western European Communist Parties in 1976, the possibility that the Partito Comunista Italiano would come to power in Italy following major advances in the elections of 1974 and 1976 and the publication of Santiago Carrillo's *Eurocommunism and the State* (1977), where the leader of the Spanish Communist Party openly identified with and advocated an alternative strategy, provided the momentum for Eurocommunist advance within the CPGB.

Eurocommunist intellectuals became more influential in different areas of the party's work. Martin Jacques became editor of *Marxism Today* in 1977 and Sarah Benton editor of *Comment*, the party's house journal, in 1978. Both sought, in different ways, to reorientate their journals and embarked on regular battles with the leadership over the content. New journals with a distinctively critical and Eurocommunist stance were started, notably *Eurored* (1976), *Socialist Europe* (1977) and *Red Letters* (1976). *Eurored*, which arose out of the west European subcommittee, pursued a strategic analysis of western European politics and in particular the fortunes of the Eurocommunist parties. It published articles and interviews with figures such as Claudin, Balibar, Carrillo and Berlinguer and heterodox articles which opposed party policy on the Common

Market and NATO. *Socialist Europe*, published by the 'Committee for the Study of the European Socialist Countries' carried interviews with leading Soviet dissidents (such as Roy Medvedev) and opened a debate on the 'crisis' of Soviet ideology and the Soviet system. *Red Letters* was comparably heretical in its analysis of the inadequacies of traditional Marxist approaches to literature. Generally these journals were given a degree of autonomy that was denied the more official party publications (such as *Morning Star*, *Comment* and *Marxism Today*). In addition leading Eurocommunists were appointed to the theory and ideology committee which was set up as a recognition by the leadership of the greater need for theoretical and ideological work, though the mechanisms through which this would influence the party's strategy were not clear.[44]

The rewriting of *The British Road to Socialism* for the 1977 congress amplified the political differences between the Eurocommunist intellectuals and the leadership. After securing three representatives on the British Road Commission, which had the job of preparing the drafts, debate on the commission between the Eurocommunists (represented by Martin Jacques, Pete Carter and Judith Hunt) and the leadership (represented, until his death in September 1977, by John Gollan and by George Matthews) was intense, with differences over language and who would write the final version as well as the content itself. One participant referred to it later as a 'Mexican stand-off'.[45] Outside the commission discussion of the document was more open than in previous years due to the decision by the party leadership to launch a public discussion of the draft document as well as an invitation to a film crew from Granada TV for a 'fly on the wall' documentary on the political background leading up to the congress.

The leadership and the intellectuals differed in their interpretation of the significance of the new document. The leadership saw the new edition of the *BRS* as having continuity with earlier drafts as well as a modification and updating of a revolutionary programme geared to British conditions that had been first set out in 1951,[46] while the intellectuals saw the possibilities of a major break with the past. They maintained sufficient optimism at this point to see the new edition as a key element in the transformation of the party. The changes in the draft from previous programmes included the replacement of the Anti-Monopoly Alliance with the Broad Democratic Alliance (emphasising a greater role for democracy), the recognition of pluralism through both the 'new social movements' (including the WLM and anti-racist movements) and the commitment to multiparty democracy in the future 'left government of a new type', and the 'broader' rather than 'narrower' definition of the working class (to include professionals and white collar workers), which had been discussed at some length in *Marxism Today* and on the party's sociology group.[47] Although unity existed on the surface and was most clearly evident in the face of criticism from a minority faction from the Surrey and Sussex districts (who broke away shortly before the 1977 congress to form the New Communist Party), a different concept of the party could be identified by the Eurocommunists. Indeed the breakaway itself brought different responses which indicated important differences over the future of the party. For the leadership the need was to minimise the damage created by the breakaway, to have faith in the loyalty to the party of members who might disagree with some of the fundamental changes and if possible to win back some of those who left. By contrast Eurocommunist members of the EC welcomed the departure of the 'sectarian traditions' of the party and argued that loyalty to the politics and strategy of the party must take precedence over loyalty to the party as an organisational form. Others even questioned the commitment amongst members of the leadership to the new draft proposals.[48]

The need to extend the concept of democracy in the document was important to the Eurocommunists in order to challenge deep-rooted anti-democratic practices and structures throughout different spheres of society. It was argued that democracy should be given a more fundamental significance in its own right as well as a way of unifying different groups who faced different levels of oppression. This emphasis on democracy led to the term 'revolutionary democrats' being used to describe the Eurocommunists and to distinguish their more radical position from that of the leadership. In the context of the party's strategy this debate challenged the prevailing interpretation of the leading role of the working class and gave a greater attention to the 'new social movements'. Inevitably it took on a critique of economism which was critical of an over-emphasis on the trade unions as the major source of progressive change.

The final version submitted to congress was therefore a compromise document. Gramscian in its concept of broad democratic alliances and of revolution as a process, it offered little insight into the nature of ruling-class hegemony. It accepted the 'broad' definition of the working class, though its 'leading role' left the nature of the relationship between the broader working class and the 'new social movements' unclear. While accepting the importance of 'new social movements', its commitment to pluralism did not get much beyond accepting the right of other parties to coexist after the (process of) revolution.

Discussion in the party press indicates a mixed response from the intellectuals. There were strong criticisms from feminists arguing that references to women's liberation were 'tokenistic', 'economistic', did not give sufficient attention to the ideology of patriarchy or recognise the autonomy of the WLM. Other criticisms included the general subordination of 'new social movements' to the primary role of the Labour movement, the lack of self-criticism, the lack of an independent role for the CP (and its dependency on the election of a left Labour government) and the preference for 'propaganda' over serious analysis. Although there were harsh criticisms, including from some who regarded the compromises as defeats,[49] in general there was a cautionary enthusiasm amongst Eurocommunist intellectuals, who if not ecstatic about the document saw it as a 'step in the right direction'; an essential contribution to the transformation of the party.

The adoption by the same congress of a resolution strongly subservient to the Soviet Union went relatively unnoticed by comparison, and yet, in retrospect could be seen as the most historically decisive. On the 60th anniversary of the Russian Revolution, resolution 72 acknowledged 'the great debt owed to the USSR and the CPSU for the great example and inspiration not only of the October Revolution but by the triumphs of socialism over 60 years both in peace and war'. It further recognised 'the importance to progress and peace of strong socialist countries and in particular the USSR, the mightiest country in the socialist family'. The leadership argued that this represented a celebration but did not amount to a policy statement, and therefore there would be no debate, only a formal vote. Seemingly caught unawares, Eurocommunists argued from the floor that the resolution was at odds with the party's previous statements on socialist democracy and should therefore be debated. The overwhelming endorsement of the leadership position and the carrying of the resolution (with only ten votes against and 15 abstentions) re-emphasised both the historical ties with the Soviet system but also the loyalty of the membership to the leadership.[50]

At the time resolution 72 was overshadowed by the adoption of the new *BRS*, achieved with the defeat of a Stalinist minority and seen as a victory for the Eurocommunists, a recognition at last of their long-standing theoretical critique. This partial victory led to the most audacious attack yet on the culture of the party with some Eurocommunists seeking to follow their strategic gains with a transformation of the party's structure and organisation. The 1977 congress had agreed to set up a new commission on inner party democracy to report to the 1979 congress. Eurocommunists were quick to respond to the opportunities this brought. Dave Cook, by now the party's national organiser, argued in *Marxism Today* for changes in the party's method of working: 'If ever the maxim "once the political line is decided organisation decides all" needed replacing by "involvement decides all" it is now'.[51] The response to Cook's argument from the old guard leadership indicated the extent of differences that existed over the type of party that was needed. Dave Priscott was typical of that element of the leadership who went along with the new *BRS*, but was unwilling to compromise on inner party democracy, fearing the changes referred to by Cook would 'amount to the liquidation of the party as an effective revolutionary force'.[52]

Differences over the future organisation of the party were reflected on the commission where six Eurocommunist members submitted 'alternative proposals' in addition to signing the (majority) report.[53] A different concept of the party was conceived in the alternative proposals, one of the most radical set of proposals put forward for the organisation of any Communist Party, and which simultaneously challenged the leadership's grip over the party. It proposed abolition of the recommended list and the election of the leadership by secret ballot. It condemned that part of the party's heritage which consisted of the 'anti-democratic, distorting practices which have come to be known as Stalinism'. It criticised the 'anonymous' and 'monolithic' impression of the leadership and 'the pretence of a leadership that is never wrong'. It accepted the basic premises of democratic centralism, namely that the party should act as a united force, based on collective leadership, but argued for the recognition of 'different trends and positions' in the party and the open discussion of political differences, a view which the leadership and opponents interpreted as the endorsement of factionalism.[54]

The alternative proposals got a third of the vote at the 1979 congress, a defeat which had become clear months before in the run up to the congress and confirmed a realignment between the leadership and those who had opposed aspects of the new edition of the *BRS* (and who in the strife of the 1980s largely left the party). The defeat was a signal for a wider decline in the influence of Eurocommunism within the CPGB. Key Eurocommunists lost positions of influence within the party at this time, as the leadership's distrust of the motives of intellectuals increased.[55]

The spheres of intellectual influence were also reduced. After peaking in 1977 and 1978 the CUL started to decline, ending finally in 1981, when the party's influence in student politics was also beginning to wane.

Eurocommunist journals also started to fold in this period and intellectuals involved with the official party publications had mixed fortunes. After two years as editor of *Comment* (1978–80) Sarah Benton's pluralistic and critical approach, including a controversial account of the party's links with Stalin,[56] upset the leadership, whose response further emphasised the measure of control that it was prepared to exercise in dealing with heterodox views which directly confronted the party's traditions. The practice of the party leadership to discuss and take decisions over the content of the journal without the involvement of the editor led eventually to Benton's resignation. In her resignation letter she complained of 'bureaucratic inertia' and a 'lack of collective political discussion'.[57] Martin Jacques outlined a new approach in the September 1978 issue of *Marxism Today*, arguing that the journal 'must appeal to the wider Left' and include a broader range of contributors. In the same issue the 'Forward march of Labour halted?' debate was launched by Eric Hobsbawm. This indicated a much wider purpose of analysing the predicaments of the left and the Labour movement and brought into the open differences that had previously been contained, and was later followed by the analysis of Thatcherism which was to develop in the 1980s. The transformation of the Communist Party became less of a concern for Jacques, and his own interests became increasingly bound up with the future of the *Marxism Today*.[58]

The sometimes fragile unity of the intellectuals also started to fragment as people sought different avenues of political renewal. Two of the most persistently critical intellectuals, Dave Purdy and Mike Prior, published *Out of the Ghetto*, an extended version of their criticisms of the economism and sectionalism of the British left (which included of course the leading currents within the CP) and which proved to be their 'swansong'.[59] A group of radical Eurocommunist intellectuals who had come together in the peak years of the CUL sought a wider influence and got together with non-party intellectuals to start *Politics and Power*, a quarterly journal, formed with the objective of 'bringing together intellectuals of various theoretical and political experiences who have shown an interest in creating new dimensions within the British Marxist tradition'.[60] The intention was to be a 'Eurocommunist *New Left Review*'.

External factors can be added to the Eurocommunist defeat at the 1979 congress as reasons for the exodus of large numbers of intellectuals at this time, during a period (1977–81) in which the party lost a quarter of its membership. The decline of Eurocommunism on a more global scale took away an alternative vision, while the rise of Thatcherism brought home the seriousness of the left defeat and shifted the focus of the political agenda. When the Labour left began to make some headway after the 1979 election defeat some intellectuals channelled their ideas and energy into the new possibilities that existed there. Others admitted that energy wasted on a decade of internal struggles had taken away their appetite for further battles. For those who chose to stay a much more pessimistic analysis of the possibilities for transformation prevailed, as the divisions which originated in the 1970s took on a final and more antagonistic form in the 1980s.

The relationship between intellectuals and the Communist Party in the 1970s presents a challenge to much existing research. The Communist Party had at that time embarked on a different relationship with the Soviet Union, found itself once again in the forefront of industrial militancy, yet also found itself the main beneficiary of the 1968 student generation. For a while it became identified with radical and heretical voices. It attracted some of the most innovative thinkers on the left, notably a younger group of economists who rivalled anything that any other political party could muster. For their part the intellectuals were never the isolated 'specialists' of earlier periods, neither were the compromises they inevitably made on occasions enough to dilute intellectual energy.

However the objective of transforming the party through a more prominent strategic role for intellectuals had failed. One reason for this failure must lie with the naivete in believing that the successes of the CUL and the students' movement could be replicated at the party level, with all the cultural and traditional baggage that went with it: 'the CUL wasn't the party', one recalled.[61] 'I plead guilty', another has admitted, 'to the charges of naivete, enthusiasm and intellectual voluntarism'.[62] There was not much attempt to construct an alternative Eurocommunist vision: the Broad Democratic Alliance (the 'BDA' in party jargon) always remained an internalised and abstract concept which lacked practical relevance.[63] In retrospect we must also doubt the extent of 'lost opportunities' and whether more could have been done. The challenge to the leadership over its continuing subordination to the Soviet Union at the 1977 congress was overwhelmingly defeated. When the critical alternative proposals were presented to the inner party democracy debate at the 1979 congress there was a backlash.

The ultimate failure to transform the party reflects both the specific political context of the CPGB in the 1970s and the wider question of the nature of Communist organisation. In retrospect the greater openness of the 1980s which included the broad cultural and political events associated particularly with *Marxism Today*, as well as highlighting the major divisions emanating from the *Morning Star*'s economistic editorship, confirmed in different ways the inability of the party to reform itself. The roots of the party's decline in the 1980s, with its dependence on a depleted Labour movement culture, the loyalty rather than ideological conviction of the membership and the effects of the defeat of existing Communism, can be traced to the preceding decade. The Soviet heritage lasted well into the 1970s, confirmed by the 'Gollan speeches', 'resolution 72' and – as we now know – Moscow Gold, paid to the party until 1979. Its other outward loyalty to the trade unions remained, guaranteeing a strong place and influence within the political culture of militant unionism which it was not prepared to risk by having a serious debate over industrial strategy. At the same time an entrenched leadership, whose three leading members – Gordon McLennan, Bert Ramelson and Reuben Falber – had clocked up over 100 years full-time service between them by the end of the 1970s, presided over an internalised culture of decline and routinism which in its own logic could justify the freezing out of invention.

Acknowledgement

I am grateful to the following for sharing their reflections with me: Sarah Benton, Jon Bloomfield, Jude Bloomfield, Doug Bourne, George Bridges, Genia Browning, Pat Devine, Jackie Heywood, Sally Hibbin, Steve Iliffe, Martin Jacques, Monty Johnstone, Alan MacDougall, Chris Nawrat, Mike Prior, Dave Purdy, Geoff Roberts, Sue Slipman, Ken Spours, Graham Taylor and Willie Thompson.

Notes

1. N. Wood, *Communism and British Intellectuals* (Gollancz, 1959), p. 218.
2. See N. Wood, *Communism*, pp. 172–3. For an account of the complexities in Harry Pollitt's relationship with intellectuals see K. Morgan, *Harry Pollitt*, (Manchester University Press, 1993), pp. 123–5.
3. Founding Communist signatories of the Radical Students Alliance in 1966 included Martin Jacques and Alan Hunt, CPA.
4. Mike Prior interview, December 1993.

5. Monty Johnstone interview, November 1993.

6. Martin Jacques interview, December 1993. His arrival on the EC coincided with his 'great political change'. During late 1967 and early 1968 all his orthodox ideas were challenged.

7. Letter from Bill Carritt (cultural committee member reflecting on the event) to Brian Simon, chair of cultural committee, 24 June 1969. Cultural committee box, CPA. Martin Jacques' later *Marxism Today* article (October 1971), 'Notes on intellectuals', was based on a discussion at this event.

8. Martin Jacques has admitted being an 'inveterate faction organiser' from the time of his arrival on the EC. Interview December 1993.

9. The twofold objectives of the Party Group were: (i) 'to develop alternative, more Marxist and more revolutionary analyses and strategies than the revisionist ones now dominant in the Party and (ii) to disseminate such alternatives throughout the Party', 'Report of committee on future policy of Party Group'. The group published two editions of a journal for selective circulation and distributed regular discussion papers. I am grateful to Mike Prior, a former member of the Party Group, for letting me see his papers.

10. B. Warren, 'The British road to socialism', *New Left Review*, 63, September–October 1970, pp. 27–41.

11. The Welsh Secretary Bert Pearce's article 'the strategy for socialist revolution in Britain', *Marxism Today*, January 1971, was picked out for particular criticism and initiated a series of critical papers by members of the group. See also M. Prior, 'Discussion', *Marxism Today*, May 1971.

12. 'Report of committee on future policy on Party Group', Mike Prior Papers.

13. Prior papers.

14. Members included later Eurocommunists as well as Ken Gill and Mary Davies who became identified with the rival group around the *Morning Star* in the 1980s.

15. *Red Rag*, no. 4, 1972.

16. EC and PC notes on *Red Rag*, EC box, CPA, 1972.

17. NSC Box, CPA, 1972, and Willie Thompson interview July 1993.

18. NSC meeting 29/30 April 1972 records 14 out of 15 members opposed to Cook's appointment, an indication both of a pro-Nicholson majority and – from correspondence between Reuben Falber and other NSC members – discontent with consultation procedures. NSC Box, CPA, 1972.

19. NSC minutes, NSC box, CPA, 1973.
20. See 'What is the Broad Left?' Communist student leaflet, Broad Left box, CPA. The Broad Left continued until 1979 when it was succeeded by Left Alliance.
21. K. Spours, 'Students, education and the state', *Marxism Today*, November 1977.
22. Jon Bloomfield, 1974–7; Ken Spours, 1977–8 and Sally Hibbin, 1978–80.
23. See K. Spours, 'Students, education and the state'; Jon Bloomfield, 'A democratic strategy for post-school education', *Marxism Today*, October 1976; A. Pearmain, *Towards an Educated Democracy: A Strategy for the Democratisation of Post-School Education* (Education Office, Manchester University Union, 1977), NSC box, CPA,1977.
24. Sue Slipman interview, April 1994.
25. CUL box 1, NSC box, CPA, 1969.
26. At the height of the CUL in 1978 there were 18 committees which were involved in running specialist courses. Theory and ideology committee box, CPA.
27. Ken Spours interview, August 1993.
28. See debate in *Times Higher Education Supplement* October–November 1975.
29. Interviews with CUL organisers: Geoff Roberts, August 1993; Steve Iliffe, November 1993; Chris Nawrat, November 1993 and Sally Hibbin, August 1993.
30. *Morning Star* 13 July 1977; CUL box 2, CPA.
31. CUL records consistently show this. CUL box 2, CPA. According to Willie Thompson, one of its organisers, the Scottish version of CUL ('Festivals of Marxism'), had a consistently more working-class composition. Thompson interview, July 1993.
32. *About Marxism: A Communist Party Introductory Course* (CP Education Dept, January 1974). I am grateful to Michael Stephen for this suggestion.
33. See 'On the internationalisation of capital and the nation-state', *New Left Review* (NLR) 68, pp. 83–8; 'Capitalist planning and the state', NLR 72, March–April 1972, pp. 3–29; 'Imperialism and capitalist industrialisation', NLR 81, September–October 1973, pp. 3–44; 'Recession and its consequences', NLR, 87/88, September–December 1974 (double issue) ('Discussion').
34. See Dave Purdy, 'Some thoughts on the party's policy towards prices, wages and incomes', *Marxism Today*, August 1974. Other major articles in this debate included Pat Devine, 'Inflation and Marxist theory', *Marxism Today*, March 1974 and Dave Purdy,

'British capitalism since the war' (parts I and II), *Marxism Today*, September/October 1976. Bill Warren and Mike Prior, *Advanced Capitalism and Backward Socialism* (Spokesman pamphlet, 1975) was the most radical statement of the critical position and was apparently considered too 'reformist' for NLR.

35. See for example Mike Prior, 'Discussion on inflation and Marxist theory', *Marxism Today*, April 1975.

36. For similar arguments elsewhere on the left see Stuart Holland, *The Socialist Challenge* (Quartet Books, 1975); Institute for Workers' Control bulletins and pamphlets including 10th Anniversary Conference, (Spokesman pamphlet, 1978), in which Arthur Scargill, Audrey Wise and Mike Cooley were in debate, Mike Rustin, 'Workers' plans and industrial democracy', *Politics and Power*, 2 (Routledge & Kegan Paul, 1980).

37. Dave Purdy interview, December 1993.

38. Purdy interview.

39. For example Martin Jacques and Monty Johnstone.

40. EC member Sue Slipman had taken a bolder (though, on her own admission, 'a bit kamikaze') approach in confronting the leadership, particularly over its industrial strategy. Beyond the EC Geoff Roberts, Chris Nawrat and Alan MacDougall, who had come together in the peak years of CUL (1977–8), also argued for bolder approaches. Interviews with author.

41. G. McLennan interview with Peter Avis, *Morning Star*, 4 July 1977.

42. Former student organisers Dave Cook became national organiser 1975, Jon Bloomfield secretary of the Birmingham party 1976.

43. See Willie Thompson, *The Good Old Cause* (Pluto Press, 1992), pp. 170–2; John Callaghan, *The Far Left in British Politics* (Blackwell, 1987), pp. 179–80.

44. Set up in 1976 its terms of reference were to 'encourage and promote the development of Marxist thought and study ... To be responsible for the activity and development of [the] specialist groups.' It remained an advisory committee to the EC. Theory and ideology committee box, CPA.

45. Jacques interview. *Decision: British Communism* (D:BC), Granada TV, 1977.

46. Gordon McLennan traced its origins to Harry Pollitt's *Looking Ahead* (CPGB 1947), *Morning Star* interview with Peter Avis; see also James Klugmann, *Comment*, 5 February 1977.

47. See Alan Hunt (ed.), *Class and Class Structure* (Lawrence & Wishart, 1977) and earlier debates in *Marxism Today* (June 1970, March/October 1973).

48. Sue Slipman and Pete Carter contributions in EC discussion, 11 September 1977; D:BC.

49. Prior interview. Slipman interview.

50. See D:BC for behind the scenes disputes over this.

51. *Marxism Today*, December 1978.

52. *Marxism Today*, February 1979. See also Mick Costello, *Marxism Today*, June 1979.

53. The six were: Dave Cook, Pat Devine, Josie Green, Maria Loftus, Veronica Luker and Joanne Richards.

54. 'Alternative proposals' to *Report of Commission on Inner Party Democracy* (CPGB, 1979).

55. Martin Jacques came off the PC in 1979 and Dave Cook's job as national organiser was 'redefined' by the PC, providing him with less responsibility and more mundane work.

56. For example the January 1979 EC referred to the 'Stalin front cover' as a 'crude representation of the Party's policy and its publication was an error of judgement'; reported in *Comment*, 3 February 1979.

57. Sarah Benton, *Resignation letter to the Executive Committee* CPA, 6 November 1980.

58. Jacques interview.

59. *Out of the ghetto* (Spokesman, 1979). Earlier distribution of the document in draft form at CUL in 1977 earned a mild rebuke for breaching party rules in the run up to congress. Prior interview; Purdy interview.

60. Founding statement. The group were Geoff Roberts, Chris Nawrat, Alan MacDougall and Ken Spours. Routledge published four editions, but the journal ceased following internal divisions on the editorial board.

61. Jacques interview.

62. Nawrat interview, November 1993.

63. For an exception see D. Fernbach 'Eurocommunism and the ethical ideal', in M. Prior (ed.), *The Popular and the Political* (Routledge & Kegan Paul 1981).

Further Reading

There is a dearth of material on the CPGB's last period. There were three books published from papers given at CUL: Jon Bloomfield (ed.), *Class, Hegemony and Party* (Lawrence & Wishart, 1977); Sally Hibbin (ed.), *Politics, Ideology and the State* (Lawrence & Wishart, 1978) and Ros Brunt and George Bridges (eds), *Silver Linings* (Lawrence & Wishart, 1981). For other contributions from participants see Mike Prior and David Purdy, *Out of the Ghetto* (Spokesman, 1979). Mike Prior (ed.), *The Popular and the Political* (Routledge & Kegan Paul, 1981).

Afterword

Eric Hobsbawm

One of the last decisions of the then still undivided CP Historians' Group in 1956 was to press the party leadership to authorise a genuine history of the party. If I remember correctly, Brian Pearce and I were selected by the group to sit on the committee which met to discuss this at King Street. As might be expected, it led nowhere. Harry Pollitt, who attended, was against the project. He clearly did not believe that a realistic history of the party was possible at all or that any history of the party was desirable, except something like a regimental history, designed to inspire the lads and lasses with stories of heroic battles and devotion to the cause. Palme Dutt recognised what we are after and, in principle, approved it. A proper history of the 'party line' and its changes was needed. No doubt it would be written in due course. We could see immediately that this meant 'not in the foreseeable future', since Moscow still blocked a free discussion of the two episodes in the history of the party line most in need of realistic revision, the 'Third Period' and 1939–41. James Klugmann, who should have spoken his mind, said nothing. In the end it was he who was given the impossible task of writing an official history of the CP that would satisfy both Moscow and those who did not believe in such a history. Not surprisingly, it had not reached the first of the controversial periods by the time he died. He should have had the courage to refuse. Of the two Historians' Group delegates, one left the party and pursued his researches into party history among the Trotskyites and the other stuck to the nineteenth century.

As this books shows, the situation today has been totally transformed, if only by the disappearance of both the USSR and the British CP. This has done two things. In the first place, it has begun to make available the major written sources accumulated in Soviet offices and archives. This constitutes the real 'opening of the books'. Although the papers in this volume do not make much use of these sources, they are indispensable, for example for the realistic study of the financing of the CP, as Kevin Morgan's study of the *Daily Worker* shows. In the second place, the affairs of the CP are no longer discussed on what was essentially a political and ideological battlefield. It can now be seen in some kind of historical perspective, even by many of those with very strong political commitments for or against it. Neither the British CP nor the USSR any longer exist. There is all the difference in the world between debates about a political organisation which is there, charged with a cargo of hopes, hatreds and fears, and discussions about the past of a body which no longer has a future because it no longer has a present. It is true that the waves of the old political storms, even those of tempests in tea-cups, have not completely subsided. Nor are they likely to, since no historian of the foreseeable future can be expected to be dispassionate about Communism. Nevertheless, a book such as this, written essentially by men and women belonging to the tradition of the Labour movement and the Marxist left, could not have been written 20 years ago.

It will naturally be read by people who also belong to this tradition. Why should it also interest others? For three, perhaps four reasons. Though small in numbers and consistently negligible in terms of electoral politics, the CP was in no sense a fringe performer on the national stage, like some other small Communist parties or, for that matter, like the Scottish and Welsh nationalists between the wars. As Nina Fishman and James Hinton show, it is impossible to understand the history of the British Labour movement since the First World War, and certainly since the 1930s, without an understanding of the organisation which in effect became the characteristic school for trade union rank-and-file activists, that is the recruiting ground for a high proportion of those who became national trade union leaders after the Second World War. Hence 1956 is a crucial date in the history not only of the CP, but of the British trade union movement. It marked the beginning of the end of the CP hegemony of the trade union left.

The second reason why CP history is of general interest emerges from John Callaghan's chapter. It was the Comintern's main conduit into the British Empire, and – at least initially – provided both theoretical leadership and actual organisers for the Indian Communist movement. The study of this aspect of British Communism still has some way to go. The role of the 'colonial groups' in the student movement of the 1930s awaits a fuller study – they formed not only later leaders of Third World Communist parties, but persons who later played a central role in the governments of the Nehru dynasty in India. We need more attention to the dogs that did not bark: not only to the weakness of Communism among West Africans, discussed by Hakim Adi, but to the turning away from Soviet Communism of the active and distinguished inter-war group of English-speaking Caribbean Marxists – Padmore,

James, Williams, Arthur Lewis and others. In this they differed, at least at the time, from the French-speaking Caribbean leftists like Césaire and the Haitians. Why?

The third reason is the influence of the CP on British intellectuals and therefore British intellectual life. This is perhaps of more restricted interest, since it affects primarily one period, and the intellectuals formed or matured within it – the 1930s and 1940s. (The party's role in, and as a beneficiary of, the student radicalisation of the 1960s–70s was more modest, if only because, by international standards, the British student radicalisation, unlike the much less political counter-culture, was a modest affair.) Essentially it forms part of the world history of the era of the great slump and anti-fascism, a cause which mobilised intellectuals (including the influential contingent of journalists) earlier and more profoundly than others. The problem here lies not so much in the impact of the people attracted to Communism on British culture, but in the relation of the party to them, on some aspects of which this book throws light. It may safely be said that the CP, somewhat taken aback by its unexpected appeal to the intellectual and sometimes rather well-born young, did not quite know how to handle them. Yet, unlike the American CP, it did not drive a significant body of them into Trotskyite or other ideological dissidence, and, unlike the ferociously *ouvriériste* French CP it did not tell them to drop intellectual activities and do proper party work. How are these differences to be explained? In short, there is still room for more research in this field.

The final reason why non-left readers might take an interest in CP history is that, as Alan Campbell's and Henry Srebrnik's chapters show, it can throw light on the history of the lesser components of the multi-ethnic nation-state of Great Britain. The role of Communism was no doubt disproportionately great in Scotland, Wales and among the British Jews, as indeed was that of the Liberal and Labour parties, presumably out of opposition to the dominance of Conservatism among the majority people of the UK, the English. Nevertheless, the differences between the radical politics within the minority peoples are significant, and the chapters in this field – Campbell's perhaps more than Srebrnik's – can form the starting-point for an instructive comparative analysis. Thus Campbell throws light on a question which goes far beyond the local politics of the Scottish coalfield. Why, in spite of the obvious and persisting communalist tension between Catholic and Protestant, Orange and Green, in industrial Scotland, has it been possible in that country – unlike Northern Ireland and, for so much of its history, Merseyside – to build a unified movement of the political left across sectarian boundaries?

These are some of the reflections which occur to at least one reader of the present volume, which demonstrates both the potential of Communist Party history, and the high quality of those who practise it today.

Notes on Contributors

Hakim Adi teaches in London and has written a number of articles on the history of Africans in Britain. He is a founder member of the Association for the Study of African, Caribbean and Asian Culture and History in Britain. He is currently researching the African and Caribbean membership of the CP during the 1940s and 1950s.

Geoff Andrews teaches at the Open University, the University of Westminster and Kingston University, where he is researching the social composition, ideology and strategy of the CPGB in the 1970s. His other research interests include recent developments in social and political theory and he edited *Citizenship* (Lawrence & Wishart, 1991). He was a member of the CPGB between 1985 and 1991.

Sue Bruley teaches Historical Studies at the University of Portsmouth. Her PhD thesis, on women and Communism in Britain between the wars, was published in 1986 by Garland Press. Her interests focus on women in twentieth-century Britain, particularly from an oral history perspective.

John Callaghan is Professor of Politics at the University of Wolverhampton. His publications include *British Trotskyism: Theory and Practice* (Blackwell, 1984), *The Far Left in British Politics* (Blackwell, 1987), *Socialism in Britain since 1884* (Blackwell, 1984) and *Rajani Palme Dutt: A Study in British Stalinism* (Lawrence & Wishart, 1993).

Alan Campbell lectures in the Department of Economic and Social History at the University of Liverpool. He is currently writing a book on trade unions and politics in the Scots coalfields, 1874–1939.

Andy Croft teaches Literature and Creative Writing in Middlesbrough for Leeds University's Department of Adult Continuing Education. A CP member from 1983 to 1991, he was secretary of the party's Middlesbrough and Teesside branches and of its Northern district. He has recently edited (with Graeme Rigby) Harold Heslop's autobiography *Out of the Old Earth* (Bloodaxe, 1994) and is currently writing a biography of Randall Swingler.

Richard Croucher is the author of *Engineers at War* (Merlin Press, 1982) and *We Refuse to Starve in Silence* (Lawrence & Wishart, 1987). He works for the Workers' Educational Association and is international secretary of the Society for the Study of Labour History.

Nina Fishman is a senior lecturer at the Harrow Campus, University of Westminster, teaching History, Politics and Industrial Relations. Her Book *The British Communist Party and the Trade Unions, 1933–45* was published in 1994 (Scolar). She is currently working on the CPGB, trade unions and the cold war.

James Hinton has written extensively on Communist Party history. His previous publications include *The First Shop Stewards' Movement* (Allen & Unwin, 1973) and *Labour and Socialism* (Wheatsheaf, 1983). He is a Senior Lecturer in the Department of History at the University of Warwick.

E.J. Hobsbawm was born in 1917 and educated in Vienna, Berlin, London and Cambridge. A Fellow of the British Academy and the American Academy of Arts and Sciences, with honorary degrees from universities in several countries, he taught at Birkbeck College, University of London, and since retiring at the New School for Social Research in New York. In addition to *The Age of Revolution* and *The Age of Empire*, his books include *Primitive Rebels*, *Labouring Men*, *Worlds of Labour*, *Industry and Empire* and *Bandits*. His most recent book is *Age of Extremes: The Short Twentieth Century 1914–1991*. All have been translated into several languages.

Michael Kenny lectures in the Department to Politics, University of Sheffield. He is the author of *The First New Left, 1956–62: British Intellectuals after Stalin* (Lawrence & Wishart, 1994).

Kevin Morgan lectures in Government at the University of Manchester. He is the author of *Against Fascism and War: Ruptures and Continuities in British Communist Politics 1935–41* (Manchester University Press, 1989) and *Harry Pollitt* (Manchester University Press, 1993). He is currently researching the attitudes of the British left to jazz and modern architecture.

Henry Srebrnik is Assistant Professor of Political Studies at the University of Prince Edward Island, Canada. A specialist in comparative politics and radical ethnic movements, his publications include *London Jews and British Communism, 1935–1945* (Vallentine Cunningham, 1994).

Mike Waite was a member of the CPGB from 1987 until 1991, serving on the party's last north-west district committee. His articles on youth issues have appeared in a number of journals including *Young People Now*, *Critical Social Policy* and *New Times*. He is a member of the editorial team of *Socialist History* which is published by Pluto Press.

A Note on Archival Sources

The Communist Party's own archives are now accessible to researchers at the *National Museum of Labour History, 103 Princess Street, Manchester M1 6DD*. Party archives were not kept in any systematic fashion until the Second World War, but for the post-war period there are extensive records of the party's executive, International Department, Organisation Department, Historians' Group, National Cultural Committee, National Students Committee, the Young Communist League and other leading bodies. In the pre-war period, the main CP records were sent to the Comintern in Moscow and are now accessible at the Russian Centre for the Storage and Study of Documents of Contemporary History (RTsKhIDNI). Microfilms of some of this material, mainly Central Committee and Political Bureau records from the 1930s, are already with the British party archives. Financial backing is now being sought for a further microfilming project to complete the holdings available in this country. Materials for this earlier period will also be found in a number of the individual collections held by the archives, including the papers of R. Palme Dutt, Harry Pollitt and Ivor Montagu. Other important individual deposits include papers of John Gollan and Bert Ramelson. The archive also has materials relating to a number of front organisations or campaigns instigated by the CP.

A number of other archives hold important collections relating to Communist activities. The *University of Hull Library, Cottingham Road, Hull HU6 7RX* has papers of several relevant individuals and pressure groups including the anti-imperialist activist Reginald Bridgeman and the historians John Saville and R. Page Arnot. Collections at the *University of Warwick Modern Records Centre, Coventry CV4 7AL* focus mainly on industrial activities, including papers of the Austin shop stewards' convenor Dick Etheridge and the Fife socialist and miners' leader Lawrence Daly. Among the centre's many trade union deposits, the files on Communist activities among the TUC's records are of particular interest. A notable individual collection is that of R. Palme Dutt at the *British Library Manuscript Collections, Great Russell Street, London WC1B 3DG*. While very much complementary to the Dutt papers at the NMLH, this collection for many years provided most historians with their only real glimpse of internal party documentation.

All of the above institutions have good collections of Communist pamphlets and periodicals. Other important sources for printed materials are the *Working Class Movement Library, 51 Crescent, Salford M5 4WX,* which also has strong trade union holdings, and the *Marx Memorial Library, 37A Clerkenwell Green, London EC1R 0DU*. During the cataloguing of the Communist Party archives, the Marx Memorial Library received from the archives large quantities of duplicate CP materials including minutes, circulars, leaflets and ephemera. These are to provide an alternative research collection accessible in London.

The results of the considerable oral history work on the Communist Party are scattered among a large number of collections including all those mentioned. Particularly successful projects were those on the Spanish Civil War held by the *Imperial War Museum Department of Sound Records, Lambeth Road, London SE1 6HZ* and the South Wales coalfield held by the *South Wales Coalfield Library, 50 Sketty Road, Swansea*. Mike Squires of the Socialist History Society is compiling an inventory of all relevant materials which will be available, along with recordings and transcripts where possible, at the *National Sound Archive, 29 Exhibition Road, London SW7 2AS*. Anybody wishing to carry out their own oral history work should consider seeking the advice of the NSA, which can recommend equipment and useful publications and also holds regular free training days. The archive will also make available to researchers any copies it receives of recorded materials.

Bibliography

Attfield, John and Williams, Stephen (eds), *1939: The Communist Party and the War* (Lawrence & Wishart, 1984).

Bell, Tom, *The British Communist Party: a Short History* (Lawrence & Wishart, 1937).

Branson, Noreen, *History of the Communist Party of Great Britain: 1927–41* (Lawrence & Wishart, 1985).

Callaghan, John, *The Far Left in British Politics* (Blackwell, 1987).

Callaghan, John, *Rajani Palme Dutt: A Study in British Stalinism* ((Lawrence & Wishart, 1993).

Challinor, Raymond, *The Origins of British Bolshevism* (Croom Helm, 1977).

Childs, D., 'The British Communist Party and the war, 1939–1941: old slogans revived', *Journal of Contemporary History*, vol. 12, 1977.

Dewar, Hugo, *Communist Politics in Britain: The CPGB from its Origins until the Second World War* (Pluto Press, 1976).

Fishman, Nina, *The British Communist Party and the Trade Unions: 1933–45* (Scholar Press, 1994).

Fishman, Nina, 'The British road is resurfaced for New Times', in Martin Bull and Michael Heywood (eds), *Western European Communist Parties and the Revolutions of 1989* (Macmillan, 1994).

Francis, Hywel, *Miners Against Fascism* (Lawrence & Wishart, 1984).

Fyrth, Jim (ed.), *Britain, Fascism and the Popular Front* (Lawrence & Wishart, 1985).

Hinton, James, *The First Shop Stewards' Movement* (Allen & Unwin, 1973).

Hinton, James and Hyman, Richard, *Trade Unions and Revolution: The Industrial Politics of the Early British Communist Party* (Pluto Press, 1975).

Hinton, James, 'Coventry Communism: a study of factory politics in the Second World War', *History Workshop Journal*, no. 10, autumn 1980.

Jupp, James, *The Radical Left in Britain 1931–1941* (Cass, 1982).

Kendall, Walter, *The Revolutionary Movement in Britain: 1900–1921* (Weidenfeld & Nicolson, 1969).

Kenny, Michael, *The First New Left: British Intellectuals after Stalin* (Lawrence & Wishart, 1994).

King, Francis and Matthews, George, *About Turn: The Communist Party and the Outbreak of the Second World War*. The verbatim record of the Central Committee meetings, 1939. (Lawrence & Wishart, 1990).

Klugmann, James, *History of the Communist Party of Great Britain*, vol. I 1919–24; vol. II 1925–6 (Lawrence & Wishart, 1968 and 1969).

Macfarlane, L.J., *The British Communist Party: Its Origin and Development until 1929* (Macgibbon & Kee, 1966).

McIntyre, Stuart, *Little Moscows: Communism and Working-class Militancy in Inter-war Britain* (Croom Helm, 1980).

MacIntyre, Stuart, *A Proletarian Science: Marxism in Britain, 1917–1933* (Cambridge University Press, 1980).

Martin, Roderick, *Communism and the British Trade Unions, 1924–33: A Study of the National Minority Movement* (Oxford, 1969).

Morgan, Kevin, *Against Fascism and War: Ruptures and Continuities in British Communist Politics 1934–41* (Manchester University Press, 1989).

Morgan, Kevin, *Harry Pollitt* (Manchester University Press, 1993).

Newton, Kenneth, *The Sociology of British Communism* (Allen Lane/Penguin, 1969).

Pelling, Henry, *The British Communist Party: A Historical Profile* (A. & C. Black, 1975).

Samuel, Raphael, 'The lost world of British Communism', parts 1–3, *New Left Review*, 154, 156 and 165, 1985–7.

Saville, John and Miliband, Ralph (eds), *Socialist Register 1976* (Merlin Press): John Saville, 'The 20th congress and the British Communist Party'; Malcolm MacEwen, 'The day the party had to stop'; Margot Heinemann, '1956 and the Communist Party'; two interviews with Jean Pronteau and Maurice Kriegel-Valrimont and Rosanna Rossanda; Mervyn Jones, 'Days of tragedy and farce'.

Saville, John and Miliband, Ralph (eds), *Socialist Register 1994* (Merlin Press): '1956: Edward Thompson and the Communist party'.

Squires, Mike, *Saklatvala: A Political Biography* (Lawrence & Wishart, 1990).

Srebrnik, Henry, *London Jews and British Communism, 1935–45* (Vallentine Mitchell, 1994).

Thompson, Willie, *The Good Old Cause: British Communism 1920–1991* (Pluto Press, 1993)

Werskey, Gary, *The Visible College: The Collective Biography of British Scientists and Socialists in the 1930s* (Allen Lane, 1978).

Wood, Neal, *Communism and British Intellectuals* (Gollancz, 1959).

Woodhouse, Michael and Pearce, Brian, *Essays on the History of British Communism* (New Park, 1975).

Index